LOST
WONDERLAND

L O S T

WONDERLAND

THE BRIEF AND BRILLIANT LIFE OF
BOSTON'S MILLION DOLLAR AMUSEMENT PARK

STEPHEN R. WILK

 BRIGHT LEAF
BOOKS THAT ILLUMINATE

Amherst and Boston
An Imprint of University of
Massachusetts Press

Lost Wonderland has been supported by the Regional Books Fund, established by donors in 2019 to support the University of Massachusetts Press's Bright Leaf imprint.

Bright Leaf, an imprint of the University of Massachusetts Press, publishes accessible and entertaining books about New England. Highlighting the history, culture, diversity, and environment of the region, Bright Leaf offers readers the tools and inspiration to explore its landmarks and traditions, famous personalities, and distinctive flora and fauna.

ISBN 978-1-62534-558-5 (paper); 557-8 (hardcover)

Designed by Jen Jackowitz
Set in Adobe Garamond and Univers
Printed and bound by Books International, Inc.

Cover design by John Barnett, 4 Eyes Design
Cover art: *Entrance to Wonderland, Revere Beach, Massachusetts*, ca. 1920–1935, from the Tichnor Brothers Collection, Boston Public Library.
Courtesy of Digital Commonwealth.

Library of Congress Cataloging-in-PublicationData
A catalog record for this book is available from the Library of Congress.

British Library Cataloguing-in-Publication Data
A catalog record for this book is available from the British Library.

TO MY FATHER, JOSEPH S. WILK

CONTENTS

PREFACE

Wonderland

That was the word, written in bold block letters, next to the black dot at the end of the blue bar representing the subway line. It was 1976, and I was taking time out from my undergraduate classes to visit the beach. I had grown up in New Jersey, and to me "the beach" was a broad expanse of fine sand, bordered on one side by the Atlantic Ocean and on the other by a strip of raised boardwalk, one side open to the beach, the other side filled with booths of spinning wheel games, nickel throws for glassware, fish pond games, basketball throws, and other games of chance and skill. There were pizza stands, ice cream stands, lemonade stands, miniature golf, kiddie rides, and adult rides such as roller coasters.

I expected much the same from Revere Beach, which the city proclaimed "the first public beach in America." I could get there by taking the Blue Line subway from Boston to its extreme end, the Wonderland stop. On the walls of the subway, the routes were marked by broad primary-color lines on a schematic map that distorted geography in the service of easy-to-understand stylization, with all the routes shown as lines bent at 45-degree angles.

When I got out there, though, I was disappointed to see—nothing. It was midweek and a bit early in the season for bathers, but that never kept the booths on the New Jersey boardwalks closed. But here there was no boardwalk. There were no booths with games of chance. No miniature golf. No kiddie rides. No roller coasters. There was a vast emptiness. I walked up and down the boulevard, past bare pavilions with benches for looking at the ocean, past a vacant bandstand, looking for something— anything—in the way of the usual beach diversions. There were none.

Much later, I read that the last of the Revere Beach attractions were destroyed by the awesome blizzard of 1978. But in reality, there really wasn't anything for the blizzard to destroy. Two years earlier, Revere Beach was virtually a ghost town. I apparently missed the last days of the Nautical, which had an indoor arcade of some sort, and miniature golf in the basement. The nightclub The Frolic was still active, but I wouldn't have counted that as a beach attraction. I was quite right about the lack of rides—the kiddie attractions and the Dodge 'Ems (which I would have called bumper cars) had folded up shop years earlier, along with the other rides. The Cyclone, the impressive wooden roller coaster built by the legendary Harry Traver's company in 1925, had lasted until 1969. It was partially destroyed by fire in 1971, and the last of it was torn down in 1974, two years before my visit.

Since then, I've tried to visualize Revere Beach as it must have been at various times in its heyday, though I had a hard time imagining where the attractions seen in pictures from the 1900s through 1970 could have existed. This is what started my "urban archaeology" interest in Revere Beach.

The name "Wonderland" seemed particularly unsuited to this wasteland. There was a Wonderland Ballroom and a Wonderland Greyhound Track, and I assumed that one or the other of these was responsible for the name. I was wrong, of course. "Wonderland" was, I found, the name of an amusement park built just off the beach. Reference works said that it lasted only from 1906 to 1911, but it gave its name to the area. (This turned out to be an error—Wonderland Park actually closed at the end of the 1910 season.) At over twenty-three acres, the park was the biggest in New England—bigger, in fact, than any of the Coney Island amusement parks that inspired it.

A great many postcards of Wonderland survive and are in library collections, as well as reproduced in books and on the internet. These images, often hand-colored, show what an exotic world Wonderland was, and still appears to be to modern eyes. But I didn't realize just how exotic it was until I started researching it. The most interesting details and stories aren't reflected in those gaudy postcards. Many images escaped being fossilized that way, and postcards can't tell you the story of the people who built the park. These stories are fascinating and dramatic. It's altogether amazing that this cadre of creative people could be drawn together from so many places in so short a time to produce this short-lived palace of wonders, and then disperse again. The park seemed to have almost kidnapped some of them, so radical was the change. Some flourished and thrived on the exposure, and went on to changed lives, while others were traumatized by the experience. But here it is, set out for the first time, the story of the Mystic City by the Sea, built in a marsh. The Wild West shows, the incubators full of premature babies, the balloon ascents, the swimmers and divers and daredevils, the wild animals, the circus and vaudeville acts, the sky rides and the Shoot the Chutes, the Descent into Hell, the Scenic Railroad, the (what we would today call) virtual reality rides, the roller coasters, the Fairy Tale Musical Extravaganzas, the Fire Fighting Spectacular, and the Scintillator. All brought back to life for you, in these pages, for one low price of admission.

℘

I must place a cautionary note here. Times have changed, and attitudes have radically altered in the past century. We are more open in our discussions of sex and relationships, which makes many of the contemporary records seem coy and evasive. We have been made more aware of our ethnocentricity and our attitudes toward people of different ancestry, and the casual racism and assumptions of cultural superiority exhibited in Massachusetts in the first decade of the twentieth century appear crude and offensive today. The terms "midget" and "Dwarf" were applied without concern for the individuals who exhibited themselves for a living. I have frequently quoted the words of newspapers and souvenir books without any attempt to censor them in order to be accurate. I mean no offense by these, and hope that my readers will understand the intent and accept the genuine record of posterity in preference to a watered down or censored record.

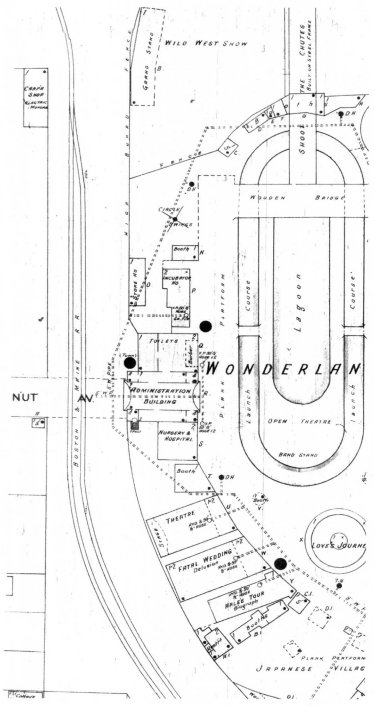

Figure 1. Wonderland map. Courtesy of Sanborn Library, LLC.

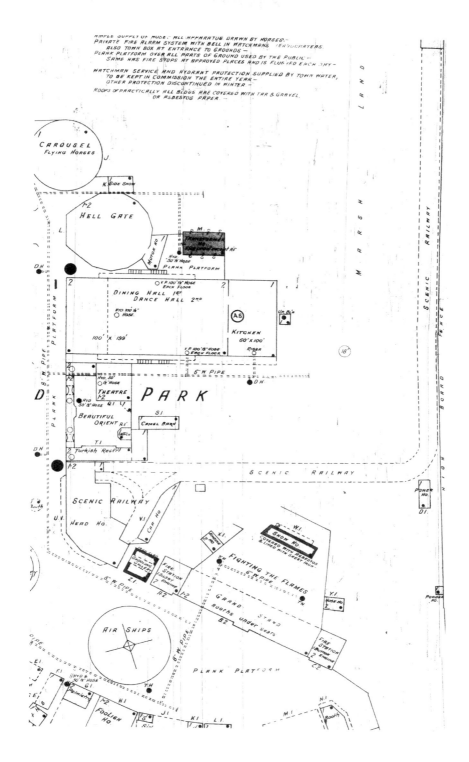

ACKNOWLEDGMENTS

I have to acknowledge the help of many people—local historians, amusement park historians, librarians, and enthusiasts. I will doubtless overlook someone. My apologies to all I missed. It was not deliberate.

First, I have to thank the Revere Society for Cultural and Historical Preservation and its many members. They showed great interest throughout this project and provided me with historical material, pictures, and postcards. They acted as an effective sounding board, discussing my latest discoveries with me and providing me with a stage where I could lecture about the park. In particular, I want to thank Dr. Toby Pearlstein, past president Mary Jane Terenzi, current president Robert Upton, and Tom Sullivan (whose huge collection of postcards and Revere Beach memorabilia helped flesh out my mental image of Old Revere).

Additional thanks to Brian McCarthy, president of Kelly's Roast Beef, who preserves much Revere Beach memorabilia and images (they decorate the walls of his restaurants) and who let me see his collection, and to amusement park historians James Abbate, Bob Kitchen, Fred Dahlinger, Mike Onorato, Stephen M. Silverman, and Jeffry Stanton.

I am grateful to librarians Janine Whitcomb (UMass Lowell), Donna Russo (Otis House/Historic New England), Lori Bessler (Wisconsin Historical Society), Julie Huffman-Klinkowitz (Cedar Falls Historical Society), Julie Tarmer (Nahant Historical Society), and others at the Saugus Public Library, Winthrop Public Library, Revere Public Library, Lynn Public Library, Boston Public Library, and Massachusetts State House library. Also thanks to the people at the Suffolk County Deeds Office, Chelsea City Hall, and Revere City Hall (especially Maggie Haney at the License

Office), and to authors Stephen M. Silverman (again), Clair Prentice, and Dawn Raffel.

A special thanks to Gail Chumbley, the granddaughter-in-law of Floyd C. Thompson, who shared family photographs and documents with me. This helped enormously in untangling the details of his life.

My thanks to Ron Morse and Carlton "Skip" Hoyt of the Lynn Photographic Society for scanning images and making them look professional.

Thanks to Brian Halley, Rachael DeShano, and Sally Nichols at the University of Massachusetts Press, and to Margaret A. Hogan, my copyeditor.

And, finally, my thanks to my wife, Jill Silvester, and my daughter, Carolyn, for putting up with me and my enforced absences during the research, writing, and editing of this book.

L O S T

WONDERLAND

CHAPTER 1
Opening Day and Background

It was the anticipated event of the summer of 1906. The newspapers had run advertisements promising the appeal and attraction of a new and huge amusement park near Crescent Beach in Revere, Massachusetts, for months. There were rides and attractions aplenty along Revere Beach, but there was nothing on the area known as the North Shore of Massachusetts to match this—an enclosed park filled with rides and attractions, all in one place. White City Park outside Worcester and Paragon Park in Hull had opened the previous year in the commonwealth, but Wonderland boasted more attractions, and it was much closer to downtown Boston.

On May 31, 1906, Memorial Day, the crowds gathered in anticipation at the main entrance on Walnut Avenue in Revere, facing south. The entrance building had four towers—two on the outside, two on the inside—each bearing a flagpole. There were two staffs at the front; one bore a U.S. flag, the other had the word "Wonderland" embroidered on it. Above the main entry was written WONDERLAND in white block letters, surmounted by an American shield with an eagle atop, wings spread majestically. It looked like the entrance to a castle, a resemblance heightened by the bridge that crossed the Boston & Maine (B&M) Railroad, as if it were the drawbridge over a castle moat, before you reached the gate.

The official opening was scheduled for noon, but the crowds had come earlier and were larger than anticipated. They could see not only the main entrance but also, to the left, a half-timbered building, like something out of Shakespeare, except that it had the non-Elizabethan words INFANT INCUBATORS in large white letters on its roof. To the right of the entrance, a metal framework tower protruded, as did four pink minaret towers in a row. The newspaper stories leading up to this day had given brief descriptions of the attractions within, but it wasn't clear which ones these fragmentary sights were associated with.

Seeing how large the crowd was, the management opened the gates early, and the people surged in. Inside, they found a boardwalk, freshly watered. Directly ahead was a huge artificial lagoon, its long east-west axis perpendicular to the entranceway, placed in the center of the boardwalk. To the left was a ramp sloping down from a tower, the launching point for the Shoot the Chutes ride that ended in the lagoon. Surrounding the lagoon on each side were canals that joined on the side opposite the ramp. In the canals were Venetian gondolas and a Mississippi River–style steamboat. Bridges allowed visitors to cross the canals, and another long bridge straddled the lagoon just at the end of the chute, so visitors could stand there and watch the boats plummet down the ramp into the lagoon and skip across it like a stone thrown into a pond. Lines strung across the lagoon from the towers of the Administration Building to towers on buildings on the other side were filled with gaily colored flags and pennants, flapping in the breeze. A series of concession booths was located underneath the tower of the Shoot the Chutes, and to one side was the Flying Horses carousel.

From all around came the shouts of the barkers, directed through large megaphones, touting the glories of each attraction: "Princess Fatima here, a full-blooded princess from the storied city of Nineveh, will dance the mystic anaconda dance, exactly as danced by Hypatia in Holy Write." "Don't miss the Fatal Wedding! Sixty laughs to the minute!" "Foolish House— cra-a-a-azy house—only a dime, ten cents, the tenth part of a dollar!" "The Foolish House, the Crazy House, the Daffy House, the Third Degree."[1]

On the other side of the lagoon was a large octagonal building with the ominous sign HELL GATE written on it in red letters. The top was crenelated like a fortress, and a broad set of stairs led up to the arched entrance. To the right of this was the ballroom and restaurant together in an elegant porticoed building. Beside that was an odd building with four minarets thrusting to the sky, each slightly different, but all of them colored with alternating pink and white horizontal bands. Between the two center minarets was a keystone-like detail, flanked by two blue "onion" domes. Lettering on the front read BEAUTIFUL ORIENT and ORIENTAL EXHIBITS and TURKISH THEATER and A CONGRESS OF STRANGE ORIENTAL PEOPLE. Written above the central portal was BAZAAR.

To the right of this was the LaMarcus A. Thompson Scenic Railway. The Thompson Scenic Railway was one of the most popular rides in America, and examples of it abounded around the country. There was, in fact, already a "Scenic Railway" nearby on Revere Beach, manufactured by a Johnny-come-lately competitor. But this one was a genuine LaMarcus A. Thompson Scenic Railway, and it promised a much longer track. The elevated, undulating surface could be seen progressing behind the Beautiful Orient, the ballroom and restaurant, and the Hell Gate off into the northwest corner of the park, where it entered another building, then returned.

Turning to the right from the main entrance, one passed a nursery for small children, a penny arcade, then the Children's Theater. Beyond that was a three-peaked building with the perplexing title THE FATAL WEDDING. Next to this was a building with a peaked top containing Hale's Tours. On the opposite side, between this and the railway was a round building housing Love's Journey.

Proceeding along, one reached the Japanese Village, complete with a sixty-foot-tall scale model of Mount Fuji, covered with "snow." Entrance to the village was through a traditional Japanese Shinto gate, a torii, which had ADMISSION FREE written across the crossbar in a very non-Japanese way. A steep-sided Moon Bridge—"The Royal Arch"—spanned the stream through the village.

Next was a building adorned with a huge human hand, the palmist's building, which also had an astrologer. This was followed by a building decorated with a huge relief carving of a ridiculous, bulbous-headed, goggle-eyed figure in a top hat. The souvenir program and the newspaper stories called this the "House of Momus" or the "House of Mirth" or, later, "The Third Degree," but the building actually originally bore the title "The Foolish House." It was the funhouse of Wonderland.

Opposite the Foolish House was that tall, pyramidal framework tower that could be seen from outside the park. It has a set of six arms that projected at an upward angle set equidistant around the perimeter near the top, from which cables descended, holding gondolas for passengers. After people got in, the top would rotate, sending the cars going in a circle that rose higher the faster it went. This was the Circle Swing.

Beyond the Foolish House was the tent housing Princess Trixie the Educated Horse, its entranceway in the shape of a horseshoe. Princess Trixie was famous in her day, and everyone know about this educated animal that could count and add and knew her letters. She had performed before the royal family in London, and now she was here at Revere Beach. Next to Princess Trixie's tent was a booth and photographer's studio, where you could have your visit memorialized.

Beyond was Ferari's Wild Animal Show in its own huge tent. Ferari's was famous from international exhibitions for its collection of wild cats and hybrids. Past Ferari's was another park entrance, which came in directly from Revere Beach along Beaver Street and over the B&M tracks on its own bridge. A ticket booth lay between Ferari's and the entrance.

Opposite that entrance was one of Wonderland's biggest and most extravagant attractions, Fighting the Flames. From the boardwalk, you could see an exterior filled with game and concession booths that gave little of the interior away, but beyond that facade was a reconstructed city block and a grandstand to hold an audience of two thousand to watch the show. Nevertheless, the show was swamped on opening day, unable to accommodate everyone who wished to see it.

Between the Fighting the Flames grandstand and the Thompson Scenic Railway was a shooting gallery. Between the scenic railway and the lagoon was the Arcus Ring, a circus-style ring home to spectacular free performances throughout the day. Across the park, barkers extolled the glories of the attractions within in stentorian voices.

In the southeast corner were the Indian Congress and Wild West show and the vertical tower of the Whirl the Whirl ride. Throughout the day there were parades featuring a marching band, which also played in a band pavilion near the lagoon.[2]

At night, the park was illuminated by over 150,000 electric lights that edged the major buildings and both the main gate and the Beaver Street beach entrances.[3] The bridges were lit up, and bright lights illuminated the minarets of the Beautiful Orient and the U.S. shield on the main gate, while searchlights pierced the sky and drew attention to the park.

Over 100,000 people attended that first day and were ready to return again to explore parts they had not had the opportunity to see, and to revisit their favorite parts.[4] Over the course of the summer, over 2 million people visited the park. Wonderland was off to a promising start.

☙

Revere Beach is a relatively placid stretch of sandy beach next to Broad Sound, within a couple of miles of Boston. Embraced by the peninsulas of Winthrop and Nahant, Broad Sound has little surf unless storms are present. The combination of shallow water and relative stillness were a great draw when urban workers began retreating to the beaches in hot summers, both for the ocean breezes and for the opportunity for a quick dip in the water. The ease of access provided by the railroads and ferries combined to make this site a natural one for recreation and one where modern beach culture was born. It calls itself America's First Public Beach.

Like many beaches along the Atlantic Coast, Revere Beach is located on a barrier island with an inland waterway behind it. In the case of Revere Beach, however, the area behind is not open water but a salty wetland called Rumney Marsh. A glacial drumlin extends out to Roughans Point, just below Crescent Beach, and at one time terminated in Cherry Orchard Island, named after the fruit trees that grew there in colonial days. The island disappeared gradually throughout the nineteenth century and now only a shallow sandbar remains. Two piers were built on this bar at different times in the past, and today it supports a jetty. Sand swept away from the island was redeposited northward along the beach, all the way up to the rhombohedral spit of Point of Pines at the northern end, at the mouth of the Saugus River. There, as the name implies, a pine forest once existed, anchoring the sand. Revere Beach is thus bracketed by geographical features named after the predominant plant life. Nearby is another—a short distance south of Point of Pines is the region called Oak Island, a name that seems odd, as there is no break in the gently curving beach and no sign of any island in Broad Sound. But the island was in the other direction—inward into the marsh, where it distinguished itself as a solid patch of ground with its own ecology and species, until creeping urbanism led to landfill solidifying the surrounding marshland.[5] Now Oak Island exists only as a street name. All three of these plant spots served, at one time or another, as retreats and amusement areas. It is only because of changing styles, some minor disasters, and quirks in human history that none of them today sports an amusement park.

The area, along with much of the surrounding land, was occupied in precolonial days by the Rumney Marsh Pawtucket Indians, who hunted and fished here. When the English began to colonize, present-day Revere

Beach was largely unoccupied. Cut off by rivers and the marshes, it was difficult to access except by sea. The nearby Saugus River held the first long-term ironworks in the Americas, but it didn't turn a sufficient profit and closed after about a quarter of a century, only operating from 1646 to about 1670. Despite its proximity to the city of Boston, the area, lacking easy access to the city, was given over to farming and harvesting of salt-grass. It constituted the northern part of the community of Winnisemmet, later called Chelsea. In the nineteenth century, the peninsula of Pullyn Point separated from North Chelsea to become the town of Winthrop, and the Rumney Marsh area of North Chelsea declared itself a distinct town as well.

While today widely recognized, Paul Revere, the silversmith and patriot, was neither highly regarded nor particularly well known outside his political and business circles in the decades after his death. His resurrection to a place among the patriots of the American Revolution began with Henry Wadsworth Longfellow's 1861 poem "Paul Revere's Ride," which later formed a section of Longfellow's larger *Tales of a Wayside Inn*. Longfellow saw this work as part of his cycle of American legends, and he knew of the historical inaccuracies in the poem, which he nonetheless hoped would foster patriotic sentiments at the start of the Civil War. Ten years after the poem's publication, Rumney Marsh adopted Revere as the name for the new town, even though Paul Revere had neither set foot in it nor had anything to do with it.

The end of the nineteenth century saw much improved access to the area, both from the mainland and by sea. A large pier extending out from near where Cherry Island had existed was erected in 1881. It was 1,700 feet long and originally named the Broad Sound Pier. It came to be called the Great Ocean Pier and was intended as a resort with its own restaurant and attractions, as well as to provide an easy way to Revere. It lasted until 1893, when it was dismantled.

Around the same time, a complex series of railways and trolleys began to snake up from Boston through the North Shore, changing hands and ownerships in a dizzying array. The first line was laid out by the Boston, Revere Beach, and Lynn Railroad in 1875. It connected in Chelsea to a ferry that came across from Boston, and it opened the beach area for the first time to easy access from Boston. Because of the three-foot spacing between tracks, the line became better known throughout its life as the "Narrow Gauge." Another railroad, the Eastern Junction, Broad Sound Pier, and Point Shirley Railroad, opened in 1882; it was run by the Boston, Winthrop and Shore Railroad in 1884 and 1885, at which point operation of the line by that company ceased. The tracks and right of way were purchased by the B&M Railroad to extend the Chelsea line southward. Another track that separated from that line and curved eastward toward the shore, running between the B&M and the Narrow Gauge was acquired from the Boston Winthrop and Shore by the Chelsea Beach Railroad, who ran it until 1897. It was acquired by the B&M, who used it mainly to store unused rolling stock. The effect of this curl of track was to isolate a section of Revere from direct access and development.[6]

The trains opened the area to people and commerce. The Point of Pines became the resort of choice, at the end of the Narrow Gauge (until a bridge was built across the Saugus River taking the line into Lynn). A huge hotel and restaurant went up there, catering to city dwellers as a getaway, catching the sea breezes, and offering a respite from city life. A few amusements and attractions went in as well, eventually extending down as far south as Oak Island. But Revere Beach developed a reputation for rowdiness, and both sides of the Narrow Gauge's track along the spine of the barrier island were lined with cheap shanties.

That all changed in 1896, when Charles Eliot, one of the proteges of famed park designer Frederick Law Olmsted, proposed making Revere Beach into a park. The city of Revere agreed to his plans, and as a result the Narrow Gauge was moved downhill and away from the highest point. Its place was taken by a broad boulevard with pavilions where people could sit and look out onto the beach. The shanties and houses along the beach were pulled down to provide an unbroken vista of Broad Sound. A traffic circle near where the Great Ocean Pier had been was named Eliot Circle.

The great hope was probably that this new park would provide a getaway for people of even modest means, where they could escape the hustle and bustle and heat of the city and perambulate in the serenity and tranquility of the beach, lulled by the rhythm of the small breaking waves. The fear was that Revere Beach rowdyism, drunkenness, and gambling would come to the fore and spoil this paradise. The reality was somewhere between these extremes. Eliot's parkland did not long remain a park.

Although nothing could be built on the beach side of the boulevard, things could be built on the other side. In spite of the steep falloff to the west of the boulevard, buildings were constructed with upper stories level with the boulevard containing restaurants and attractions to tempt the wanderer in. Revere Beach began to acquire its honky-tonk atmosphere by the first years of the twentieth century.

❧

Arguably, the amusement park craze all started with an enthusiastic, self-promoting Renaissance man named Paul Boyton. There are others who could stake a claim to the idea and practice of the modern amusement park, but Boyton has a better title than most. He was born on June 29, 1848, in the town of Rathangan in County Kildaire, Ireland, but his parents soon moved to western Pennsylvania. He supposedly joined the Union Navy during the Civil War at the age of fifteen and later served with the Mexican Navy under Benito Juarez and the French Navy during the Franco-Prussian War. He was a barge pilot, a diver in the Caribbean, and later commander of the Peruvian Torpedo Service. Captured by the Chileans during this phase of his life, he escaped from a promised execution and made his way back north. He helped to organize the U.S. Live-Saving Service. He was director of a life-saving service for the Atlantic Railroad Company in Atlantic City, New Jersey. In his two summers there he rescued seventy-one distressed swimmers. It was there that he met Clark S. Merriman, and the encounter changed both their lives.[7]

Merriman was an inventor from Iowa who had been working on a water-proof survival suit made of rubber to save the lives of steamship passengers washed overboard. He held two patents for his invention. He needed an experienced swimmer to test his suit and to demonstrate its effectiveness. Life-Saver Boyton seemed like the ideal choice.

Boyton didn't simply don the suit and show it off in Atlantic City—he stowed away on the steamship *Queen*, bound for England. When the ship was two days out from Liverpool, thirty miles off the Irish Coast, he ostentatiously donned the suit and dropped over the side. Surviving a storm, he came ashore at Trefaska Bight, near Skibbereen, and received a hero's triumphal welcome. Boyton was abruptly famous and spent the next five years demonstrating the suit by riding it down the rivers of Europe.

He received a gold chronometer from Queen Victoria and made lucrative appearances on the London stage. Then he used the suit to swim the English Channel in twenty-three hours, the second person to successfully do so. He smoked six cigars along the way—something no other channel swimmer could boast of.

He performed in Italy, in Spain, and at the Paris Exposition of 1878, where he demonstrated the capabilities of the suit and its associated gadgets by firing signal flares, releasing pigeons, catching a fish, cooking a meal, and sinking a model ship. It was undoubtedly because of this show that Jules Verne incorporated the suit into his novel released the next year, *Les Tribulations d'un Chinois en Chine* (Tribulations of a Chinaman in China). The Chinese hero of that novel falls overboard, fortunately while wearing a Merriman suit, and is able to survive for several days, catching and cooking his own meals at sea and drinking his supply of fresh water.

Boyton had a direct connection with the town of Revere: he demonstrated the Merriman Survival Suit off of the Great Ocean Pier in August 1889. He cooked, ate, demonstrated sleeping, rescued another person in the water, demonstrated a marine bicycle, and briefly "walked" on the water.[8] But Boyton's attention was attracted by another water-based activity— Shooting the Chutes. As before, Boyton did not invent the activity, but he did take the idea and run with it, with surprising results.

Shoot the Chutes or Shooting the Chutes developed from a dangerous, thrill-seeking sport indulged in by the Lachine Indians of present-day Ontario. They would make runs on the Lachine Rapids of the St. Lawrence River between the island of Montreal and the river's south shore. The rapids are characterized by large standing waves, and running the rapids is popular to this day. Running them in a birch bark canoe must have been harrowing. Early settlers called it "Shooting the Chutes," a term already used for toboggan runs in the winter.[9]

In the late nineteenth century, people began building artificial Shoot the Chutes using wooden ramps going down an existing hill from a body of water at the top to another on the bottom. Such a ride could be designed and become essentially automatic, with no need to guide the craft used. One such contraption was built at Ottawa, going from the top of the falls downward. In 1884, J. P. Newburgh of Rock Island, Illinois, built a somewhat different Shoot the Chutes on the side of a hill at Watchtower Park, in which a flat-bottomed boat rode down a five-hundred-foot-long greased wooden ramp into the Rock River, across the surface of which the boat would skip like a flat rock thrown side-hand against the surface of a pond. Here was something new and very different from shooting the rapids—the ride didn't even slide down a water chute.[10]

The idea spread to Europe, where Boyton encountered it, saw its possibilities, and acquired the rights to build them. He put one up in Antwerp for the 1894 World's Fair and another at Earl's Court in the United Kingdom for the May 1894 World Water Fair. By this time, he was using water instead of grease to ease the boats down the ramp and using a drive system to bring the boat to the top of the ramp. With a tower constructed at one end, the structure could be put anywhere, requiring no hill or water source at the top—all could be done with engines driving the chain and pumping the water.

On July 4, 1894, Boyton opened a Shoot the Chutes in Chicago, cannily putting it close to the grounds of the recent World's Fair there. A boat holding eight people was lifted to the top of a tower and sent down a chute three hundred feet long, into an artificial lake another three hundred feet long, achieving a speed of forty miles an hour and sending it skimming across the water. The design of the boat kept most of the spray outside. His passengers got the thrill of feeling the drop, acceleration to high speed, expectation of a crash, and expectation of getting wet, yet arrived safely without injury and only minor dampening. It was immensely popular.[11]

Boyton had seen the future, and he knew how to exploit it. The Shoot the Chutes ride was only part of it, however, although a big part. Boyton had seen how P. T. Barnum's circus worked in 1887, with a single admission gate and a single price for admission to an enclosed and defined area. Before that time, amusement parks (such as Connecticut's Lake Compounce) had opened with many attractions gathered together, each charging its own admission. Boyton's amusement park would be more like a circus, a set of attractions in an enclosed and defined space with a single admission fee.

He chose the up-and-coming area of Coney Island, a one-time island now connected via landfill to the city of Brooklyn, and whose beaches had become a recreational attraction to the inhabitants of Brooklyn and New York City. The area he chose was near the Elephant Hotel, a landmark in the shape of a huge elephant, on grounds previously used by Pain's

Spectacular Fireworks shows (which had put on such involved shows as "The Last Days of Pompeii"). His Shoot the Chutes ride was the centerpiece. The park also held an Old Mill ride (a "dark ride" similar to what is often called a Tunnel of Love), cages of wild wolves, a ballroom, and food outlets. For a time, the park had another innovative ride—the Flip-Flap Railway. It was a sort of roller coaster in which the track made a complete vertical loop. It was a bit ahead of its time, though; the ride was judged too dangerous and soon closed.

The park also featured Boyton's aquatic show, which had forty sea lions. Because of this, the park was dubbed Sea Lion Park. It opened on the Fourth of July—Boyton clearly saw the value and significance of the date—in 1895. Unfortunately, the weather was terrible. It rained steadily, and Boyton's opening day was not a success. But as the summer progressed, attendance rose. He kept adding new attractions to keep the park fresh. He started sending animals and other things down the chutes, including himself, riding a bicycle. He brought in swimmers and divers, and employed a band to give the park continual music. He added a river ride, which he also patented, and other attractions.

The success of Boyton's Sea Lion Park encouraged others to try similar ventures, starting with George Tilyou's Steeplechase Park in 1897, located virtually next door to Boyton's park. Tilyou's park was more successful than Boyton's. Tilyou resisted the temptation to hire "name" talent and kept the rides he created in operation for as long as required until they paid off.

Frederic Thompson was born in Irontown, Ohio, in 1872. He visited the 1893 Chicago Exposition and got a job as a janitor at one of the machinery exhibits. He was entranced by the fair and wanted to make this kind of thing his life's work. He went to the Omaha Trans-Centennial Exposition in 1898 and set up a cyclorama depicting a journey to Heaven and Hell, though the title was changed to Darkness and Dawn to mollify the religious communities. But he discovered that someone else had set up a similar attraction called the Mystic Garden. The proprietor, Elmer Scipio Dundy, who understandably went by the nickname "Skip," was the son of a federal judge, born in Nebraska in 1862. Besides their own exhibits, both men worked with Henry Roltair, a magician and ride designer who would become one of the best-known and most inspirational of all designers.[12]

Thompson did design work for Roltair and Dundy arranged financing, although the two men otherwise had nothing to do with each other.

For the 1901 Buffalo Exposition, Thompson decided to try something that had occurred to him while he was taking classes between fairs. Thinking of how patrons could cross over the so-called Chasm of Fire in his Darkness and Dawn, he had the idea of using a flying machine. But the flying machine could be an exhibit all by itself, with the appropriate destination. Thompson parlayed this into A Trip to the Moon, using a Jules Verne-esque flying machine.

Dundy was at the fair too, planning to put up his journey to the underworld, now refabricated to closely resemble Thompson's Darkness and Dawn. Thompson was furious, but Dundy pointed out that he had failed to copyright the show. Thompson tried to outmaneuver Dundy, but Dundy was able to slip out of Thompson's machinations. Thompson became convinced that it would be better to have Dundy's business and legal sense on his side and offered him a partnership in A Trip to the Moon if Dundy would drop the Darkness and Dawn show to join him. Dundy agreed, and the two continued in business together until Dundy's death.

A Trip to the Moon was a hit at the 1901 exposition, and the two men wanted to continue the show after the exposition closed. Dundy went to St. Louis to secure space for them at the upcoming 1904 exposition. But Thompson went to Coney Island and spoke with George Tilyou about putting the ride up at his Steeplechase Park for a semi-permanent home, rather than relying on the ephemeral expositions. Tilyou offered them space in exchange for 40 percent of the profits for the 1902 season.

It was an innovation—the amusement park adding to its repertoire an item first made and tested at the World's Fair midway. This was to become as recurring pattern in the years to come.

Although the ticket price for A Trip to the Moon (not included in the general admission to Steeplechase Park) was higher than usual, the ride's originality and novelty carried it through, and it was immensely popular, making a name for Thompson and Dundy in New York.[13]

Meanwhile, Paul Boyton's Sea Lion Park was failing economically. Dundy lined up investors, and he and Thompson signed an agreement with Boyton to take over the park in October 1902. Thompson drew up plans for the changes they would make, then made a trip to Europe to line up new attractions.

After the 1902 season concluded, they ended up tearing down most of Sea Lion Park but keeping the Shoot the Chutes and its lagoon as the central attraction. They built a midway that echoed the Chicago White City and the Buffalo Exposition, installed their Trip to the Moon, and called the whole thing Luna Park. Ostensibly it was named after Dundy's sister, but surely the real reason was to honor the Trip to the Moon ride.

Dundy and Thompson's park, with its novelties and original attractions, offered competition for Tilyou's Steeplechase Park just as Tilyou had offered competition to Boyton. And new competition for Thompson and Dundy wasn't long in coming.

William H. Reynolds, a former Republican New York state senator and Brooklyn developer, could see the writing on the wall regarding popular amusement at Coney Island. He bought up a large parcel near both Steeplechase Park and the new Luna Park in July 1903 and laid out his own amusement park, deliberately intending to one-up Luna Park with similar attractions, only larger and more impressive. He started the Wonderland Corporation to assemble his own amusement park, to be called Wonderland, but he soon changed his mind about the name. By the time it opened, it had been rechristened Dreamland.

Dreamland's biggest problem was that its cost was far greater than the other two parks. Reynolds's plan was to so far outclass and overpower Luna Park that it would go bankrupt in defeat, leaving Dreamland the sole victor. It opened on May 14, 1904. The stakes were high, and it was unlikely that all three parks could be financially successful at the same time—there were only so many entertainment dollars to go around. But the public was the overall benefactor in this War of the Amusement Parks, as they fought for patrons by cutting prices and offering more entertainment than their competitors.

It was this competition that made Coney Island a byword for popular entertainment, and which encouraged other cities around the country to set up their own amusement parks in response, or to revamp existing recreational outlets to more closely resemble the Coney Island parks. Over the next couple of years, a plethora of Luna Parks and Wonderlands and Coney Island and White Cities (named after a Chicago park, whose name was, in turn, inspired by the 1893 exposition) emerged. There were a half-dozen Wonderlands alone set up in various parts of the country, using the original name for Dreamland. One of these was at Revere Beach, north of Boston.

CHAPTER 2
The Boulanger of Wonderland

The early amusement parks built along the lines of those at Coney Island were something new in the world. Very few people had any experience in building such parks. Most of them were designed and organized by complete amateurs. Astonishingly, many of these executives responsible for the parks, even as little as two or three years before, were not involved in anything like this new business, had not considered getting involved in it, and were often pursuing wholly unrelated lines of business.

This applied to the management of Wonderland in Revere as much as to any of the others and began with the man who started the entire process going, and who ultimately had the greatest responsibilities in its operation over its lifetime, John Joseph Higgins. Three years before Wonderland began, he had no apparent interest in amusement parks or in Boston. He was happily ensconced in Savannah, Georgia, as the treasurer of a company making baking powder. That seems like a quiet business, but Higgins was in the midst of a war—the Great Baking Powder War.[1]

A mixture of sodium bicarbonate and an acidic powder, baking powder became a popular product at the end of the nineteenth century. It was used as an artificial leavening that took the place of yeast in the making of quick breads. There were two basic types of baking powder—those based on tartrate and those using salts of alum or phosphate.

One company in the United States, Royal Baking Powder, which had a virtual monopoly on tartrate baking powder, reorganized in New Jersey in 1900 as a trust and began seeking to monopolize the entire market. They started spreading the word that tartrate baking powders were "natural" and produced only from natural ingredients, while their competitors used "phosphate" or "alum" ingredients, which they declared unhealthy chemicals. The obvious thing to do was for the alum and phosphate manufacturers to counterclaim that they were as healthy as tartaric powder. Or better, that cream of tartar baking powder itself was toxic. This they did, but they were at a disadvantage—they were many and small, while Royal was one large company with a big advertising budget.

Enter John Joseph Higgins.[2] He was born in Savannah in 1868 of Irish Catholic stock to John and Sabina Norton Higgins.[3] He served as the secretary and treasurer of the Morehouse Manufacturing Company in the 1890s. The company was incorporated on July 19, 1895, for the purpose of manufacturing and selling "baking powder, self-raising flour, and buckwheat." They manufactured three different brands of baking powder—the curiously named Battle-Axe and Railroad brands, and the more logically named Success. All of these were alum-based.[4]

In order to combat Royal's attempted baking powder coup, the phosphate and alum companies banded together to form the American Baking Powder Association in 1899 with headquarters in New York City. They met for the first time on October 26, 1899, and elected as their permanent chairman none other than J. J. Higgins. Three days later, at the first executive committee meeting, he was named president.

Figure 2. John Joseph Higgins, onetime secretary and treasurer of a baking powder company, as he appeared the year his creation, Wonderland, opened. *Wonderland Souvenir Magazine 1906*, [14]. Courtesy of the Wisconsin Historical Society Library, Madison.

Why, exactly, is not clear. Higgins, after all, wasn't even president of his own company. When the association started bringing actions against Royal and testifying at government hearings regarding baking powder, Higgins's voice was not a significant one, and he does not appear to have been a driving force. Morehouse or one of the other manufacturers usually testified on the details of manufacture. When Higgins was called to testify, it was to state simply that the American Baking Powder Association was a protective trade organization intended to make the case for non-tartar baking powder and support certain legislation. He argued no legal cases and made no bold statements. He appears to have been reciting boilerplate that he had no hand in preparing. There was no passion for baking powder in his speech. He acted like a figurehead put there to state the obvious and gave the impression that he was doing this only because it was his job.

Whatever else it did, it got Higgins out of Savannah and staying in New York for the meetings of the association and in Washington to testify before Congress.[5] Perhaps he traveled to Boston as well. His brother certainly lived there later on. Or he might have met people from Boston along the way. What we do know, by his own admission, is that Higgins left Savannah sometime in 1903 for the city of Chelsea, north of Boston. And he left his position as secretary and treasurer of the Morehouse Company to join the real estate firm of John A. McCann and Company, a business completely unrelated to his work and life before this time.

It could have been for love, as cliched as that sounds. On the evening of November 28, 1906, Higgins married Helena Frances Welch of East Somerville, Massachusetts, in the home of her parents, Thomas J. and Ellen Welch. Helena's sister, Grace, was bridesmaid, and J. B. Maddock of Savannah was the best man. Reverend Edward F. Saunders of St. Ann's Church in the Winter Hill district of Somerville officiated. The report rather confusedly called J. J. Higgins "manager of a large business enterprise at one of the beaches," only it said the beach was in Savannah. In any event, it is certainly possible that Higgins met Welch during one of his business trips for the Baking Powder Association and moved to the Boston area to be closer to her, and once his fortune seemed established through his new business venture, to marry her.[6]

In 1905, Higgins made some land deals that were to profoundly change Higgins's already uprooted life. On May 2, 1905, Higgins obtained 27.2

acres from Daniel Poole and George S. Lee Jr., consisting of land between the two branches of the Boston & Maine Railroad in Revere. The land between these tracks had been tentatively laid out as Hanover, Otis, Beaver, and Bath Streets, all running parallel to Brewster Avenue, which was not between the tracks. Lee and Poole had apparently obtained the land from the railroad on July 8, 1903.

It was property that had been cut away from the rest of Revere, isolated by the tracks of the B&M, both the active northern line and the inactive branch that curved away to the east. That track sat mostly idle, but it continued to cut that piece of property off from the rest of the city. City maps showed it subdivided into lots, with a regular system of named roads providing access, but it was all just potential real estate. No roads existed, and none would until and unless the railroad tracks were taken out or bridged over.

Who first saw the potential isn't recorded but it was probably Higgins himself. Here were almost twenty-five connected acres of land only a couple of blocks from Revere Beach, which was rapidly filling up with rides, attractions, and commercial concerns. No one else had such a large block of unused land this close to the beach and within easy walking distance of stations on the Narrow Gauge. And now amusement parks in imitation of those in Coney Island and White City in Chicago had become all the rage. No one else could pull together so much land so easily accessible to Boston in which to erect a park. Paragon Park down in Hull was smaller and not as easy to reach. An amusement park in Revere couldn't help but be a financial success—the smaller enterprises along the beach proved that. The tiny resort at Bass Point in Nahant regularly drew in crowds, and it was much harder to get to. All it would take would be another radical change in career, another leap in the dark, and J. J. Higgins could be the next George Tilyou. And perhaps that itself was the reason—to distinguish himself. No longer would he be the figurehead and mouthpiece of the American Baking Powder Association or just another real estate speculator in the McCann firm, but a character in his own right.

The Harvard Class of 1886 at their twentieth reunion in 1906 (the year Wonderland opened) conferred a series of honorary degrees. One of these went to John Joseph Higgins, but not our John Joseph Higgins. This one was a poor boy born in Boston. In true Horatio Alger fashion he got into

Phillips Exeter Academy and then went to Harvard Law School, from which he graduated in 1890 with a Bachelor of Laws degree. The class of 1886 must have noticed the identity of names, however, because they granted a joke "Honorary Degree" to the Harvard graduate that is altogether fitting for the Wonderland Higgins, in both Latin and English:

JOANNEM JOSEPHUM HIGGINS:
Boulangerum Terræ Mirabilis, Equitem, Insulæ Misericordiæ Hominem Insanum Amentemque, Athletam, Advocatum, Anchoram, Ad Gradum
Joannis Digitis Versis
Admisimus

Upon JOHN JOSEPH HIGGINS:
The Boulanger of Wonderland, the Man on Horseback, the Maniac of Misery Island,
Athlete, Advocate, Anchor, we confer the degree
B. U. J.
(Buck-up-Johnny)[7]

As the onetime president of the American Baking Powder Association, in charge of the agent used in making quick breads, Higgins was arguably a "Boulanger," a baker of fine breads. By 1906, he was an officer and founder of Wonderland. If there is any doubt that the class of 1886 had Wonderland and its Higgins in mind when they composed this statement, it is worth noting that they paid a visit to Wonderland Park the night they bestowed this honor.

એ

Higgins needed help. He needed a board of directors for the park, with some known and respected names to help raise funds. He needed investors. He needed someone who knew about amusement parks, and he needed people with a variety of skills. There was his personal network of contacts to help him with this, and there was his real estate firm to give guidance.

The first one he found was probably Floyd C. Thompson. As Thompson had done before, and would again, he sought out a conspicuous and fashionable address. The original Wonderland headquarters in the Pemberton Building, a new upscale building on Beacon Hill, was moved to the more impressive and prestigious Boston Stock Exchange Building at

53 State Street, in the heart of the financial district and across from Boston's Old State House.[8] Again, Thompson sought out an impressive and well-connected person to act as the president of the company. With someone well-known and a respectable businessman, they could draw in more investors to their company.

Thompson's strength was that he knew how to start up a company, having started at least eight by this time, and to interest people with money to invest. He also knew the world of the entertainment industry and how to get attractions, rides, and acts. He had been involved in the Coney Island parks—exactly how, he was reluctant to say. He claimed at one point to have been the president of Coney Island's Steeplechase Park, but surely that was George Tilyou.[9] In any event, he knew his business. As he told the Wonderland board, he knew how to build an amusement park. What he lacked was capital. How Higgins and he met is not recorded, but it was a fortuitous alliance.

Their choice for president of the company was Harold Parker. A member of the Massachusetts Highway Department (and soon to be its chairman), he was also a member of the Massachusetts Forestry Commission and of the Wachusett Mountain Reservation Commission. He had been

Figure 3. Floyd Chaddock Thompson, the secretive builder of Wonderland. *Wonderland Souvenir Magazine 1906*, [12]. Courtesy of the Wisconsin Historical Society Library, Madison.

a member of the Massachusetts state legislature and held a number of offices, was director of the Lancaster Street Railroad in his hometown of Lancaster, Massachusetts, and his brother was the former attorney general for the state.[10]

Born June 17, 1854, Parker grew up in Lancaster, attended Phillips Exeter Academy, and then went to Harvard. He became an engineer, at first for the Pennsylvania Steel Company and then for the Pennsylvania Railroad. He returned home to Lancaster and cofounded the civil engineering firm of Parker & Bateman. With his father, George A. Parker, who was also an engineer, he built the Charlottesville & Rapidan Railroad in Virginia and the Zanesville & Ohio River Railroad in Ohio. At the age of fifty-one, Harold Parker was well-known, well-liked, and well-connected.

As managing director and chairman of the board, Higgins and Thompson chose Major Thomas Danellan Barroll, a dapper, balding man with a trim moustache. The official souvenir booklet of Wonderland issued in 1906 says of him,

> [He] is one of the most conspicuous figures in the group of active, energetic and serious-minded young men associated with this gigantic amusement undertaking. . . . Major Barroll is undoubtedly one of the best known and most popular personalities in Boston clubdom and Boston society, having the entrée to the most exclusive circles of both. Besides being a member of the Governor's staff with the rank of Major, he is a member of the Boston Athletic Club and other equally prominent social organizations in Boston. Before coming to Boston, he held office under the Baltimore and Ohio Railroad Company in Baltimore, severing his connection therewith to take the position of private secretary to Mr. Nathaniel Thayer. . . . He joined the First Corps of Cadets in 1885 and held the rank of sergeant, when, ten years later, he was transferred to the Eighth Regiment as inspector of rifle practice. Major Barroll was at the front during the Spanish-American War as adjutant in the Eighth Mass. U.S. Volunteers, serving at Chickamauga, Lexington, Americus and Matanzas, Cuba. The regiment was mustered out April 28 1899, and then for five years Major Barroll ranched in Colorado.[11]

This gives a somewhat misleading image of Major Barroll. (The Cadet Corps of which Barroll was an officer, was gradually reorganized as the National Guard, a process that started with the Militia Act of 1903.) He was born in Baltimore on October 21, 1862, which made him forty-three years old in 1905, somewhat stretching the definition of "young."[12] He was indeed an adjutant in the Eighth Massachusetts Volunteers, but he arrived in Havana after hostilities had ceased. His sister, Cornelia Street Barroll, had married Nathaniel Thayer III on February 1, 1881, so the two were brothers-in-law, and Thayer did not exactly call Barroll in from obscurity to be his secretary.[13] Thayer was one of the wealthiest men in Massachusetts, so this was a fortuitous match for Thomas.

Barroll had no connections with the Baltimore & Ohio Railroad (B&O)—that seems to be an error on the part of the Wonderland Park publicist, who evidently noted Barroll's railroad connections and figured that someone from Baltimore must be with the B&O.[14] In fact, Barroll was associated with the less famous Eastern Kentucky Railroad. He was one of its directors from the 1880s until the end of the 1890s.[15] The president of the company and its founder was Nathaniel Thayer II.

It wasn't only Barroll's prominent appearance in the Boston clubs and social scene that enabled him to interest other investors—they knew him personally through business and family connections. Eugene Van Rensselaer Thayer, for instance, was another director of the Eastern Kentucky Railway and president of the Osceola Mining Company in Minnesota, a subsidiary of the Calumet and Thecla, the largest copper mine in the Lake Superior region.[16] A graduate of Harvard's class of 1904, the young Eugene V. R. Thayer also grew up in Lancaster. He would become the youngest bank president in Boston in 1912, when he was elected to lead Chase National Bank.[17]

Another of Wonderland's directors was Rodolphe L. Agassiz. He was vice president of the Calumet and Thecla Mining Company in 1904, treasurer in 1906, and would go on to be its president.[18] Agassiz was also president of the Ahmeek Mining Company, the Allouez Mining Company, the Centennial Copper Mining Company, the Cliff Mining Company, the Isle Royale Copper Company, the LaSalle Copper Company, the Lake Superior Smelting Company, the Superior Copper Company, and the White Pine Copper Company.

Many of the Wonderland directors were on the boards of railroads or mining companies, which used those railroads to transport their ore.[19] One could fairly say that Wonderland was built on Lake Superior copper and Eastern Kentucky coal.

In addition to his multiple presidencies, Agassiz was an avid sportsman. He was one of the cofounders of the Myopia Polo Club in Hamilton,

Massachusetts, and one of its legendary players, still with one of the high-est ratings ever achieved.

Other directors included John T. Burnett, secretary of the Boston Ele-vated Railway; Benjamin Peirce Cheney, whose father founded what would become American Express (and the ancestor of future vice president Dick Cheney); and Quincey A. Shaw Jr., secretary of the Calumet and Thecla.

Another member of Wonderland's board, Horace S. Meese, was born to be a journalist. His father, Captain Jacob W. Meese of the 45th Penn-sylvania Infantry Company in the Civil War, took up publishing after the war. For fifteen years he was the manager of the Pennsylvania State Print-ing Office in Harrisburg, then established the Irving Press in Brooklyn, New York. He was the first business manager of the St. Paul Press. Horace attended the Harrisburg public schools, graduating in 1890. By 1904, he was listed as a clerk in New York City and within a couple of years was working for Frank A. Munsey's legendary pulp *Munsey's Magazine,* work-ing his way up to a position as Munsey's secretary.[20] Late in 1904, however, he seems to have gone into advertising. Meese also diversified into enter-tainments and theatricals as a director and manager in New York. He was working at this when he was solicited for a position as secretary of the Wonderland Company, probably by Floyd Thompson.

Perhaps the most poignant personal story is that of James Walker Jr., the assistant treasurer under Higgins. A native Bostonian, he attended the Harvard School in Charlestown and English High School in Boston.[21] He got a position on the Atchison, Topeka & Santa Fe Railroad, where he remained for eighteen years as a transfer agent, living in Somerville.

As with others of the Wonderland crew, he had joined the cadets. While there, he became deeply interested in performing onstage and did so in Cadet productions. In fact, one of his fellow cadets was Benjamin Peirce Cheney. The two of them appeared together in productions written by the cadets themselves from 1891 to 1893. Walker was performing at least through 1895.[22]

Walker's interest in the theater may have also led to a marital connec-tion with the Ring family of Roxbury, Massachusetts, who had long been performers. Grandfather James H. Ring had been with the theater known as the Boston Museum, along with his grandchildren Cyril and Frances. Young Blanche Ring, another grandchild, was a performer too, so her match with Walker seemed ideal. They were married on June 3, 1896.[23] Following a dream he had long had, Walker resigned his post at the Atchison, Topeka & Santa Fe to become a theatrical agent. He failed at this, however, and returned to his accustomed specialty, railroad accounting.[24]

Blanche Ring, however, did not want to give up on theater. After two years of apparently happy matrimony, she left for New York City and the vaudeville stage. James Walker followed her and begged her to return to Boston, to no avail. It was while she was performing in the vaudeville halls that A. H. Chamberlyn, manager of the Globe Theater, discovered her. She would, he thought, be ideal for a part in the new play he was about to produce, *The Defender*. The show, a musical extravaganza, had a trial run in Boston in May and June 1902, then officially opened at the Herald Square Theater at 1331 Broadway, New York, on July 3, 1902. It was set amid the yachts at Newport, Rhode Island, and featured Ring as "Millie Canvass," in which role she got to perform a new song by George Evans and Ren Shields, "In the Good Old Summer Time."

It was an instant and spectacular hit and raised her to what would today be called superstar status. Ring had an attractive and infectious smile, which comes through even in poor copies of her old newspaper photographs. It was she who pushed for inclusion of the song in the show, and the great attraction of it was that she encouraged the audience to sing along in the chorus—something that became a signature mark of her performances.[25]

The Defender only ran for sixty performances, closing on August 23, but Ring immediately went on to appear in *Tommy Rot* and then *Fad and Folly*. When the sheet music for "In the Good Old Summer Time" was published, it bore her face on the cover. She continued to have hit after hit, selling large numbers of copies of the sheet music, and was much sought after by composers of popular songs.[26]

On August 17, 1904, Walker filed for divorce, claiming that Ring had deserted him three years ago.[27] Reached by newspaper reporters for comment in Chicago, where she was performing in *Vivian's Papas*, Ring was surprisingly candid: "It is all very simple. I left Mr. Walker seven years ago, and have not seen him or heard from him since. I suppose that's desertion, isn't it? He charges me with desertion. That's all there is to it. I have been calling myself Blanche Ring now for seven years."[28]

People who knew both of them said that they had parted amicably. Ring's mother, interviewed by the newspapers, volunteered that she was sorry for Walker, who she called "a very devoted husband." The public was astounded—they had assumed that Blanche Ring was single.

In another interview, Ring seemed less blasé, and tried to excuse her behavior in what reads like a prepared statement:

> It is perfectly true that Mr. James Walker has applied for a divorce from me on the grounds of my desertion. In extenuation I may say that the marriage between us was one that had been arranged by our parents and which was distasteful to me. I left him some years ago and since that time I have earned my own living on the stage to the best of my ability. The whole affair is an old, old story, and one upon which I closed the covers many years ago, with the belief that the whole affair was at an end. It is only another argument against the marriage of children, in my mind.[29]

Her argument probably satisfied the audiences of the day. It might not have if they knew that she was twenty-five years old and Walker thirty-one at the time of their marriage, hardly children (though Blanche, like many performers still, shaved a few years off her age in her publicity; she claimed to be six years younger). Further, she had been married prior to wedding Walker and had a child by that previous marriage.[30]

There was no contesting the divorce, and it was granted on November 29, 1904.[31]

☙

Another addition to the Wonderland team was Eugene L. Perry, the son of a painter originally from Prince Edward Island. He was born on May 6, 1877, and at first nothing seemed to indicate he was destined for a career in entertainment. He ran a lunchroom at a railway stop, probably not far from his home on Rice Street in Cambridge. But it was a lunchroom with a difference. He not only provided food, but as a diversion for his customers (and as a way to draw people in), he had a little art gallery. He also had a piano in the shop and sold sheet music—the equivalent of selling recordings. When he could, he played music on the piano and sang. He started giving regular evening performances.[32]

Perry's love of performing led him to volunteer at charity events and community theater. His work in show business eventually drew him away from the lunchroom and into becoming a professional. In 1902, he ran the Around the World Vaudeville Theater connected with the Revere Beach Steeplechase and was so successful that the following March he was hired by them to supervise both the Steeplechase itself and the associated amusements.[33] He still had time to coach minstrel shows for other groups, and the *Cambridge Chronicle* called him "the talented pianist and musical director." When Paragon Park went up in Hull the next year, Director George A. Dodge hired Perry as secretary and advertising manager.[34] At the age of twenty-eight, he worked in conjunction with various businesses along Revere Beach, which was where the Wonderland Company found him and snatched him up to act as their excursion agent, organizing tours by large groups to the park. He was also in charge of advertising. But, in time, he would become much more.

෨

On October 12, 1905, J. J. Higgins sold the twenty-five-acre property to the Wonderland Company, of which Harold Parker was president, Floyd C. Thompson general manager and vice president, and Higgins himself treasurer. Horace B. Meese of New York served as secretary, and John T. Burnett and Eben Hutchinson Jr. were directors. The announcement was made in the *Boston Globe* on Friday, October 13, a potentially alarming date to which no one drew attention. The enterprise was to be called "Wonderland Park and County Fair," the "Wonderland" name following the one originally intended for what became Dreamland at Coney Island. "County Fair" probably intended to refer to the midway and to convey an idea of what attractions would be there, but the construction was cumbersome, and after a few announcements the directors truncated the name to Wonderland. The October 13 article went on to say that the park would open next Decoration Day, May 30, 1906, and that it had "no connection with any other schemes that have been under contemplation in Revere, but is an actual fact, the incorporation of the company having been completed and the men interested including many who are prominent in business life in Boston."[35]

෨

The two problems Wonderland had to face first were fire and water. Fire was the bane of rides and popular amusements, as poor fireproofing had allowed the destruction of many amusements. Much effort would be put

into making Wonderland as fireproof as possible. A more immediate problem was water. One critic later remarked that Wonderland "was built in
a swamp."[36] That was not really true. Wonderland was built on the edge
of Rumney Marsh. The Whitman and Howard map of Revere ominously
shows a "Marsh Line," indicating the boundary between solid ground and
water-soaked marsh, running near the proposed Walnut Avenue entrance
of the park, with virtually all of the park sitting on marshland except the
southeast corner. Something would have to be done or patrons would find
themselves walking through mud at hightide.

There were basically two solutions: the builders could bring in extensive amounts of landfill to pack the ground solid or they could build a
boardwalk. Pedestrian boardwalks at amusement places went back at least
to the Atlantic City Boardwalk, which first went up in 1870 as a seasonal
structure, taken down at the end of each summer. In 1885, a permanent
boardwalk, built on pilings driven into the beach, was set up. Both temporary boardwalks and permanent ones began to be put up at Atlantic Coast
beaches in New Jersey, Delaware, and Maryland.[37]

The White City Amusement Park that opened in Chicago in 1905 had a
boardwalk, and the *White City Magazine*, a regular publication populariz-
ing the park, had a feature entitled "Advantage of a Boardwalk" (subtitled
"The Result of Experience Proves Plank to Be Superior to Either Cement
or Brick"), which gave the reasons they used such a surface:

> Many visitors have asked why cement walks have not been used in pref-
> erence to plank walks. The reason is obvious to those who have practical
> knowledge of both materials.
>
> The board walk in White City is elevated four feet above the ground; the
> planks are laid with one-half inch crevice between them. All the dirt and
> dust sifts through this crevice and the plank walk is always clean.
>
> The water mains, sewer mains, electric wires, and gas mains are under this
> walk and can be altered or repaired without inconveniencing the public by
> tearing up the walk.
>
> The plank is much cooler than either cement or brick, it is never damp
> and is much better for pedestrians. The board walk was the first thing erected
> in White City, and as all buildings front on it, they were built from the walk,
> and upon this walk all the trusses and mill work were framed.
>
> By its use the workmen avoided the mud which is ever present about new
> buildings and their work was more expeditiously handled.[38]

Maps and diagrams show that this was the case for Wonderland as well—the boardwalk ran throughout the area of pedestrian foot traffic, filling all the space from the lagoon out to the entrances of the surrounding buildings.[39] The Wonderland boardwalk was erected two to three feet above the marshy ground to fit the conduits underneath and allow easy access for repairs.

The buildings themselves required driven-in pilings for construction and landfill so that basements were not waterlogged. Spruce pilings were driven into the ground to provide firm anchoring for the buildings and boardwalk. Undoubtedly, the land where the Wild West and Fire and Flames shows were to go would also be landfilled, since dry, packed ground was required for the horses and fire engines in these shows. Likewise, the lagoon would have to rest on a firm foundation, not on boards. Caissons were placed where the lagoon would go.[40] Some of the other attractions, like the Scenic Railway, could be built on pylons driven into the ground.

The other worry was fire. As experience had shown, and as would be made clear many times over the coming decades, fire could be the most devastating thing at an amusement park, destroying huge areas in a very short time. On Revere Beach only a couple of years earlier, a popular ride, the Old Mill, had caught fire and burned to the ground. The buildings to one side of it burned as well. On the other side, however, was the Johnstown Flood, an attraction housed in a building said to be absolutely fireproof. It not only survived but it saved the other buildings on its side from the fire as well.[41] Nevertheless, the next year this "fireproof" building itself burned to the ground.[42]

Wonderland was not going to take chances. Its owners made every effort to protect themselves from fire. Gorham Dana of the Underwriter's Bureau of New England laid out the fire protection plan. A fire insurance trade magazine, *The Standard*, set out the precautions taken and the practices invoked in the name of fire safety. "When completed," the magazine wrote, "Wonderland will undoubtedly be better protected than any similar park in the country." Shellac and varnish were to be used sparingly, and fireproof paint was preferred. Electric lights and power equipment were built to code, with transformer rooms of fireproof construction. The plans called for the installation of automatic sprinklers, especially in kitchens and restaurants, supplied by town water through six-inch pipes. Fire extinguishers and fire alarms would be provided at regular intervals, and a system of fire hydrants installed throughout the park. No gasoline was to be stored on the premises.[43]

The buildings were made of light frame covered with tar paper and asbestos sheeting. The fire hydrants had eight-inch mains and were connected to a forty-thousand-gallon tank on a seventy-five-foot trestle—the top of the Shoot the Chutes ride, in fact. The boardwalks were to be flushed daily.[44] The precautions were good and reasonable ones, approved by the insurance companies, and during the years of its operation, Wonderland never had a serious fire or fire emergency.

Wonderland had its own fire department, one completely separate from the "show" fire department that was used for the Fire and Flames show. It consisted of fifty firemen, former members of fire departments in Boston, New York, and Brooklyn, among other places. The department had two modern fire engines, two hose wagons, one combination wagon, an aerial truck, a chief's wagon, a fire and police patrol, and an ambulance. It had twenty-six horses not associated with the show. For the first year the chief was J. A. Lankin, who had been with the Lynn Fire Department. The second year James D. Fitzgerald, who had retired from the Boston Fire Department, took over.[45]

A plan for Wonderland and a preliminary design had been worked out by November 1905, and the Wonderland board contracted for a "bird's-eye view" illustration of the park that they could use to explain the park to investors and the public. The image shows a railroad station in the foreground on the west side of the park, away from the ocean. This would have to be a new stop on the Boston & Maine Railroad, since none existed at that place. Just inside the park were eight long buildings arranged so that they radiated outward from a center, circular courtyard. These, it would appear, were the buildings that made up the County Fair portion of the park. Unlike the bucolic farm show that the name implies, this was intended to be a showplace for manufacturing and industrial exhibits from near and far, much like the displays of the new and original inventions at the various World's Fairs and expositions. But this was on a smaller scale. A story in the December 2, 1905, issue of *Billboard* displayed the image of the park and touted its greatness:

The County Fair Exhibition in Wonderland is a new departure for park enterprises, and from the enthusiasm with which this manufacturing and industrial exposition is meeting, there is no doubt as to its success. Applications are coming in from all over the country for spaces in these exposition buildings. New England being noted as a purely manufacturing center, New England manufactures alone could considerably more than fill the spaces allotted. In order to make the exhibition representative, however, great care is being taken in approving applications so that all sections of the country and all branches of the manufacturing industries will have opportunity for representation.[46]

Among the attractions was the LaMarcus A. Thompson Scenic Railway, depicted in the background of the view, as well as the hit of the 1904 St. Louis Exposition, Henry Roltaire's epic ride Creation. This ride had been immensely popular, a combination boat ride and walking tour that showed the viewers panoramas of the natural world and various illusions before leading them into a great central dome that had panoramic views of a representation of the six days of creation. To see the entire ride at the St. Louis Fair purportedly took three hours. The ride had been purchased by William Reynolds for his Coney Island Dreamland and put up on Surf Avenue, with the entranceway marked by a twenty-four-foot white plaster statue of a bare-breasted woman. This ride only took about an hour to view, which kept people going into the ride at a faster pace and thus improved the revenue. Roltaire had signed a contract with Wonderland in November 1905, so his ride was an assured thing.

In addition, the painting indicates the placement of a Fire and Flames show, which had already proven to be a big hit in Coney Island and elsewhere—both Luna Park and Dreamland had their own versions. There was a roller coaster in one corner, and several buildings and tents of unspecified purpose. One of these was surely the restaurant and ballroom, which planned to have a dance floor measuring one hundred by two hundred feet. And, of course, there was a Shooting the Chutes ride, such as every park had as a centerpiece, with a lagoon that would also host other boats of all kinds. There were to be villages filled with exotic people, just as there had been at the World's Fairs—a Japanese village, a Moorish enclave, an Irish village, and a company of Igorotte tribesmen

from the Philippines.[47] A tall tower showed an airship ride, while overhead
in the sky sailed two dirigibles. The T. B. Moore Construction Company,
described as "widely known as one of the leading amusement construction
firms in the United States," was already at work in early December 1905
putting the park together for the summer of 1906.[48]

It was an exciting and intoxicating image, but there were barriers to
the realization of this promise. Possibly the park as advertised would
have been too expensive. Perhaps the Wonderland Company was unable,
despite the tantalizing come-on, to secure enough exhibits to fill all those
eight long buildings. Maybe it could not afford the hefty price tag for Creation and still have enough for the other planned attractions. Undoubtedly, the T. B. Moore Construction Company was not really "one of the
leading amusement construction firms in the United States." In fact, it
didn't yet technically exist. It wasn't formally incorporated until February
17, 1906, by T. B. Moore, Edward L. Shea, and Henry B. Aldrich. Less
than three months later, Aldrich announced a meeting to discuss the dis-
solution of the company.[49]

A radically new plan emerged by the beginning of February, only two
months after the release of the painting. The County Fair was dropped
from the park's name. An entirely new and different bird's-eye view picture
was issued, depicting the park from the other side, looking at it with the
ocean behind the viewer. Gone were the eight fair buildings. The Shoot
the Chutes ride now occupied a bigger and more central part in the park,
ringed by a variety of attractions. The Thompson Scenic Railway was still
there, as was the Fire and Flames show and the roller coaster. There was a
grand entrance (also housing the park's administration offices) on Walnut
Avenue in Revere, with a bridge to bring people over the unused spur of
the Boston & Maine Railroad. The illustration depicts a fountain in the
park, a ballroom/restaurant, and a couple of gardens, along with a number
of buildings no doubt housing interesting attractions.

No one mentioned Roltaire's Creation anymore. Instead, there would
be a ride called Hell Gate. There was also a Japanese village (with restaurant), an illusion called the Fatal Wedding, a Wild West show, a dog and
monkey circus, a shooting gallery, a pony track, a Whirl the Whirl, a Circle
Swing, the House that Jack Built, a Living Picture Show, a free circus ring,
an Airship Tower, and a carousel.

It was clear that the owners were still deciding what to put in the park. Some accounts mentioned the Igorottes, a ride called the Razzle Dazzle, and an ostrich farm.[50] The park was now to be constructed by the firm of Aldrich & Shea, although their firm wouldn't be incorporated until October 1906 (after Wonderland had closed at the end of its first season).[51] Gone was T. B. Moore from the roster, his place filled by an electrical contractor, D. J. Buckley.

The new bird's-eye view would be reproduced on the cover of a Wonderland souvenir book and on postcards sold at the park, many of which still exist today. Confusingly, the original November 1905 bird's-eye view was also reproduced as a postcard and sold at the park, even though it bore no resemblance to the Wonderland that would be constructed. Of course, the park as it would eventually be built differed from both images, but it was close enough to the later one not to matter.

A radical change in design, the loss of one of the major attractions, and a new and cobbled-together construction firm could have been a recipe for disaster. Surprisingly, it was not. The construction proceeded at a brisk clip through the late winter and spring of 1906 as the designated opening on Decoration Day neared, with no major problems or setbacks from this point onward. The Wonderland Company's publicity department sent out a regular stream of press releases reporting how well the construction was going and keeping the public informed, whetting appetites with descriptions of the attractions to come, along with the occasional photograph of the work in progress. Easily the biggest outlet for these stories was the *Boston Post*, but the *Boston Globe* also ran several stories, as did *Billboard* out of New York City. The newspapers of the surrounding towns ran pieces as well—the *Cambridge Courier*, the *Portsmouth Herald*, and the *Revere Journal*.

ꚍ

Edward L. Shea, forty-six years old when he began work on Wonderland, had been born in Quebec. He had been superintendent of docks and wharves in Newfoundland under Sir Ambrose Shea, the Newfoundland politician and onetime governor of the Bahamas, who may have been a relative. Edward Shea moved to New York City to become a builder and general contractor, constructing several notable buildings with a variety of

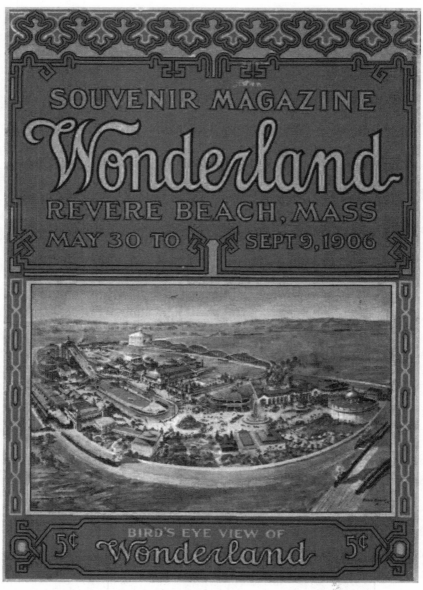

Figure 4. The Wonderland Company's February 1906 conceptual painting of the park as the builders imagined it would appear. The park did resemble this image in most respects, and it was used in postcards, souvenir booklets, and elsewhere. Courtesy of the Wisconsin Historical Society Library, Madison.

partners. His importance to Wonderland was his experience in building amusements. He had worked on the 1904 St. Louis Exposition, and he had built Creation and the Fighting the Flames structures for Coney Island's Dreamland. Shea also joined Thomas B. Moore's construction company to build a Boer War exhibit (where veterans of the Boer War fought out battles twice a day for the amusement and edification of crowds) at the new Brighton Beach Park near Coney Island.

Henry B. Aldrich was thirty-three in 1906. He started as a bicycle manufacturer in New York, then became active in Brooklyn politics, which is how he met William H. Reynolds, a New York State representative in Brooklyn. When Reynolds decided to build Dreamland in opposition to Luna Park, he hired Aldrich to be in charge of construction.[52]

Aldrich and Shea chose D. J. Buckley as their electrical engineer. Buckley had worked with the two men back in 1894 when they constructed the World's Fair Scenitorium or Scenograph, first at Madison Square Garden in New York, then later at the Cyclorama building in Boston.[53] This was a 1/60 miniature replica of the 1893 World's Columbian Exposition in Chicago—the "White City" World's Fair. People unable to attend the real thing eagerly visited this replica, which was fully illuminated with 600 miniature lamps using 122 different circuits.[54] Buckley's prior association with Aldrich and Shea brought him to Wonderland, and he joined them as a director of the Aldrich & Shea Construction Company when it finally did incorporate. For Wonderland, he secured the largest transformer in New England.[55]

As the artistic designer, Aldrich and Shea hired Attilio Pusterla, an Italian artist who had emigrated to the United States and become a citizen in 1900. He had been born in Milan in 1862 and attended the Accademia de Belle Arti de Brera, a public academy of fine arts in Milan.

Pusterla came to the United States and seems to have worked painting murals for cycloramas and exhibits at World's Fairs. He started designing rides and amusements himself, and in 1899 registered the first of many patents. He patented several variations on water rides and, in particular, whirlpools. He appears to have been present at the St. Louis 1904 Exposition, possibly working on murals for Roltaire's Creation. When Dreamland purchased Creation for its new season, it also purchased one of Pusterla's patented rides, Descent into the Hell Gate. In 1905, Pusterla incorporated the Island Amusement Construction Company to build his new rides.[56]

Possibly the Wonderland board approached Pusterla because they had just lost Roltaire and his Creation; thus, they perhaps went to the creator of the other new ride at Dreamland and secured the (presumably less expensive) rights to Hell Gate.[57] At the same time, the founders obtained the services of the ride designer to act as a decorative artist. Exactly what he did, and how he interfaced with the architect and designers of the other attractions, isn't clear. It is possible that the title was mostly honorary, giving Pusterla a boost and allowing Wonderland to brag that it had the services of an Italian-trained artist contributing to its park. Pusterla seems to have been pushing for another of his rides to be used at the park, because an announcement from March 18, 1906, for a ride designed by him called the Razzle Dazzle appeared in the *Boston Post*. "It consists of four monster discs," says the report, "capable of carrying 80 people each, which revolve in a big basin of water. When the discs are set in motion they complete five different motions. These several motions have an exhilarating effect upon the passengers, which is decidedly fascinating. It will be the razzle-dazzle jag this summer when the discs are operated."[58]

This may be the ride Pusterla patented under the name Water Carousel, but it was never installed at Wonderland. Perhaps it was thought to be too expensive, too experimental, or too dangerous. In any event, it was never mentioned again in any park announcements or literature.

Construction actually began by about the second week of February 1906, and within three weeks the exteriors of most of the buildings were up, thanks to a workforce of 726 workmen. At this time, Martin Couney, the genius and innovator behind the incubator exhibit, was brought in to inspect the arrangements.[59] Couney was a perfectionist, and as there had been problems with a previous effort to display incubators on Revere Beach, his approval was essential to the exhibit's success. He did certify the effort, with no recorded reservations, so that stage was cleared.

At the beginning of March, Thompson set up the Manning & Armstrong Company for the pair that was arranging the Fire and Flames show for Wonderland.[60] A piece in the *Boston Post* a few days later described the grandstand for watching the show.[61]

By March 11, Aldrich estimated that construction was 75 percent complete. He described the Japanese Village as being well along.[62] It was being built by the Japanese Construction Company of New York City, which had made a business of constructing such villages. Otherwise known as the F. U. Shuichi & Kengyo Mortya Company, it constructed similar villages for the Pan-American Exposition at Buffalo in 1901 and the St. Louis Exposition in 1904, and advertised that they also did theatrical scenery and provided tea ceremony demonstrations.[63]

By April 8, the *Boston Post* announced that construction was almost complete. One hundred more workers had been added to the rolls, and a temporary railway was put in to haul away the dirt as they excavated the central lagoon. Most of the buildings were finished, with only interior decorations to be added. Still lacking was the garage to be added outside the Walnut Avenue entrance, an extravagance in a time when most patrons were expected to arrive by railroad or trolley. The *Boston Globe* on the same day reported on the beach-side entrance at Beaver Street, still to be constructed. Spanning the little-used B&M tracks that paralleled Revere Beach, it required a variance from the city of Revere. Made of iron, and fifteen feet high at its tallest point, twenty-eight feet wide, and seventy-five feet long, the bridge cost $10,000.[64] Although the published plans did not show it, the beach end of the bridge would have an arch with WONDER-LAND written on it and would be fully lit by electric lights.

A piece in the *Portsmouth Herald* only a few days later remarked that there would be 150,000 Edison electric lights, powered by six fifty-kilowatt transformers. That was more, the *Herald* observed, than the electricity provided to Somerville and Cambridge combined.[65]

On May 6, the *Globe* described the park, and a similar piece, with pictures, appeared in the *Post* on the May 17.[66] On the May 19, the wild animals for Ferrari's Animal Show arrived by train. They were kept in their transportation crates outside the park while the builders put "finishing touches" on the park.[67] On May 27, the *Globe* ran a major spread with many pictures. The *Boston Post* ran a picture of two cross-breed panther-leopard cubs that had just been born at the park, named "Wonder" and "Land" in its honor.[68]

Three days later was Decoration Day, and all was in readiness for opening day.

CHAPTER 3

Year One—1906
(The Northern Half of the Park)

Some 100,000 people visited Wonderland on its opening day.[1] Revere Beach would not see a crowd so large again until 1921. Reportedly, more people entered through the Beaver Street entrance (the one opening onto Revere Beach) than through the larger and more imposing Walnut Avenue entrance that led into the heart of the park.

The first one to enter Wonderland—the first "Wonderlander," as the papers called him—was Edwin G. Smith, an East Boston businessman who had sold Wonderland the spruce pilings to support the boardwalk. He bought two admission tickets so that he could frame one.

The *Boston Globe* reported the next day on the succession of strange sights: "Once inside, the visitor was in the midst of a scent [*sic*] of indescribable animation, with an open-air circus in the middle of the plaza, accompanied by a brass band, Moorish women riding camels, a band of genuine redskins in war paint and feathers parading about with a brass band from their own numbers, genuine cowboys and 'cowgirls' whose volleys of musketry made noise enough to have represented Custer's last stand and which sent the average small boy into spasms of delight."[2]

An interesting dissenting voice came from Rollin Lynde Hartt, a Congregational minister turned journalist and surprisingly cynical observer who wrote about the Coney Island parks and Wonderland. His observations serve as an antidote to the relentlessly positive press releases that emerged as newspaper stories. He compared the new amusement parks to the international exhibitions that inspired them:

A hot boardwalk replaces the delicious lawns and shrubbery, tinsel architecture the exquisite façades, a few plastic fol-de-rols the lavish sculpture-groups, a heartrending "lagoon" the iris-bordered waterways, a jargon of ill-combined hues the gracious harmonies of color, and a crudely magnificent illumination the sweet poetry of radiance that once—ah, so rapturously!—turned plaster to opalescent glory. And yet, if you dismiss those visions of supreme loveliness, you call the place very pretty, while to those for whom it is it is particularly designed it represents a jubilant paradise of beauty. Indeed, it contributes not a little to æsthetic education.[3]

✦

In the center of the main courtyard stood the Shoot the Chutes with its lagoon and surrounding canals. The Shoot the Chutes had become the primary attraction at just about every amusement park that went up in the first decade of the twentieth century. It certainly wasn't the first to go up in the Boston area. Twenty years earlier there had been one at Massachusetts Avenue and Huntington Avenue, about where Symphony Hall now stands in the Back Bay.[4] But Floyd Thompson had scored a major coup with this one—it was possibly the largest one in the world (both tallest and longest), it had two tracks on it (so that it could launch two boats at the same time), and it was the one that had stood on the midway at the 1904 St. Louis Exposition. Its tower stood 83 feet tall, and the chute itself was 340 feet long.

Following the exposition, it had been taken apart for transportation to Wonderland and loaded on eleven railroad cars. During the spring of 1906 four of those cars had gone missing, causing some frantic times as tracers were sent out to locate them. But they were found and assembled in time for opening day.[5]

Passengers got on board the boats for the ride at the base and were drawn up the incline by the machinery. At the top the boat pivoted around, giving the riders a view of the park from the highest point they could reach, as well as a view down the slope. The boat was then released, sliding unrestrained down the slope, picking up speed until it hit the water and went skimming across the surface of the lagoon, leaping into the air as it ricocheted from the water's surface, passing under the bridge that spanned the lagoon and out into the water until the boat ran out of momentum.[6]

"It is noticeable," wrote the *Wonderland Souvenir Magazine 1906*, "that nearly all that try the Shoot the Chutes are not satisfied until they have taken a second ride, often several more. A common remark, especially of

Figure 5. A boat caught in midair as it skips across the surface of the lagoon, having come down the ramp visible on the left. The conical building on the right houses Louis Bopp's Flying Horses carousel. Shooting the Chutes—Souvenir Program from Wonderland Featuring Pawnee Bill, Revere Beach, Mass., 1908. Courtesy of Historic New England, Boston.

girls who take the ride, is 'I'm going down again, and keep my eyes open this time.'" The literature also assured prospective riders that neither they nor the spectators would get wet, and that the ride, although exhilarating, was perfectly safe.[7]

On either side of the central lagoon were two canals in which various boats could run. These seem to have been copied from the expositions, which also had canals, though generally not flanking a central lagoon. A pedestrian bridge, just like the one at the Shoot the Chutes in Coney Island's Dreamland, crossed the ride just beyond where the skiffs splashed into the water, letting spectators view the ride without getting wet.

At the end of the lagoon was the Arcus Ring, which featured a continually changing roster of circus acts—trapeze artists, tightrope walkers, acrobats, contortionists, and so on. In its first year, the Arcus Ring was superintended by Fred A. Bennett, who acted as ringmaster, announcer, stilt-walker, and impersonator.

On the side of the lagoon was a circular building containing a merry-go-round—Louis Bopp's Flying Horses.[8] It was housed in a round building with a conical top, so that it could run regardless of the weather.

Next to the merry-go-round was the Descent into the Hell Gate, usually called simply the Hell Gate, the name written in red over the entrance. This was Wonderland's edition of one of the hit rides from Dreamland's second season. The Dreamland version had an enormous devil appearing to peer and reach over the entrance, but Wonderland's was a relatively sedate building. From the front it appeared octagonal, but beyond the facade it became a polyhedron, essentially a circle 104 feet in diameter.[9] The front looked like a medieval castle, made up apparently of massive stone blocks with a crenellated top. There was a long flight of steps going up to a dark entrance.

For once, the description given in the newspapers was not simply the same as the one used in the souvenir book. Both descriptions waxed positively and even literally poetical about the ride. Curiously, they don't say much about the physical layout of the ride, but they do illustrate the visual and visceral impact it had. From the 1906 souvenir booklet:

"Leave all hope behind, ye who enter here"—Dante

That familiar line with which the Latin poet begins his immortal *Inferno* is in no sense applicable to Wonderland's patrons who enter the portals of Hell Gate and descend the maelstrom which carries them in gondolas around giant whirlpools, down steep rapids, to the underworld.

Hell Gate at Wonderland is one of the most popular, novel, and sensational of the twentieth century amusements.

The journey is made by water, a striking adaptation of the classical river Styx. Only in this case, the Styx is a spiral river instead of a straightaway. During the trip various demons of the lower world are seen, plenty close enough to create mirth, but not so close as to destroy the allegorical illusion. Slowly at first, the boat, with its precious burden of subterranean-bound pilgrims. Moves on around the outer rim of the whirlpool, gradually gaining impetus as it approaches the centre, until finally it is drawn, with a mad rush, down the chute, out of sight into the underworld, where, at first, it passes through a region dark as Erebus.

Now come the scenic effects. From vast caverns, out of the dim recesses of which strange vegetation, the like of which was never seen on earth, appears, and such forms and faces as people of vivid imagination, monsters

Figure 6. The fortress-like entrance to the Descent into the Hell Gate ride. Riders walked up the steps and under the arches to board the boats. They probably exited through the tunnel under the ticket booth. Hell Gate—Souvenir Program from Wonderland Featuring Pawnee Bill, Revere Beach, Mass., 1908. Courtesy of Historic New England, Boston.

and midgets, harlequins and hobgoblins, peep forth or strut about amid the weird surroundings.

A feeling of awe begins to possess the mind, but before even the most timid have become really fearful of the situation, light breaks once more upon the scene and the boat itself approaches the bank of the river Styx. There an emissary of Satan awaits you and the last lop of the journey is made on foot. There sits his Satanic Majesty, and circling about him are the members of his royal court. You may or may not make obeisance to Satan. No harm can come to you in either event. Pass on, and, before you are aware of it, indeed, the moment you leave the kingly presence, you emerge into the light of day—or the electric glare of night—at Wonderland, amid the ever-moving, ever-laughing throng of sightseers on the Board Walk. The Descent to Hell Gate is then a memory.[10]

The ride was designed by Attilio Pusterla, and his patent fits the description of Descent into the Hell Gate perfectly.[11] There is an upper level with a spiral basin going in toward the center. Constant pumping of water into the outer track keeps filling in the water, but a hole in the center continually draws the water in, so that each successive ring is lower than the one outside it, and the constant current moves the boats along without any need for a track. There is a tall structure in the center (a lighthouse in the patent, although it might have been a pinnacle of "rock" in the Hell Gate ride) that obscures the view of other passengers and keeps them from seeing clearly what is going on.

Once in the center, the boat rapidly descends on a chute to a ring one level below and the same diameter as the outer spiral above. The boat goes three quarters of the way around the circle then is pulled up a ramp of rollers to its starting point. By this point, however, the passengers have disembarked, and the boat that goes back up is empty.

☙

Next to the Hell Gate was the Wonderland Restaurant, with a ballroom upstairs. Every amusement park needed a restaurant, of course, and at that time, they all had ballrooms. Dancing to live music was one of the chief attractions of an amusement area. Revere Beach was already studded with ballrooms competing with each other for attention. The front of the Wonderland building was adorned with balconies and decorations that smacked more of Pusterla's European background than of Wonderland architect John Lavalle's more utilitarian architecture. The building itself measured 125 feet wide by 20 feet deep and had 100 windows. Reports differed on the number of tables in the restaurant and its seating, but it had about 250 tables and seating for about 1,000. A picture of the restaurant interior—one of the few of Wonderland building interior—shows anglebraced wooden beam construction and ceilings covered with incandescent lamps in a diamond latticework pattern.[12]

At the front was a confectionary, a cigar counter, and a soda fountain. The restaurant was under the supervision of Dudley S. McDonald, a caterer turned restauranteur whose establishments were noted for catering to Boston's female shoppers. His restaurant at 131–132 Tremont Street in Boston, overlooking Boston Common, had opened less than four years earlier. The specialty at the Wonderland Restaurant was the Shore Dinner, featuring clams, fish, and lobster.[13]

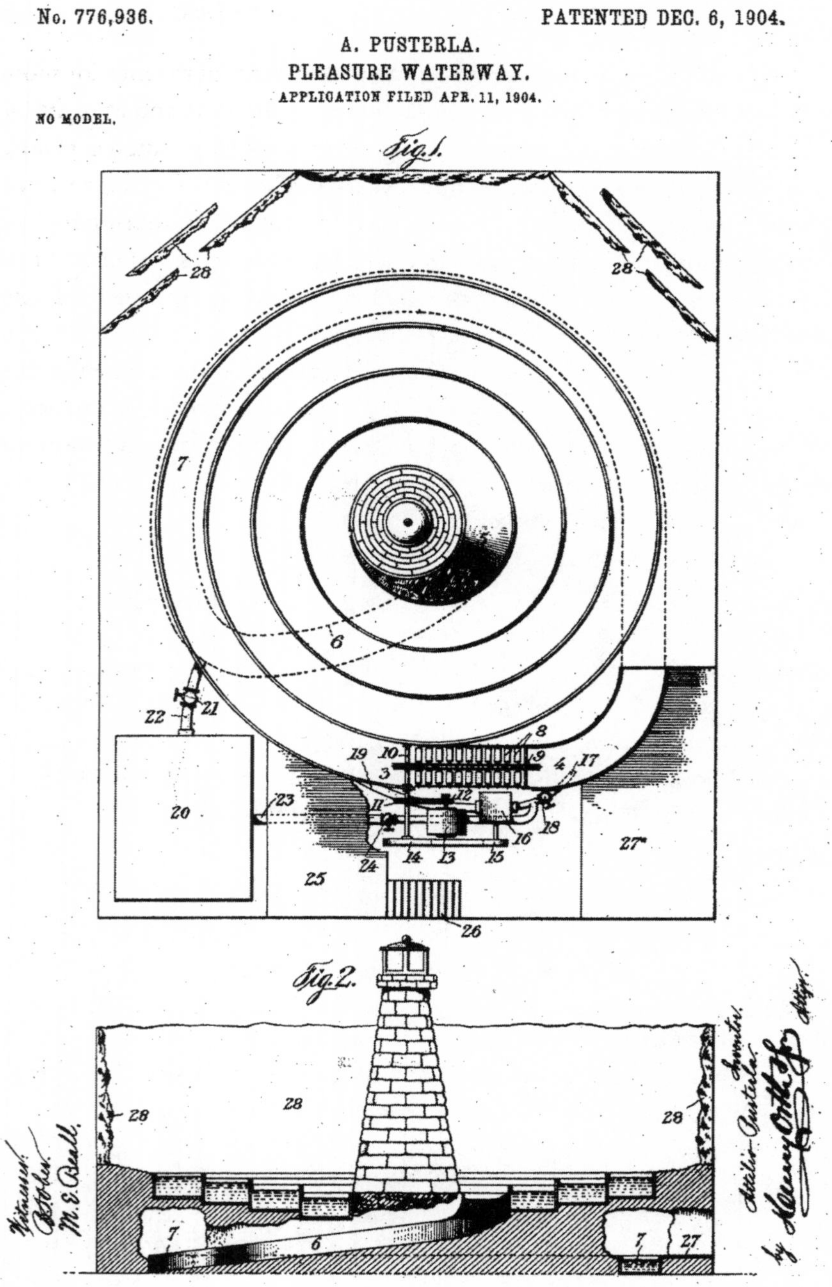

Figure 7. The patent drawing for Attilio Pusterla's Pleasure Waterway ride, which became the Hell Gate at Coney Island and Wonderland. Courtesy of the U.S. Patent Office, Washington, DC.

The upstairs was devoted to the ballroom. Postcards of the interior show it to be a broad open area, illuminated by many windows and at night by incandescent bulbs set in X patterns. There were many hanging plants, and the walls were adorned with hand-painted scenery. The floor was of polished white maple. In addition, there were cloakrooms, retiring rooms, and a veranda. It could accommodate a thousand dancers and claimed to be the largest in New England. The music was provided by Louis S. Poole and his orchestra, who had performed for years in Boston. The company appointed Harry E. Munroe, a mustachioed, well-groomed man who had been a dancing instructor for the previous twenty-six years, as manager of the ballroom, tasked with giving directions as necessary and insuring everyone danced.

౿

Another attraction, Wonderland's Beautiful Orient, was constructed and managed by one J. S. N. Maloof.[14]

The 1906 souvenir magazine offered a heavily atmospheric description:

Out of the storied East!

The fascination of the Orient ever obtains. This is with all due respect to Tennyson's line:

"Better Fifty years of England than a cycle of Cathay."

Maybe so, but has not Kipling said:

"W'en you've 'eard the East a callin', then you won't 'ear nothin' else."

We Occidentals are Kiplingites, so far as interest in the Orient and its people go. The Orient is old, so mystic, so suggestive of ancient peoples, of curious customs, or [sic] habits and manners that Time itself has not changed.

Here is a bit of the East set down in the heart of Greater Boston. There are interesting Oriental men, women, youths, maids, and children. There is the camel whose padded hoofs trod the sands of Persia and Arabia when people thought the world was flat and when America was an unknown quantity.

In strange contrast to the lively schottische and the giddy two-step with which the American girl is wont to whirl away her dancing hours are the slow, languorous dances of the Eastern people, as shown in the Beautiful Orient. The graceful movements of limbs and body that delighted the rulers of ages long ago are shown by beautiful Oriental girls, to the sonorous music of queer Eastern instruments.[15]

Clearly they were banking on the allure of "Muscle Dancing" (which today we would call "belly dancing") to draw in the customers. But in addition the advertisements spoke of a Turkish restaurant, a café, a fortune-teller, a Turkish cigarette factory, and an Oriental bazaar with 125 performers. There were a dozen camels, "one of which is big enough to carry 15 men at a time." The camels had their own barn in the back of the building.[16]

Many fairs and parks had "Turkish Dancers." Their presence dated back to the Philadelphia Centennial Exposition of 1876, but they had become ubiquitous in the wake of the Chicago 1893 Exposition and were a common feature of the Streets of Cairo/Beautiful Orient exhibits. Wonderland featured Rosina, doing "the dance of Damascus," along with "a dozen dancers of the land of Hindu."

The design of the exhibit was pretty unusual, with four pink minarets, each in a slightly different style, and banded exteriors. In addition there were two smaller "Onion" domes and a keystone-shaped device in the center. Each of these bore a spar with a Muslim-style crescent at the base. Wonderland's coral-pink fantasy looked as if it came from Hieronymus Bosch's *Garden of Earthly Delights*.

⁊

LaMarcus Thompson is known as the Father of the American Roller Coaster, although he neither invented it nor claimed to.[17] He was, however, a tireless popularizer of the gravity-powered railway attraction, especially in the form of the scenic railway. Even during his lifetime, his rides were criticized as too gentle and insufficiently exciting, in comparison to the enormous drops and twisting turns of the newer breeds of roller coasters. But Thompson had no need to worry. There were already two of his scenic railways operating at Revere Beach when Wonderland was being planned. Another would open on the beach later, as well as one across Broad Sound at Bass Point in Nahant, in addition to those in other Boston-area parks. Clearly, he was not in danger of market saturation.

The key to Thompson's success was probably that moderation. The gentle undulations of the track provided enough of a thrill to riders of all ages, and the slow speed allowed them to view the dioramas set up along the route. There were no sudden accelerations or turns, and the riders really didn't want them.

Seen on the bird's-eye views of Wonderland, the tracks seem unreal, like a schematic of a ride, with small undulations of about the same height. To modern eyes, familiar with large and sudden changes in height, the track doesn't look real. But photographs of the Thompson Scenic Railways verify that this was, indeed, what they looked like.

The railway ride started at a large building next to the Beautiful Orient, at the angle between the court defined by the lagoon and Shoot the Chutes ride and the midway that paralleled the beach. The train pulled out northward, along the direction of the midway, but was shielded from it by the scenic railway station building and the backdrop of the Fire and Flames show. It then turned left, to the west, undulating up and down until it reached another building, which housed the scenes. Thompson's rides typically featured grottos lit by blinking lights and tableaus depicting foreign scenes or biblical subjects. After going around inside this building, the train returned on a track parallel to its original route to the main building.

The 1906 souvenir book described it as follows:

Thompson Scenic Railway

An Enchanting Ride in Swift Moving Cars Up Hill and Down Dale

"Let's go around again" is the chorus of the passengers who have just made a trip over the hills and dales of the Thompson Scenic Railway and around again they go! The popularity which was instantaneously won on the opening day of Wonderland has never waned and the capacity of the road is still inadequate to accommodate the people who desire to ride.

The experience of a first ride is always a new sensation, and when the fascination of the fast motion takes hold of you, it becomes inspiring; it astonishes; it exhilarates like a draught of champagne.

Entering the pavilion we find awaiting us a comfortable train of cars in charge of an experienced gripman; we are seated and the ride begins. Drawn by cable up a long and steep incline the crest is reached and from here we get a magnificent view of the Ocean and the inland country. Hesitating but a moment, the train dashes down the slope in front. Faster and faster with ever increasing speed it flies, until after reaching the bottom it is carried by its own momentum up the opposite hill. Here on the crest it hesitates a moment. Then another dash downward. On! on! Faster and faster. Up and down, down and up, over hill and dale. Involuntary screams and shouts spring to the lips and the joyous sensations are indescribable. The merriment and excitement run higher each moment until finally the famous Scenic

Grottos are reached. Entering there the train slows up and winds its sinuous course through beautiful and awful scenes that call forth "ohs" and "ahs" to the lips of all. Once more the train reaches the open air and speeds away towards the sea. The pavilion is reached and again the train starts away on another trip around. More climbs, more dashes downward, more hills and dashes, and then these dimly lighted tunnels—opportune tunnels—and on past more scenes. "The Grand Canyon," "Venice" and others, all masterpieces. Out again into the daylight and away on the home run. The first hill is pretty steep, the second a little steeper, but the third is the best of all. There is a double jump at the finish that is great. One last dash down and after three miles of throbs, thrills, and unalloyed pleasure have been passed in absolute safety you alight feeling that you have had the time of your life.[18]

The line about "absolute safety" was clearly there to reassure the timid that, exciting as the ride might be, they would have no cause for alarm. Despite the claim about "three miles," measurement of the track lengths on the 1906 Sanborn Fire Insurance Map shows that the length of the ride, even with twists and turns, could not be even a mile in length.

℘

Not far from the end of the lagoon was a circular attraction called Love's Journey. At first glance, it appeared to be another Tunnel of Love ride, but as a story in the *Boston Globe* observed, it was "an amusement feature which is not only new in Boston, but is new to the entire amusement world. Wonderland will see the first journey of the kind. It is the invention of Herbert H. Pattee and is being constructed under his personal direction."

Wonderland succeeded in getting this brand-new ride before anyone else had. Herbert Horton Pattee of New York City had filed his patent application for an amusement device only in March 1906.[19]

Who was Pattee? He was born in 1866 to Captain M. J. Pattee, a clerk in the Life Saving Service of the U.S. Treasury. Herbert started out as an actor and achieved some measure of fame, playing Hamlet and other notable roles. He appeared on Broadway in *Richard Savage* in 1901.[20] And then, like so many others who ended up associated with Wonderland, he made a very abrupt and radical career change.

In 1902, Pattee quit the stage to go into furniture manufacturing. But he was waylaid by his own love of invention.[21] Pattee had already been granted a patent for a combination chair and couch in 1899 and for a new kind of hinge, among other projects.[22] He probably decided to go into furniture manufacturing on the basis of these sorts of designs. But his designs veered off into the direction of amusements as he started to design rides. He patented The Planets or The Ball Coaster, a roller coaster that placed the passengers not in a train but in a spherical cage that could roll along on a special track.[23] It was, perhaps fortunately, never built. He designed and patented a carousel and a very unusual Ferris wheel. And he came up with the amusement device that would become Love's Journey.

The ride consists of a circular structure that is free to rotate on rollers, from which are suspended a series of cars. The cars are suspended at each end by two chains or cables, rather like hammocks (although the cars are rigid). A number of these go completely around the ring—the patent shows eight of them, but the number can be varied, depending on the size of the track and the cars. As the ring rotates, so do the cars. But there are additional features. The cars can be bumped upward or sideways by arms with rollers on them. These can be fixed, or they can be operated by mechanical or pneumatic actuators, so that all the cars can bump upward or sideways every time they reach that point or at the discretion of the ride operator.

Furthermore, there are other rollers with levers that can be activated by the approach of the car to lower a door in front of the car. Above the cars there is intended to be a covered tunnel, so that when the car bumps open one of these doors, the car finds itself isolated in a room that can be decorated to taste. The room might even have a tank of water in it on which the car rides. Pattee's patent shows the ride either half or completely on such a water track (the cars are designed to ride either suspended in air or riding on the water). In use, the cars pass through a succession of "rooms" that are each decorated in a different way, can be hanging or in water, and can be bumped abruptly. The ride owner can have it constructed with any combination and can change them over time.

A description in the *Boston Globe,* clearly citing a press release from Wonderland, gives some details of the ride: "Twenty cars, each holding two persons and each overhung by a figure of cupid, go on a circular course, which is described as 'crazy, sentimental, and sensational.' The cars enter a tunnel with trick doors which are opened automatically, and in the course of the journey pass through four doors, each of which reveals a surprise, the final incident being a whirlwind and a snowstorm of confetti."[24]

Pattee even filed a design patent for the individual cars. Each bore a huge Valentine heart on the side. An advertisement shows the ride with its two passengers, a cupid on the side of the car, and "Love's Journey" written across the back.[25]

The ride was an immediate success. Pattee set up a company to construct it at other parks, located in New York and later in Revere and Providence, Rhode Island. His company boasted that the ride generated $9,000 in gross receipts in the first eleven weeks and $15,000 in gross receipts in its first twenty-six weeks of operation at Wonderland. Pattee created an illustrated booklet to describe the ride to potential buyers and applied for patents in Canada and Mexico. Copies of the ride went up all over the country, including the new Golden City amusement park where Kennedy Airport now sits on Long Island, New York.

Pattee stayed on in Revere Beach to supervise the ride, probably watching to see how people reacted and what changes or improvement he could make. But more happened than he expected.

According to friends, Pattee stated that he would never marry. Two weeks later, at Wonderland, he spotted a woman in a blue princess gown and white plumed hat and announced that this was the girl he was going to marry. She was Maybelle Scott Symonds of Swampscott, a North Shore town a few miles from Wonderland, and she was attending the park that day with her boyfriend. Pattee arranged to be introduced to her and got her to ride Love's Journey. The third time she did, he joined her and apparently persuaded her to let him be her suitor.

Her mother disapproved, probably in part because, at forty, Pattee was more than twice Symond's age of eighteen. But by October 1906, he had convinced Symond's mother, and Pattee took Symonds to see his relatives in New York.

They were married on New Year's Day in St. Stephen's Episcopal Church in Lynn.[26] Their honeymoon took them to several cities, including the site of the upcoming Jamestown Exposition in Hampton Roads, Virginia, where Pattee oversaw the setting up of another Love's Journey.

So, in storybook fashion, the inventor and builder of Wonderland's new innovative Tunnel of Love wooed his bride on his own invention. Their son, Herbert Eldridge, was born on September 25, 1907.[27]

Probably the most prominent ride after Shoot the Chutes was the Circle Swing. Standing in front of the another attraction, the House of Follies/Third Degree, it rose to a height of eighty feet, a massive construction of braced, galvanized steel girders, a six-sided pyramidal tower like an oil derrick, but instead of a drill, there was attached at the top a rig six braced arms sticking out, each protruding from the center about one-sixth the height of the tower. From each arm hung a set of cables supporting a car in the shape of a boat made of light, woven rattan that could hold eight passengers each.

The ride was driven by a central, four-inch steel shaft that rotated all the cars simultaneously. As the cars rotated faster and faster they began to draw away from the central shaft, each car hanging at an angle that increased as the speed did. The passengers had the odd feeling of being tilted with respect to the ground yet feeling right-side up. Each ride lasted several minutes, after which the rotating slowed until the cables were again vertical. At night the tower, cables, and cars were all illuminated with incandescent bulbs, and when the attraction spun it created an incredible sight.

The souvenir book, which was excerpted for news accounts, described it as such:

Circle Swing

Is there a man or woman who does not remember the fun enjoyed in childhood by having a rope suspended from a tall, stout pole and swinging clear of the ground around the post as long as the centrifugal motion would keep up?

The Circle Swing is the modern development, with the aid of ingenious machinery and of the inevitable law of gravity, of this childhood swing.

Watch those heavy cars start. As the circle of swings revolves, slowly at first and then faster and faster, seeking their natural goal of the horizontal plane. By the time the apparatus is speeded up to its limit the cars are whirling fast around the circle and seemingly standing out straight from the vertical centre-pole.

Then the reverse follows. The cars go slower and seek the ground level till they come to a stop in their original position.

The Circle Swing is cooling. It is stimulating. It affords an unsurpassed view of Wonderland from all sides.

The Circle Swing was the invention of Harry Guy Traver. One of seven children in a farming family in Illinois, the family moved to Davenport,

Nebraska, while he was still in school. After he finished his education, he briefly became a schoolteacher. Subsequently, he apprenticed to a mechanical engineer and went to work for General Electric, then the Denver Tramway Company, and the Harris Safety Company of New York, which made firetrucks.[28]

At the age of thirty-four he worked his way to Europe on a cattle boat, planning to see the coronation of King Edward VII in 1902 and to recuperate from an attack of diphtheria. As he told the story, it was on the way back to the United States that he found himself staring up at the seagulls circling the ship and conceived of the idea of an amusement ride in which people circled in the sky. This led to his designing the Circle Swing, his first big hit among the many rides he would design and develop.[29] He applied for a patent for an "Amusement Apparatus," a first draft of his device, on October 3, 1902, and it was granted on April 26, 1904. He applied for two more that more closely resembled his final device on May 1, 1906, for a "Roundabout" and on January 28, 1905, for a "Circle Swing." Both were granted on September 11, 1906. Prior to this, Traver installed his first one at Luna Park in Coney Island for the 1904 season.[30]

Traver's Circle Swings went on to be big business. He sold them in three sizes—eighty feet, sixty feet, and a collapsible version for traveling shows.[31] The proceeds from the Circle Swing fueled Traver's other amusement innovations. He went on to devise many that were used for years at amusement parks—the Tumble Bug, the Caterpillar, and others. But Traver became most famous for his roller coasters. Three of these, the Giant Cyclone Safety Coasters, are notorious, even today, for their high speed, steepness, and sudden turns—the Cyclone at Crystal Beach, Ontario; the Cyclone at Palisades Amusement Park in New Jersey; and the Lightning, which was erected at Revere Beach in 1927 and ran for six years.

✌

William C. Manning was born in Louisville, Kentucky, in 1862. He became a jockey—not surprising given the place and time—and was exercising a horse in 1878 when it fell on him, smashing his right leg so badly that it had to be amputated several inches above the knee. For many people, this would have spelled the end of a vigorous athletic career, but Manning was one of those people who faced challenges head-on. For him, it was only the beginning.[32]

He trained to be a wrestler and gymnast, becoming an expert on the double horizontal bars. He began exhibiting his wrestling at fairs and shows, eventually working the big cities and taking on two-legged competitors at Kansas City, Cincinnati, and St. Louis. In an 1886 news story, he issued a standing challenge to any one-legged wrestler in the world, for any amount of money. He bragged that he had never been thrown, despite having wrestled many two-legged men.

He had a heavy-browed, determined stare that comes through even in an 1886 drawing and even more in an 1889 photograph taken by the Brenham Art Gallery in Texas.[33] In the photograph he stands confidently on his one leg while dressed in an ornamented gymnast's leotard, barely braced by one arm leaning on a chair, as if to say that all he needed was his one leg.

He headlined at the California Dime Museum in Los Angeles in September 1888:

First Appearance of the Gymnastic Wonder

W.C. Manning

Two great novelty acts. The only known one-legged triple horizontal bar expert in the world. Work Graceful and Easy. Aerial Horizontal Bar and Flying Spanish Rings, finishing with terrible Flights through the Air.[34]

About 1899, he met and teamed up with acrobat Louis DuCrow, who was also missing a leg—the left, in DuCrow's case.[35] He had lost it, according to Manning, because it was struck by a large stone. "This convenient deprivation of locomotor members," wrote the *Sandusky Ohio Daily Star*, "makes it possible for the two gentlemen to perform many turns which would be impossible if two left or two right legs were missing." Some people apparently thought that one or the other of them might have deliberately had a leg amputated so as to be part of the act.[36]

Manning and DuCrow performed extensive, intricate routines on the horizontal bars, exchanging jokes and patter with each other, and were insanely popular. Their advertisements called them the "Marvelous Monopedes" and "The Greatest Novelty Act in Vaudeville." One reviewer called their act "the best of its kind," which is actually faint praise, since, as their own publicity observed, they were the "only act of its kind in the world." They played all over the country, including at the Howard Athenaeum in Boston, and worked continuously at least up through 1904.[37]

By that time Manning was in his forties, and his performances and schedule would have been grueling for anyone of his age, no matter how many legs he had. He was beginning to think of getting out of performing and into management. For a time he had his own Inter-Ocean Amusement Company, booking summer park attractions. He started working as a manager at the Albert Sutherland Amusement Company in 1904.[38] He then went to work for the famous Broadway agent and producer James J. Armstrong around 1904, becoming his eastern manager.[39] *Billboard* noted that Manning was "now a manager, but never forgetting that above everything else he is a performer and consequently always doing everything in his power to further the interests of those who risk their lives to entertain the public."[40] Armstrong and Manning moved into new offices at 121 West 42nd Street in Manhattan in May 1905 and began advertising for acts to be used for amusement parks.[41]

James Armstrong, who was born on Christmas Day in 1854 in New York City and had previously been a printer, spent thirty years as a theatrical agent, occupying every rung of the ladder, starting out with Michael Leavitt's companies in Los Angeles in 1883. A 1909 profile of Armstrong called him "the oldest in service of vaudeville agents of today."[42]

Possibly because of their advertisements in the trade publications in 1905, Manning and Armstrong were contacted by Wonderland, probably by Floyd Thompson, about setting up a Fire and Flames show for the new park. Thompson organized the Manning and Armstrong Company for this purpose, with offices in the Boston Stock Exchange Building at 53 State Street, where the Wonderland Company office was also located.

The Fire and Flames or Fighting the Fire shows grew out of International Fire Fighters competitions and exhibitions, which dated back to the 1890s. George C. Hale, who later invented Hale's Tours, took first place in one such competition at the Royal Agricultural Hall in London in 1893 and also participated in one in Paris seven years later.

There was an International Fire Exhibition in Berlin in 1901 (Internationale Ausstellung für Feuerschutz und Feuerrettungswesen or International Exhibition for Fire Protection and Fire Rescue), which featured displays of equipment and demonstrations of technique, but it was the 1903 International Fire Exhibition at Earl's Court in London that really brought out the firefighting show as public entertainment.[43] The exhibition had displays and demonstrations of firefighting equipment and techniques used since the days of the Roman Empire. Its main attraction, held in the Empress Theater, was "The Superb and Realistic Demonstration of 'Fighting the Flames.'" This didn't merely demonstrate equipment and techniques but integrated them into a dramatic narrative on a set built to appear—and burn—like a city street. "Not Imitation, but Stupendous Realism" boasted the programs and advertisements.

The very next year, George C. Hale created a similar spectacle with the same name (but no other apparent connection to the London show) for the 1904 St. Louis Exposition. It showed the firemen receiving an alarm, sliding down the firepole, driving to the scene, and performing recues of people in a burning six-story building. It was the hit of the fair.

Even before the St. Louis fair opened, the Coney Island parks were building their own versions. Luna Park had its Fire and Flames show operating by July 1904. Dreamland, not to be outdone, had Fighting the Flames at its opening in May 1904. It too had a six-story building on fire. A cast of 2,000, including 120 firefighters, staffed the show, and a grandstand seated 1,500 spectators. The next year, the park expanded the scene to include a block of buildings.

Other amusement parks around the country saw the draw of the show and hastened to put together their own. Thompson, who had been in Coney Island during the opening of the competing fire shows, was certainly aware of it, and there was simply no question that Wonderland would also have to have its own firefighting show. If Coney Island could put these shows together on their own, then so could Wonderland. Manning got H. L. Messmore, who also constructed Electric Park in Detroit that year, to build Wonderland's Fire and Flames set.[44] Fire engines were obtained from the Combination Ladder Company of Providence, Rhode Island, which had supplied the engines for the firefighting shows at the Coney Island parks.

There is no evidence that Armstrong himself ever came to Wonderland. Very likely he left the organization of the show to Manning, who had shown himself capable of organizing shows while on tour.

Exactly what the show was to be called was never precisely pinned down. Newspaper accounts called it both Fire and Flames, the name of the Luna Park show, and Fighting the Flames, the name of the London, St. Louis, and Dreamland shows. The names were essentially used interchangeably in the popular mind. The name of the Wonderland attraction was given as Fire and Flames in the brief blurb at the front of the Wonderland souvenir books and on a separate attraction souvenir book. But in a longer piece inside the Wonderland guidebook, it was called Fighting the Flames. That name also appeared on a picture postcard sold at Wonderland. For practical purposes, both names were apparently used about equally.

A Fire and Flames souvenir book from Wonderland for 1906 lists forty-four fire and police officials and forty-three named actors and actresses, in addition to numbers of extras and unnamed fire and police. Twenty-five horses and 250 people were employed in the show, with retired firemen from Boston, New York, and elsewhere serving in that capacity.[45] The overall stage manager was M. B. Pollock, an actor who had appeared onstage in both Boston and on Broadway. It needed the skills of an actor to superintend the players, who provided the background against which the firemen worked. The announcer was William Judkins Hewitt, a thirty-one-year-old press representative and speaker.[46]

The 3,500-person grandstand facing the Beaver Street entrance not only held the audience for the show; it also hid the performance from anyone who had not paid admission. At first people could see nothing when they sat down—a curtain was drawn across the front of the grandstand. When it was pulled aside the admitted spectators looked out on a city square formed at the intersection of two streets, holding an ellipse of grass with a streetlamp at each end. Almost parallel to the grandstand was part of a block with four buildings of varying heights, two with decorated roofs. Perpendicular to this was part of another block with six buildings of up to four stories.

The Fire and Flames souvenir book describes the action:

In a surging mass, men, women, and children from the various walks of life throng the crowded sidewalks. In the crowd the push-cart of the huckster gets upset and the hungry urchin proves himself a real son of Adam by partaking of the forbidden fruit, and during the confusion a lively row starts in a bar-room, and the police take legal and active part, which is followed by the Police Patrol and the Ambulance—those essentials of every modern city.

No sooner does the Ambulance turn the Corner and the police are again away from the scene than fresh excitement is aroused by a disturbance in

Figure 8. The Fire and Flames show as depicted in a painting used in a souvenir book and on many postcards. Courtesy of the author.

the store of Ike Cohen, caused by some boys who insult Ike by offering him two cents for his whiskers. To resent the offered insult he dashes at the boys, one of whom has lighted a match and as they separate the lighted match is thrown, and, as "great oaks from little acorns grow" so great fires from little matches glow. With the speed and vigor of the Furies the flames spread, and the excited and unthinking crowd deafen the ears with the wild cry of "Fire! Fire!! Fire!!!" A prudent and vigilant patrolman hears the cry and, seeing the flames, rushes to the near-by box and sounds the alarm. The crowd in wild excitement separate as they see the first engine coming "like mad" down the street, followed by a hose wagon and a ladder truck, sounding unceasingly its bells of warning to "clear the way," while from another side a belching engine dashes down through the dense and stifling smoke, followed by a police patrol; the danger lines are marked, the streets are roped off, and fearless of results the brave fire fighters dash into the building to save life and property. Busy housewives are caught by the flames in the third and fourth stories; some are rescued by the firemen on ladders, while others are forced to jump into the nets from the upper stories. Eight pieces of fire apparatus, worked by skilled firemen, add to the intense excitement of the realistic scene.[47]

The journalist Rollin Hartt once again, however, angled his description to deflate the park's ballyhoo:

> Half a million dollars invested in tinder-boxes necessitates expensive fire-fighting apparatus and a large squad of firemen, and the park makes the people pay for them. Seated in a huge grand-stand, you look out upon a tenement street, which swarms with such improvident Thespians as have laid by no money for the summer. As guttersnipes, factory girls, policemen, pawnbrokers, Chinese laundrymen, newsboys, and roisterers, they enact a travesty upon the life of the quarter, and what with fights, ambulance calls, robberies, arrests, and the clangor of patrol wagons, they do it full justice. But see! A wisp of smoke curls upward from Cohen's pawnshop! Then flames, and more flames. The alarm rings out, shouts rend the air, and in a moment the Department, with two steamers, a hose cart, a chemical, and a hook-and-ladder truck, comes charging through the throng, and attacks the conflagration, which has spread to adjoining buildings, at whose windows some forty women stand screaming. But the spectators—missing the point, as usual—forget that those who climb and those who leap have had long training either as firemen or acrobats, and that the only people really in mortal danger are the unfortunate Thespians. How they dodge the rushing engines, that Providence which watches over inebriates, babes, and play-actors alone knows.

The show stage covered four acres, larger than the size of the shows at Dreamland and Luna Park or at White City in Chicago, or even the show at the St. Louis Exposition.

⁂

One feature of Wonderland that had no fixed location, at least in the first year, was the band. As the *Wonderland Souvenir Magazine 1906* described them, "The management of Wonderland and its patrons are extremely fortunate in securing the Salem Cadet Band, a musical organization second to none in the country, and the one which has for years met with the unqualified approval of all who have listened to its superb concerts. Its repertoire is practically unlimited and its instrumentation a joy and a revelation. These band concerts are free to all."[48]

This was not hype. John Philip Sousa was still conducting and composing, and would continue to do so for many years. One of Wonderland's performers, Fred A. Bennett, had an act imitating Sousa and band leader Giuseppi Creatore—an act that would have been pointless unless he could expect his audience to be familiar with the styles of both. One critic described a Creatore performance thus: "Creatore starts the band in a mild, entreating way. A simple uplifting of the arms. Then suddenly, with a wild shake of his shaggy head, he springs across the stage with the ferocity of a wounded lion. Crash! Bang! And a grand volume of sound chocks the hall from pit to dome."[49] Bennett likely reproduced this wild style, given the popularity of marches and military bands.

The Salem Second Corps of Cadets Band had been organized a quarter of a century earlier, and since 1878 had been led by Jean Missud, a French musician from Nice who not only conducted but also composed his own pieces for the band. A collection of his waltzes had been published in 1881.[50]

The band had about forty members, who both marched and played at concert halls. The newspapers frequently printed the pieces they would play that week at Wonderland. These sets included marches, waltzes, fantasias, and even operatic overtures.

At some of the booths, the park sold sheet music especially written for Wonderland. Walter Jacobs, a well-known Boston-based music publisher, got an exclusive right to sell music there, and produced "Wonderland," a waltz, and "Take Me Down to Wonderland," a march. Both of these were written by a Natick-born violinist and composer Thomas S. Allen, whose picture appeared on the cover of each. Jacobs's exclusive contract must have been for a given period, because two years later a Boston competitor, G. W. Setchell, published "Wonderland, That's the Place for Me!" by Bert Porter.

These sheet music pieces served much the same purpose as advertising jingles played on the television or radio have today. In that pre-broadcast era, people made their own music and were eager for sheet music, even if the songs themselves were unabashedly commercial.

℘

The park was alive with specialized types as well. Uniformed young women sold and collected tickets to the attractions. Barkers called out their spiels to lure customers in. Food was sold throughout the park—Lowney's Chocolate Bon Bons, Sparrow's Empress Chocolates, and Schrafft's Chocolates were all sold at the park. Visitors could purchase Fox Brand snacks—salted peanuts, peanut brittle, "walnut slice," potato chips, salted almonds, and pecans. For drinks there were Coca Cola and Daggett's Orangeade, Vineland Grape Juice ("the only grape juice sold in Wonderland Park"), and Mount Washington Cold Spring drinks—plain and carbonated water and flavored beverages. The Spring Water Carbonating Company had a contract to build booths and dispense soda water. The New England favorite Moxie had a stand in the park shaped like a giant Moxie bottle, located near the Arcus Ring. And after all that there was ice cream from the Neapolitan Ice Cream Company as well as ice cream sandwiches and ice cream cones, both recent developments made popular at international expositions. Vendors of popcorn were given special license to walk about the park selling their goods, as well as in the grandstands at both the Fire and Flames show and the Wild West show.

In addition to these items, there were small booths scattered about the park, running around the edges and filling in the spaces between major attractions, even set underneath the ramp of the Shoot the Chute ride, between the Wild West show and the carousel, and underneath the Fighting the Flames grandstand. These booths sold a surprising variety of goods and services. There was a tailor, a barber, a manicurist, a check room, a portrait sketcher, a set of small lunch rooms where you could eat if you wanted a quick snack, and shops selling ladies' toiletries, wire jewelry, postcards, cigars, flowers, photo buttons, and souvenirs. These, like the restaurant, were run by Dudley McDonald. A full-service photographer was located opposite the Fighting the Flames show, between Princess Trixie and Ferari's Wild Animals.

There were games too. A shooting gallery was located next to the Fire and Flames show.[51] A card-cutting booth allowed the patron to take a chance on winning a prize. A typical card-cutting operation was basically a gambling game where the patron would place a bet against the chance of the operator cutting a deck of ordinary cards three times and coming up with at least one face card. Of course, gambling was not allowed in Revere, but one could take the chance of winning some souvenir or stuffed animal. The probabilities were deceptive—the odds of getting at least one face card in three fair cuts of a standard fifty-two-card deck is actually about 54 percent, so in the long run the stand profited.[52]

Another game was Box Ball. This was a sort of miniature bowling game, invented by the Box Ball Company of Indianapolis in the early 1900s. The game was popular with traveling shows because it could easily be packed up and transported, and didn't take up much space. A typical lane was thirty feet long by three feet wide, with a gutter on either side like a standard bowling alley. Instead of ten pins in a triangular array, there were five pins placed across the width of the alley, all attached by cords to a bar across the top. No doubt knocking all the pins down resulted in a prize.[53]

Another game was a Pipe-Cane Rack, run by one John Osborne.[54] These were ring-toss games in which the patron tried to toss a given number of rings—typically three—so that they encircled the shaft of a cane or pipe.

One other attraction marked a huge difference between 1900s culture and modern sensibilities—the African Dodger. The stand was run by Arthur H. Adams, although Jack Everhart (who, with his wife, ran many of the other booths) later took it over. The African Dodger was a game in which patrons paid to throw hard balls at the head of a man's head, which was sticking through a hole in a sheet of canvas. As the name implies, the target was an African American individual, whose job was to provoke the throwers by shouting derogatory comments about the throwers or their abilities, and then to duck his head out of the way. If you struck his head, the typical prize was a cigar.[55]

Shockingly, this was once an accepted form of public entertainment, not only at amusement parks and fairs but at church fundraisers and the like too. The *Boston Post* of July 24, 1909, related an account of one such booth at an open-air bazaar at the home of a prominent Boston socialite, intended to benefit, ironically, the Massachusetts Society for the Prevention of Cruelty to Children. They boasted an actual African dodger from "Gwana Tumbo Land."[56]

The balls used looked like standard baseballs but were smaller and lighter; nonetheless, people would deliberately sneak in actual baseballs, and baseball pitchers were known to try to strike accurately and hard. There were reports of severe injuries to the dodgers, including broken jaws.

The practice of the African Dodger, which appears to have started around 1880, continued into the 1930s and beyond, and depictions of it showed up in drawings, comics, and cartoons long after 1906. Not everyone took a neglectful attitude toward these stands. Under pressure, Massachusetts towns started banning the practice in the 1910s. The African Dodger came to be replaced by stands using carved human heads as targets (although invariably of Black individuals). Around 1910, what has come to be called the Dunk Tank was introduced, where the patrons threw baseballs at a target connected to a seat on which a person sat. Although definitely more humane than the original African Dodger, it was still a degrading situation and subtly sent a message about the inferiority of Black people.[57]

CHAPTER 4

Year One—1906
(The Southern Half of the Park)

At the southwest corner of the park, in a spread covering three acres surrounded by a high fence, the William H. Kennedy Wild West Show and Indian Congress sat. The name might not be familiar to people a hundred years later, but his Wild West show was one of the first, and it gave early jobs to cowboy stars Will Rogers, Gabby Hayes, Hoot Gibson, Buck Jones, and Tom Mix.

Kennedy was born in Lexington, Illinois, on March 19, 1870. With his brother James and Charles they began the Kennedy Brothers Wild West Show in 1893 in Illinois. The show toured the country, beginning to pick up acts and attractions that didn't always fit in with the theme. The Kennedys had riding and marksmanship demonstrations, rope twirling, and vignettes of "Western" life like hunting a horse thief, an American Indian camp, a recreation of the Mountain Meadow Massacre, and a Roman Hippodrome race. In 1902, they moved their base from Bloomington, Illinois, to Perry, Oklahoma Territory. William was the manager, Charles the treasurer, and James the "doorkeeper." In the act, Charles and James raced each other in chariots, and William, as "Lucky Bill," was the trick rider, knife thrower, and clown.[1]

The Kennedy brothers performed in Massachusetts in the summer of 1905, working at Paragon Park at Nantasket Beach in Hull.[2] This may be where the Wonderland crew took notice of them and spoke to them about appearing at Wonderland the following year. James and William renamed their show the Wild West Show and Indian Congress in 1906 and split it into two parts. James took the western unit to a park named Coney Island in Cincinnati, Ohio, while William took the eastern half to Wonderland.[3]

A story reported about William Kennedy and his wife, Bess, that may have been a fabrication for publicity purposes (since the Kennedys actually grew up in Illinois), or perhaps merely an elaboration on the facts, would be wonderful even if only mostly true:

> A number of years ago [William and Bess] were school children together at a little schoolhouse on the plains near Houston, Texas. Bill Kennedy, as the boy was known, used to ride 15 miles from his father's ranch to school every day. There he used to meet Bessie Cook, whom he used to call "The Prairie Wild Flower." When their school days were over Bill Kennedy and Miss Cook separated, and saw nothing of one another until [1898] in Providence, R.I.
>
> The schoolgirl had grown into a handsome woman, and was famous as the crack rifle shot in the southwest, and was traveling with a show. Bill Kennedy had grown up as one of the proprietors of Kennedy Bros.' Wild West Show and Indian Congress.
>
> At Providence the two shows happened to be exhibiting at the same time. Mr. Kennedy thought he recognized the crack shot, and one evening after the performance asked her if she did not formerly live in Texas, where a sweetheart called her "The Prairie Wild Flower." They were married in a short time and are now with the one show. . . . Mrs. Kennedy is not only an expert with the rifle, but is also an accomplished horsewoman.[4]

Certainly much contained in that piece was true. Bess and William Kennedy continued to perform together for decades afterward. Her part in the show consisted of a sharpshooting act and a race against another female jockey.

The Kennedy brothers first got together an "Indian Congress" for their show in 1902. Such gatherings of Native Americans had become a standard at international expositions, so it was a natural addition to the show. They were credited with being the first to bring Oklahoma Indians to the East in these shows, and soon expanded to Natives from other tribes. For the upcoming Wonderland show, Kennedy contracted with a company of Cheyenne Indians from Oklahoma Territory. They stopped in Buffalo en route and toured Niagara Falls in full regalia, much to the joy of the local newspapers. The papers interviewed Chief Toughfeather, who spoke through an interpreter.

> "Why do you leave your country?" [asked the reporter from the *Buffalo Morning Express*]

"We get white man's money," said the chief slowly, glancing about at his tribesmen. They all nodded approval with grunts.[5]

The interview was undoubtedly condescending (the report continued, "It is probable that his untutored brain did not grasp the design of the paleface to reduce *heap big roaring mountain roaring water* to a millrace in the hunt for the almighty dollar"), but it also captured the true reason for their participation—the work paid. The Indian's "untutored brain" certainly appreciated that, just as he stated, white men paid rents to live on his tribe's land back in Oklahoma Territory.

The 1906 Wonderland souvenir book gives this description of the Wild West show:

"Wild Bill" has assembled at Wonderland a troupe of ninety people. Forty of them are bona-fide Indians—Apache, Sioux, Tuscarora, and Cheyenne—all under the immediate charge of Chief Toughfeather. The latter is a fierce old warrior who is distinguished in the West as being a survivor of the Custer massacre at Little Big Horn.

There is an equal number of cowboys from the ranches of the Cattle Country. They are the fearless, danger-loving type which Mr. Owen Wister has so heroically portrayed in his celebrated novel. "The Virginian." They can ride hard and fast, shoot quick and straight, and can do things on a galloping broncho which an ordinary man would hardly dare to attempt on a saw-horse.

Not the least in the Wild West are the five "cow girls," if the expression may obtain. They are daring maids of the West, graceful riders and admirable examples of the fearless Western girl.

Every performance of the Wild West is preceded by an imposing parade through Wonderland which alone is better than the best Indian and cowboy parades ever given in any circus.

The performance is preceded by an exhibition of fancy riding which is very inadequately described by the word "fancy." Everyone loves a good horse. The combination is irresistible, whether the man be white or red.

The riding of bucking bronchos, lassoing feats, pursuit and execution of a horse-thief by the swift and terrible Western method, riding long-horned Texas steers, and the exhibition of marksmanship are added to the programme.[6]

The space for the show included a track a quarter mile long, which was probably used for the female jockey race and a Roman chariot race. The grandstand here, against the park's outer wall, seated two thousand people. The show ran every afternoon and evening, reportedly at intervals of thirty minutes.

On July 19, 1906, Bess Kennedy and a Mrs. Dickey were engaged in the lady's race when Bess's horse stepped in a hole in the track, throwing her and then falling on her. Dickey was able to leap her horse over Kennedy's and avoid further accident, but Kennedy was badly injured. They took her to the Wonderland hospital, where Dr. Charles A. Oak, the Wonderland Park physician, treated her. The newspapers did not report on her prognosis, but evidently she recovered.[7] Her husband hosted a media event the next week with reporters from several newspapers, as well as the mayor and other Revere city officials, serving beef barbecued by Chief Toughfeather and cakes baked by the cowgirls, and does not seem to have been concerned about his wife.[8] She does appear to have been out for the remainder of the season, however.

To replace her, William Kennedy brought in Annie Shaffer, whose act was described by the *Fitchburg [Massachusetts] Sentinel* as follows:

On Monday last the pure breath of the Western plains was brought to Wonderland in the person of Miss Annie Shaffer of Texas, better known as the "queen of the cowgirls," a title which she has fairly won by her intrepid feats of equestrianism, coupled with her other deeds of valor and her life in general on the Western border. A few hours after Miss Shaffer's arrival at Wonderland a car load of wild bronchos from Oklahoma put in an appearance there, and on Monday afternoon several of them felt saddle and bridle for the first time when the "queen of the cow girls" placed her foot to the stirrup and gave the first of her marvelous performances in the Wild West show at Revere. She brought with her to Wonderland the most valuable and also the most vicious as well as the tallest bucking horse in the world. He is known as "Sky Rocket." Miss Shaffer laughingly admits that when she took him from the Link Four Ranch in Oklahoma she paid $11 for him. Since then she has been offered as high as $5000 for her prize, but invariably has refused. At Wonderland this week, with Miss Shaffer in the saddle, "Sky Rocket" was seen to clear the earth from four to six feet, when bucking, turn half around while in the air and light twice on his hind feet without ever touching his fore-feet to the ground. In riding him, Miss Shaffer never once touches her hand to any part of the saddle, saying that would be "pulling leather," and that she "had rather get thrown off 'Sky Rocket' than pull leather."[9]

Shaffer, the wife of Wild West performer George Hooker, had started performing the previous year at White City in Chicago. She went on to join Buffalo Bill's show in 1907.[10]

In addition to this show, a nearby Indian souvenir stand and an Indian archery booth, where patrons could try their hand at hitting a target, brought in additional money. The Kennedy Wild West show had its own barkers, J. Kelley and J. C. Warren. The show was immensely popular.[11]

∾

Next to the Wild West show enclosure was the Whirl the Whirl. This ride is a little obscure. It appears in no Wonderland postcards nor are there drawings of it in any Wonderland stories, though it appears in the backgrounds of photographs of some other attractions. It is not described in any of the news articles about the park, which sing the praises of other rides. The only description of it we have is from the 1906 souvenir book:

Whirl the Whirl

It creates a whirlwind of mirth and merriment while revolving in mid-air.

Among Wonderland's many thrilling and thoroughly enjoyable lodestars is the Whirl the Whirl. This amusement enterprise, the property of Mr. Lewis Bopp, is a novel form of the revolving swing. The mechanism is attached to a tall pillar of steel which is capped by a huge ball of electric lights, seven feet in diameter and ninety three feet from the ground. At night the big ball gleams brightly and the lights on the fast-traveling cars add to the splendid effect.

Louis Bopp (the usual spelling of his name) was born in 1864 in New York City and started as a sculptor, apprenticing at the Looff Company carousel works at Coney Island. He became a manufacturer and owner of carousels himself, first in New York City, then in Jamaica for the 1891 exposition there. He moved to Revere Beach and opened carousels and eventually other attractions. His Rough Riders became one of the big attractions at the beach. Bopp also owned and operated the carousel at Wonderland, which similarly does not appear in any contemporary photographs. Perhaps these two attractions, both owned and operated by Louis Bopp, were not considered wholly part of Wonderland. In any event, his are two of the least-known rides in the park.

Fortunately, we do know something more about the Whirl the Whirl from its first appearance at Luna Park and from its patent. The Whirl the Whirl was the creation of J. Harry Welsh, the master mechanic of Luna Park. Welsh was both a mechanical and an electrical engineer. While not much his known about him, one story gives an idea of his abilities and duties. In 1906, when a child poked Jim, Luna Park's nine-foot alligator, with a board, the alligator turned and snapped at the board. It closed its jaws over a large nail protruding from the board, driving the nail through the roof of its mouth. Frederic Thompson, one of the owner/managers of the park, had workmen jam a board into the animal's mouth to prop it open, and then Welsh reached in through the bars with "an enormous pair of tweezers" and pulled out the nail. The alligator then snapped its jaws a few times, as if to test them, and promptly went to sleep.[12]

Welsh's design of the Whirl the Whirl is a rare case of a major attraction being developed from within a park. He applied for a patent for his "Aerial Whirling Tower" on February 27, 1903, and it was granted almost a year later on January 19, 1904. The ride was constructed at Alhambra Court in Luna Park and was ready for opening day in the 1904 season.

For some reason, descriptions of the ride appeared in newspapers in the Midwest in late 1903 and spring of 1904. They were much more detailed than the one in the Wonderland guidebook:

A New Coney Island Thriller

There will be a brand new thriller at Coney Island next summer. It is called the "whirl the whirl."

The whirl the whirl is made of steel. The tower is seventy-four feet high, and the arms, of which there are four, are twenty-five feet long. Cars capable of holding from sixteen to twenty people each are attached to the end of the arms. When loaded, the machinery is started and the arms begin to revolve around the tower at the rate of eight revolutions to the minute and gradually climb to the full height of the tower, where a number of revolutions are made before the return trip is begun. It has been estimated that the trip up and down the tower will cover a distance of 6,520 feet, almost a mile and a quarter.[13]

The ride was an immediate hit, and the management did what they could to accommodate more people and streamline waiting times. Welsh founded the Whirl the Whirl Company to build franchises at other parks, but Wonderland appears to have been the only other park to operate the ride under the name Whirl the Whirl.

∾

Wonderland was not just a collection of rides. It presented exotic experiences and interesting sights from around the world. The Beautiful Orient introduced the visitor to a bazaar from the Middle East, the Japanese Village offered a tea ceremony, and the Wild West show gave people contact with American Indians, while Ferrari's highlighted wild animals from around the world. Like the other large amusement parks that opened around this time, Wonderland sought to be a type of permanent exhibition or World's Fair, bringing natural and technological wonders before the public, entertaining and educating them in addition to giving them the visceral thrills of rides.[14]

This explains the purpose behind an exhibit that looks strange to modern eyes: the Baby Incubators, which had its own attached hospital. On the surface, this seems as out of place in an early twentieth-century amusement park as an intensive care unit would be today in Disneyland. But, when considered as an item of technological process, it fits in precisely with the "World's Fair in Miniature" that Wonderland was striving to be.

Dr. Martin A. Couney's Infant Incubators first appeared at the 1896 Great Industrial Exposition in Berlin, then at the Victorian-era exhibition at Earl's Court in London the next year. They made their U.S. public debut at the 1898 Trans-Mississippi Exposition in Omaha, Nebraska, and then again three years later at the 1901 Pan-American Exposition in Buffalo. It was immensely popular, with a constant line of people streaming into the building, urged by a carnival-style barker. The babies within were premature infants who required the special care of the temperature- and humidity-controlled environment of the steel-and-glass incubators.[15]

Couney did not invent the incubator—the idea had been implemented and patented decades before. But the devices were not generally accepted by hospitals in the early twentieth century. Couney was a man on a mission, seeking to popularize the concept and bring it to people who needed it. He charged admission and used a barker to lure in customers, but the money was ploughed back into subsidizing the high cost of running the incubators. Couney, despite the honky-tonk setting, strove to keep the incubators clean, efficient, and respectable. The incubators also appeared at the 1904 St. Louis Exhibition, and after that at Luna Park, which ran for many years. He likewise put in an exhibit at Dreamland on Coney Island.

While Couney's exhibits at Coney Island attracted of the most attention, they also appeared at small events, and he arranged to have his units placed in other amusement parks around the country.

Couney's incubators actually appeared in Boston three years earlier, at the Merchant's and Manufacturer's Exposition at Mechanics Hall in October 1903.[16] The incubators were the hit of the expo. Probably inspired by this, Austin and Stone's Dime Museum in Boston's Scollay Square brought in their own incubator exhibit in May 1904, without the cooperation of Couney. They were in the charge of Charles W. G. Rollins, who claimed that his father, Dr. S. W. Rollins, had brought the first incubators into the United States some nine years earlier.[17] The incubators used were not the model used by Couney but ones from Paris. After a month at Austin and Stone's, the incubators were moved to Revere Beach in June 1904, where they were displayed at Crescent Gardens, a hotel and ballroom not far from where Wonderland would go up two years later.[18] They were promptly shut down by two agents from the State Board of Lunacy and Charity. According to the *Boston Globe,* "The action of the agents was taken under the law which requires that a boarding place for infants shall not be operated without a license from the state."[19] They were, in essence, shut down on a technicality. The real reason was no doubt because, despite its popularity, many in positions of authority saw the incubator exhibit as exploitation of defenseless children. Certainly the kind of ballyhoo exhibition that Rollins's incubators represented was precisely the opposite of what Couney wanted. He went out of his way to show that the highest standards of professionalism and decorum were met. He might, of necessity, be operating in an amusement park, but his was a true medical exhibit and a class act.

So when Thompson arranged for an Infant Incubator exhibit at Revere's Wonderland, he also made sure that it met the needed criteria. Wonderland got the permits. It is probably also why the infant incubator exhibit was attached to a fully functional hospital.

The Wonderland souvenir book called the Infant Incubators "Wonderland's most scientific exhibit." The babies were placed on wire netting inside steel and glass boxes that controlled temperature and humidity.

They were wrapped in blankets and had a blue or pink ribbon to indicate sex. The incubators were attended and monitored by uniformed nurses, and a rail kept the onlookers at a safe and respectful distance. Dr. Christopher C. Egan was in charge of the day-to-day operations.[20]

Some of Couney's incubator exhibits in other parks continued to operate for decades. The ones at Coney Island and Atlantic City, for instance, were still open into the 1940s. Ironically, it turned out that, although Couney had attended medical school in Germany and taken the title "doctor," he may never have actually acquired a formal medical degree—or a college degree of any kind.

∽

Next to the incubator building was the Walnut Avenue entrance building, which also housed the administration office on its upper floors. On the ground floor were the restrooms and a children's crèche, where parents could leave their young children while they toured the park. Attached to the administration building was a penny arcade, which was not quite ready in time for opening day. The attraction opened on June 2 instead. Such arcades were actually a very new innovation in 1906; the term "penny arcade" first appeared about 1900. They were a development from the phonograph parlors that had been set up to promote Thomas Edison's sound reproducing machine. People could come into these booths, pay a coin into a slot on the device, and hear music through a set of headphones. Putting the pay phonographs in an enclosed setting minimized vandalism and theft.

Edison also tried to introduce his motion pictures into these spaces in the form of his kinetoscope, in which a long loop of film ran over a series of reels, with an illuminated film visible by the single viewer who had paid a coin into the device to watch it, rather like a pay "Moviola" machine. But Edison's device was complex and liable to breakage, and his long films tended to break under repeated use, requiring frequent splicing. An ex-employee of Edison's, William K. L. Dickson, set up a simpler device that achieved much the same result with fewer moving parts and fewer breakdowns—the Mutoscope. He printed out each frame of the film onto heavy card stock and placed them, secured by their bottom edges, onto a rotating cylinder. This was placed in a clamshell holder with a lightbulb to

illuminate the cards, one at a time, as they were retained by a metal "fin-
ger" at the top. The patron paid a penny into the slot and turned a handle
to turn the drum of cards, which acted like a "flip book." This was such
a reliable device that many have survived to the present day, with their
drums of photo cards still intact and usable.

Today we think of the Mutoscope as a quant piece of old-time nostalgia, and many modern amusement arcades have one or two around. In
their heyday, however, in larger cities the now-renamed penny arcades had
them by the dozens. Mutoscopes were immensely popular. The private
nature of the viewings offered, and the risqué advertising used to entice
viewers, led to moralists' condemning the shows. Nevertheless, existing
Mutoscope reels are pretty tame, not having anything that would generate
above a modern "G" rating. An article from 1906 on penny arcades for
Trolley Parks explained that a typical penny arcade would contain about
fifteen Mutoscopes, eighteen phonographs, a so-called perfume machine
(likely a perfume dispenser), a stick candy dispenser, a gum dispenser, a
penny scale, a punching bag, a "test your strength" hand gripper, a "test
your strength" lifter, a mechanical fortune teller, an "Uncle Sam" machine
(another "test your strength" machine—a statue of Uncle Sam extended
his hand for a shake; the patron had to squeeze all the fingers together), a
"Home Plate" (presumably a baseball game machine), a postcard machine
(which dispensed postcards with messages from an imaginary sweetheart),
an engraving machine, and a cashier.[21] The Wonderland Penny Arcade,
according to the park ledger, hosted between twenty and twenty-five
Mutoscope machines, leased from the Mutoscope Company at a cost of
two dollars per week. The proprietor was Nat Burgess.[22]

෴

Next to this was the children's theater, an auditorium capable of seating six
hundred people. At the start of this first season, it ran Edward Gillett's Dog
and Monkey Circus, one of numerous such circuses operating at that time.
Gillett's featured "singing" dogs and a monkey bowling act. Two chimpan-
zees, Adam and Eve, competed using monkeys as the bowling balls. The
monkeys rolled up into balls and were "bowled" at pins. Monkeys also
acted as the pin boys that set them back up again.[23]

The show operated for only six weeks, closing abruptly on July 10. It was replaced by the revue "The South before the War" for the rest of the summer.[24] This was a popular musical show with idealized, idyllic antebellum scenes. A show called "The South before the War" had played at Austin and Stone's Dime Museum in Boston in 1901–2. Another show of that name was produced at Paragon Park in Hull, Massachusetts, south of Boston, in 1905. The Wonderland show might have been the same one and was run by Arthur B. Fullis.

☙

The next building over was the scene of the Fatal Wedding. This was an attraction literally brought over from Luna Park in Coney Island, where it was run by Charles Pelton in 1905. Both Pelton and the attraction itself were brought to Wonderland, presumably by Floyd Thompson.[25] It had originally been part of the 1901 Pan-American Exposition in Buffalo, New York. And what was this oddly named amusement? The description given in the 1906 souvenir book offers a little help in understanding the attraction:

The Fatal Wedding

The old Egyptians would introduce a skeleton at a banquet to remind the guests, in the midst of their good cheer, that life was but fleeting and death inevitable for all.

But the people of the pyramids never conceived of any such grim and ghastly contrast as is offered by Wonderland's Fatal Wedding.

The very atmosphere of the interior, before the curtain rises, breathes a gloomy solemnity. The walls are festooned with sobs, sighs, and tears. Did you ever see a sigh on a wall? Did you ever see mural decoration consisting of heart-breaking sobs and scalding tears? These are a few of the weird features of the Fatal Wedding—even before the nuptial ceremony begins.

After the brief but intelligent explanation by the lecturer of the nature of the show, the curtain rises. The stage is shrouded in black. Then the lecturer's real task begins. He has to persuade two people, a man and a woman, or a youth and a maid, to volunteer from the audience to be married. When the volunteers are obtained they are stood up together for the service, both draped in white covering. Suddenly they disappear and in their place stand two grinning skeletons which in turn give way to the flesh and bone couple again. Other features are the ghost lunch, spirit food, and similar accessories.

The Egyptian custom of having a skeleton at a party has real roots—it comes from Plutarch's *Moralia* (ca. 100 CE), in "The Dinner of the Seven Wise Men," where they are discussing things done at such gatherings. As for the illusion itself, the description of another Fatal Wedding show identified it as "mechanical," but the above description sounds more like an optical trick, and a description of the 1905 Coney Island performance confirms this.[26] A notice in the *New York Press* observed that "a new illusion called 'A Fatal Wedding' will provide lots of sport for the friends of 'spooney' couples."[27] One imagines that the volunteers were often "volunteered" by their friends and embarrassed by the attention.

The likely illusion used was one called Pepper's Ghost. The basic idea was that with proper control of lighting, an ordinary pane of glass could act either like a mirror or like a transparent sheet of glass, depending on where the lighting is placed. The couple would be brought up and placed each in their own coffin, standing up and facing the audience through the huge glass pane (whose presence would not be known to the audience). The lights on the couple would slowly dim while lights illuminating a pair of skeletons in identical coffins were brought up. The glass would now act like a mirror, and the couple would thus appear to have turned into skeletons. The process was reversed to "restore" the couple.

✢

George Consider Hale was already an established figure in 1902 when he retired as the fire chief of Kansas City at the age of fifty-two. A prolific inventor, he held over sixty patents, mostly for firefighting equipment, but he continued inventing after his retirement. One of the new attractions at expositions and amusement parks was the Phantom Ride (what we would today call a virtual-reality ride), in which effects contrived to convince the passengers that they were going somewhere while they were actually not moving at all. Shaking train cars with painted scenes rolling outside the windows could suggest a train journey without any motion.[28] Hale added the very novel idea of using motion pictures projected on the wall of a duplicate railway carriage to give the illusion of being aboard a train. In this way, operators could, by changing the film, provide a vast number of different journeys.

The idea caught on immediately and was incredibly successful. Marketed as Hale's Tours, the ride debuted at the St. Louis Exposition in 1904. Shortly after it appeared at Coney Island and then in hundreds of other cities across the country. That Floyd Thompson and Wonderland should have snapped up such a new attraction was almost guaranteed. The Wonderland souvenir book describes the experience:

Hale's Tours

Did you know that you could go direct from Wonderland to Spain?
   Or across the continent? Or to Mount Vesuvius?
   Hale's Tours, under the Brady-Grossman Management, are wonderfully ingenious in their adaptation of moving picture mechanism to modern illusion. The conductor calls "All aboard," you step into a Pullman car. The bell rings, the whistle blows, and the car starts. The passenger gazes with fascinated, almost awesome, interest as the car travels and the country flies by at express speed. "Look out for that curve!" The car rocks and sways as cars do. At the end of the curve the car takes the tangent with the usual jar.
   The moving pictures show a trip to Colorado and a mix-up among passengers of the Deadwood sleeper. Or, there is the trip to Spain and the bull-fight at the end. Again, the passenger is in Italy and sees Mt. Vesuvius in eruption, with scenes of awful devastation. These are some of the sights observed on Hale's Tours, starting from Wonderland.

Journalist Rollin Hartt, typically, was not impressed: "To be gulled, to know you are gulled, and to know that the people who gull you know you know they're gulling you,—ah, the bliss! Here at the park a mimic railway carriage, with biograph pictures at its farthest end, takes you spinning along the funicular 'up Mt. Vesuvius.'"

☙

Beside the Hale's Tour building was the Japanese Village. There was a Japanese village at Luna Park in Coney Island in 1903, and inevitably other parks copied it. Wonderland's Japanese Village featured an entrance through a traditional *torii* gate (with the very un-traditional words "Japan" and "Admission Free" written on the crosspiece). There were low bridges and a high Moon Bridge, pagodas and gardens, and, in the back, a miniature Mount Fuji sixty feet tall, made of painted canvas over a wooden framework. Several booths with different attractions and souvenirs lined either side, and in the back a small restaurant served patrons "with Japanese Tea and other light refreshments by Daughters of Nippon clad in Japanese Costume."

A better description than the guidebook's was given the next year by the *Boston Post:*

> The section of any big recreation park known as the Japanese Village is usually an assemblage of catch-penny devices with lanterns, wind bells, pagodas and the like to give it as much of a presumably oriental aspect as possible. On the whole, however, the usual Japanese Village is, to say the least, somewhat disappointing. At Wonderland the Japanese Village has always been a place of the deepest interest, and this year it is the real thing. The interior of the great Fuji mountain has been transformed into a typical dwelling place, reproducing a home of the best class of Japanese. There are ten rooms in the suite—hall, kitchen, private chapel, waiting, tea, dining, sewing, bed, and reception rooms, with specially imported furniture. In front of the hall, on the door stoop, arranged in a room, are pleasant and stormy weather shoes, apparently left outside by the occupants of the house or visitors, for, as is well known, no Japanese wears shoes in the house. A straw raincoat, bamboo umbrella and pan hat are near at hand. And so on all throughout the premises. Every room has its own appropriate, curious furniture. The ladies will be particularly interested in the furnishing of the kitchen and the bed room, the latter with its wooden pillows and bed upon the floor, while gentlemen visitors will note with particular interest the facilities for entertaining guests. The cleanliness and simplicity of it all is striking. A beautiful garden surrounds the house with a placid stream winding its way through the village. Quaint bridges span the water and miniature flower beds dot the grassy banks of the tiny stream. There are pagodas upon all sides where tea, ices, and rice cakes are served.[29]

Rollin Hartt brought this breathless description crashing down to earth:

> You cross the threshold of Fair Japan, that "revelation and perfect, unabridged realization of the Kingdom of the Mikado and the Chrysanthemum." Later, though, you find it a very agreeable psychological lark, since the people are obviously undismayed by American girls in Japanese costumes, or by wisteria reproduced in paper, or by shabby little pools bordered with Portland cement; and as for vermilion gateways and the crudest and most inartistic of decorations, not the jiu-jitsu performance gets a serener acceptance as "the real thing."

Figure 9. Postcard showing the theaters and attractions at the end of the lagoon from midsummer 1906. From right to left you can see the penny arcade, children's theater (with "The South before the War" banner), Fatal Wedding, Hale's Tours, and Beautiful Japan. Courtesy of the author.

Besides the tea rooms and jiu-jitsu demonstrations, there was also a show or lecture about the Russo-Japanese War.[30] This would have been of particular interest in 1906. The Japanese victory at the Straits of Tsushima the previous May had effectively finished the war, and the Treaty of Portsmouth concluding it was initiated by President Teddy Roosevelt and signed at the Portsmouth Naval Shipyard, a mere fifty miles from Wonderland, on September 5, 1905.

&

The next attraction you came to, immediately to the north of the Japanese Village, was the Temple of Palmistry, housed in a building with a huge open hand on the front. There had been a Temple of Palmistry at the 1904 St. Louis Exposition, so, of course, it was copied here. Little information exists about the feature. Hartt threw in only a few lines about it: "For illusions *par* excellence commend me to yonder fat and sleepy pythoness, who sits within the Temple of Palmistry and between yawns deludes the eye of faith. There is something magnificent about those yawns." We know the names of two of the practitioners because a publicist took an irresistible photo of them "reading the palm" of an incubator baby, which one of them holds. The palmists, Virginia Knapp and Estelka Daly, were dressed in "Gypsy" garb.[31]

❧

Exactly what to call the Wonderland funhouse, next to the Temple of Palmistry, was apparently not clear. One early account called it the House That Jack Built, although that name was not used until much later. Another called it the House of Mirth. Most called it the House of Follies or the Third Degree. The insurance map, the 1906 park ledger, and a drawing in Hartt's book *The People at Play* call it "The Foolish House."[32] Maybe because the name wasn't solidly pegged down, a lot of newspaper accounts didn't name it at all. One simply called it "the funny, freakish, foolish house."[33]

The name might be important and hold special significance, though. Funhouses were a feature of exposition midways and amusement parks of the period, and you could find Houses of Mirth and Third Degrees all over the country. Most were operated by the same organization—the Keystone Amusement Construction Company of Pittsburgh, Pennsylvania.[34] Significantly, they operated one House of Mirth at Dreamland on Coney Island. Their houses seemed to have a steep staircase going up in the front and distorting mirrors inside, along with sometimes a mirror maze. At one point, the company changed the names of the funhouses to the Third Degree. Photographs and postcards of the park all called the funhouse the Third Degree, which was the name of the concessions run by Keystone.[35] Perhaps Wonderland leased it to them after it had been built.

The entrance to the house was through the spread legs of a huge, grotesque man, rendered in high relief. He was dressed in a suit, with a top hat and monocle, but his face was that of an idiot—huge splayed teeth, a broad nose, goggle eyes. It looked somewhat like the face of an older Alfred E. Neuman, the mascot of *Mad Magazine* from over half a century later but one derived from illustrations and advertisements contemporary with Wonderland. (The resemblance is heightened by the one missing upper incisor, the absence of which this figure shares with Neuman.) Clearly, both were intended to represent dim-witted boys. The figure in the Third Degree had two outstretched hands held by elegantly dressed women who also carried bouquets of flowers. Possibly this was intended to suggest that the hapless figure was betrothed to both women at the same time. Very similar entrances were used for the fun houses of other amusement parks of the time.

Our only real description of the interior comes from Rollin Hartt:

It is vague and mysterious,—without, a blend of the awesome and the comic; within, well, let's see! Darkness, a winding passage,—innocuous enough, but wait! Next moment a frolicksome tornado has all but knocked you senseless. The floor wallows and shakes. Horrifying bumps confront your feet. What with tempests and earthquakes and night and labyrinthine confusion and stumbling-blocks combined, you wish yourself dead. Then relief! A crystal maze, humorous but not alarming. A row of concave and convex mirrors, showing you yourself as Humpty Dumpty, or as that gracefully attenuated celebrity, Jack the Beanstalk. Five minutes of laughter. After that, you bravely run the gauntlet of supplementary distresses, and when you emerge it is with a shining countenance as of one newly initiated by the "joiners."[36]

ↄ

Next to the funhouse on the midway at Wonderland was a tent devoted to Princess Trixie, "The Equine Paradox," as her owner, William Harrison Barnes, put it in an advertisement they took out in the pages of the Wonderland souvenir book.

The advertisements in the newspapers described her accomplishments:

Wonderland

HAS PRINCESS TRIXIE

The Bernhardt of the animal kingdom—An actress in the truest sense—A horse miraculously endowed with a human brain—Delights in human companionship—Can spell your name, add, subtract, and multiply, tell colors and pick out the prettiest girl at a moment's notice—She is

Wonderland's Star Performer[37]

The entrance to Trixie's tent was decorated with a large horseshoe with "Trixie" written on it framing the entrance, pictures of the famous horse, and a rack with press notices that the people could take with them. There was also a listing of her feats—"Plays Musical Instruments, Goes to School, Works National Cash Register."

Her act consisted of a number of physical and mental feats. Trixie could do simple arithmetic—adding, subtracting, and multiplying—spell out words, work a cash register on a special stand (giving out proper change in amounts up to two dollars), read a watch and give the correct time. She could tell colors.

Trixie had a basket of blocks with letters and numbers written on them, and she could use them to spell out words shouted out by the audience. Asked which woman in the audience was the most beautiful, Trixie would pick out colored items from her basket and arrange them in front of the winner, matching colors to those of the woman's dress and hat.[38] She could balance herself on a chair, lie on her back and have a "spasm," and bow to the audience.

Trixie was not confined to her tent. She participated in the daily Wonderland parade around the lagoon. In the morning, Barnes would exercise her, putting on a bright red harness and hitching her to a light cart for a trot up and down Revere Beach Boulevard. It was not only good exercise; it was also good advertising.

Trixie was just one of a number of "educated horses" making the rounds on the show circuit—Beautiful Jim Key, Bonner, Prince Albert, and others. Barnes saw them as the competition. He made standing challenges to them and recorded the results on the front of Trixie's tent and in newspaper ads.

She had an "autobiography," actually written by George L. Handin and recently republished in 2015. The 2017 book *Great American Horse Stories,* edited by Sharon B. Smith, also includes her story. A lengthy article on *The Horse's Mind* by Major N. Birch, commandant of the riding establishment at Woolwich, in the *Cavalry Journal* in 1907 described Trixie's training by Barnes and speculated about the advantage of subjecting horses for the military to similar training to develop their intelligence: "Most of the following 'tricks' have already been taught [to horses] in the Army, but no soldier will deny the desirability of the horse being able to perform them by word of command alone if required."

Unfortunately for these hopes of super-intelligent horses and superior horse-training, Trixie and her competitors were examples of the "Clever Hans" phenomenon, named after a horse owned by German mathematics teacher Wilhelm von Osten, who worked to teach his horse Hans mathematics and calculation and believed that he had succeeded spectacularly. Hans did evidently display the ability to calculate, tapping out his answers with his hoof on the ground. He could seemingly perform other prodigious mental feats as well. Osten started exhibiting Hans in 1891, and the horse became a sensation, inspiring imitators such as Mahomet, a horse exhibited by an American in Britain, and a decade later Trixie and her ilk.

But Hans was investigated by several scientists, most notably psychologist Oskar Pfungst in 1907, who was able to demonstrate that Hans was not calculating. The horse was merely extremely adept at picking up non-verbal cues of body language from Osten, who was unaware he was providing them. If Osten knew the answer, Hans looked to him to know when to stop tapping out the answer on the ground.

This affected Trixie's credibility as well. Even though her stint at Wonderland preceded Pfungst's study, his was by no means the first to question these special horses. Professor Carl Stumpf of Berlin University had come to the same conclusion several years earlier, as had many others, writing in *Scientific American*, *Nature*, and other journals. Today, the "Clever Hans Effect" is a well-known psychological effect, and it has implications for testing involving animals and people. It is one reason for the use of double-blind tests, where no one involved knows the correct result, and thus cannot inadvertently "signal" the correct result.

ↄ

Next to Trixie's tent was the baroque, carved, triple-peaked front of Joseph G. Ferari's Trained Wild Animals. At first glance the show appeared to be just another animal menagerie playing small venues and start-ups like Wonderland, but there was much hidden below the surface.

Joseph Giacomo Ferari and his brother Francis "Frank" Ferari were born in Leeds, England, in 1868 and 1862, respectively, to a family of Italian extraction. Their father, James Ferari, was a showman. Joseph and Francis partnered with Frank Bostock, whose family had been running menageries in England since the beginning of the nineteenth century. All three came to America in 1893–94 and established the touring carnival business in America. They also established a permanent base at Coney Island.

The Ferari Brothers separated at some point from Bostock to pursue their own traveling show. They went through several different company

names, at one point becoming the Ferari Brothers Company operating out
of New York. There were as many Ferari Brothers as there were Ringling
Brothers, and the company included, besides Joseph and Francis, brothers
Charles, William, and Antonio.

Only Joseph and Francis performed, however, styling themselves "Colonel" Francis Ferari and "Captain" Joseph G. Ferari. They justified their titles
due to their "battles with wild animals."[39] They adopted the quasi-military
costume that has become stereotypical of lion tamers, and not only displayed animals but engaged the creatures in performances, showing how
well-trained they were. The brothers had lions named Caesar and Brutus,
but their specialty became hybrid giant cats. They had, for instance, one
beast that was, they said, one quarter jaguar, one quarter leopard, and one
half lion. They produced non-hybrids for other shows and zoos as well.
They donated the two leopard cubs "Wonder" and "Land" to Wonderland
just before the park's opening.[40]

They split off a portion of their business for Wonderland and put it in
charge of Joseph Ferari. In previous years they had split the company into
two units, one under Francis and the other under Joseph. The division
of work was successful as it helped to get their feet in the door for future
shows at parks and expositions. The 1906 Wonderland souvenir book
reports that their show featured "Lions, Leopards, Hyenas, Bears, Monkeys, etc. All finely educated." They also featured hybrid leopard-panther
cubs. Their own advertisement in the book called their exhibit "The Largest, Cleverest, and Most Comprehensive Caravan in the World." A news
story about the arrival of the animals at the fair prior to the opening listed
"six lions, six bears, two leopards, two panthers, and a puma," although
that was surely not the whole contingent of animals.[41] A later story mentioned elephants. Likewise, one of the features of the show was a "Happy
Family" display, where they displayed two bears, two Russian boar hounds,
two pumas, a panther, and a jaguar all resting in the same cage, without
any apparent conflict.[42]

വ

Professor Joseph La Roux and his wife, "Tiny," began making balloon
ascents above the park in June 1906, an act that evolved from less ambitious beginnings. They came down by jumping from the balloon and using

parachutes to land, an iffy proposition. They were at the mercy of the winds, and at times came down miles away, up the beach, or among the beachgoers.

"Professor" Joseph La Roux was actually Joseph Kray from the vicinity of Glens Falls, New York. He started out as an acrobat, wire walker, and "all-around athlete," then took up ballooning, at which point he changed his name to the more exotic-sounding "La Roux" and adopted the title "Professor," as many balloonists did.[43] He performed along the eastern circuit, taking up a balloon that had a trapeze bar suspended from it instead of a basket. Once aloft, he would perform on the trapeze, higher than any circus tent. Eventually he added a descent by parachute from the balloon at the end of the act.

On August 17, 1894, some six thousand people watched as La Roux and acrobat Ella Nelson got married in an odd ceremony that started with Ella sewn up in a large sack, the opening sealed with wax, and magically released without breaking the seals in a rendition of the "Hindoo Sack Trick."[44] They then ascended a platform to the Wedding March from Richard Wagner's *Lohengrin* and were married by Justice Nathan Pulver of Luzerne, New York. Then Professor La Roux seated himself on the trapeze bar of his balloon. Attached to this was a parachute, from which hung a second trapeze on which Ella Nelson sat. The sudden start following the release of the balloon's ropes unseated the new Mrs. La Roux, and she dangled head downward, presumably holding on by her knees. Good acrobat that she was, she soon regained her seat.

Joseph La Roux pulled out a Roman candle from a sack of fireworks he was carrying and lit it, sending out a shower of sparkling ejecta and light projectiles. Unfortunately, he had not taken precautions to protect the bag of fireworks from sparks, and the entire bag caught fire "and for a few minutes he was enveloped in a pyrotechnic shower," as one account put it. "His right hand and wrist and the left side of his face were badly burned."

When the balloon reached a height of three thousand feet, he cut away the rope holding the parachute and the lower trapeze bar, and Ella La Roux drifted down, landing in a field. Joseph himself descended by slowly releasing the gas from the balloon's valve, alighting within four hundred yards of his bride. As it was dark by this time, he claimed that this was the first night-time parachute descent from a balloon. After this they recuperated with a trip on the steam ship *Mohican* on Lake George.

You would think that once would be enough, but less than a year later year La Roux got married again. At the end of June 1895, he married to Ida M. Hart in a balloon tethered to the ground, which was then allowed to ascend. "Hm! We thought the Professor was married in a balloon here last summer!" mused the *Glen Falls Daily Times*. Then, they recalled the joke about the parishioner who showed up multiple times to be confirmed, and who explained that he thought the bishop's laying on of hands was good for his rheumatism. "Perhaps he thinks it is good for his rheumatism," commented the *Times* dryly on La Roux's remarriage.[45]

Perhaps La Roux did think so, because only three years later he was back for a third go at it. In 1898, he married Christina "Tina" Davis, who was inevitably nicknamed "Tiny." Davis was seventeen at the time. Originally from Portugal, she also performed burlesque and ballooning, and thus fit in perfectly with La Roux's professional activities. This time the marriage stuck, at least for a bit longer, because "Tiny" was Madame La Roux when they came to Wonderland. Joseph La Roux named his airship "Tiny Davis" after her.

Their standard act became a double parachute leap from the balloon. A specially wide balloon carried two trapeze bars slung from the bottom, one for each of them, with the parachutes attached fully open near the top of the balloon, rigged so that they could be released with the jerk of a rope. The parachutes could not deploy from a folded state so close to the ground, and even in this unpacked state needed a few thousand feet to fully open.[46] For their performances at Wonderland they used a balloon christened "Wonderland," which they claimed was "the largest ever constructed for parachute jumping purposes."[47]

July 25, 1906, was an unusually exciting day at Wonderland. Shortly after 5 p.m., preparations were being made as usual for the balloon ascent by Amelia Garvin and Tiny La Roux. (Joseph La Roux would be staying on the ground.)[48] The balloon was filled in the space behind the Hell Gate ride, only this time there would be a difference. Instead of Garvin going up and descending by parachute, the one accompanying Tiny La Roux would be Floyd C. Thompson. Thompson himself insisted on doing this, having seen the arrangements and the operation. Only a few minutes before the act, he sent a message to the La Rouxs of his intentions.

The Wonderland stockholders who were present were horrified. They protested, but Thompson insisted on going up. He replaced his straw hat (which would have blown off) with a light cap. After he climbed onto the trapeze bar, his hands were tied to the parachute ropes. This precaution probably saved his life.[49]

At the moment of readiness, a pistol shot signaled the release of the ropes. The balloon shot skyward with such suddenness that Thomson promptly lost his cigar from his mouth, his cap from his head, and his hold on the trapeze. It was very much like what had happened to Ella Nelson at Joseph La Roux's first wedding, except that Thompson was no acrobat and was saved not by his fast response but by being tied to the parachute ropes.[50] He clung to the rope, coached to do so by Tiny La Roux, who knew that letting go too soon would be fatal, as the parachute would not be able to open and arrest the fall at too low an altitude.[51] It was not until they reached a height of 2,500 feet that it would be safe.[52]

Once it was clear from the length of the tether rope that the balloon had ascended to a sufficient height, Joseph La Roux fired another pistol shot, the signal to Thompson that he should let go and parachute to earth. Nothing happened. La Roux fired again, and again Thompson didn't go of the rope. La Roux fired again, and finally Thompson released his hold and dropped to earth. It seemed at first as if his parachute would not open, but seemingly at the last moment it suddenly spread wide, and Thompson, still holding on by one hand, drifted to earth.

But even having seemingly escaped death twice, he found himself in peril again, because his parachute was drifting down onto the railroad tracks of the Boston & Maine Railroad—the active tracks that ran behind Wonderland, and on which a train was now running. Thompson was settling right in front of it, but a gust of wind pushed him over the tracks, and he came down safely on one side of them.

Thompson was in shock, his arm strained and practically paralyzed, and his hands scraped raw. He was brought back, carried as if in triumph by the crowd on their shoulders, to the Wonderland Administration Building for treatment by a Dr. Oakes.[53] Fortunately, he suffered no serious injury. Madame La Roux rose 1,000 feet higher. After she jumped, she didn't touch the ground until she was in the nearby town of Chelsea.

Interviewed by a reporter for the *Revere Journal*, he put a brave face on the experience:

> "I thought it was all off with Thompson when I slid from that seat," he said, referring to himself in the third person, "but it was a great thing that they had tied my hands. I hung there comfortable enough. When I found that I wasn't going to be killed I began to enjoy the sensation, and was sorry when I heard Mrs. La Roux shout for me to cut away. It seemed as if the parachute would never open. Then there was a report like a cannon, and the great parachute snapped open. That scared me blue until I remembered that the professor had told me just before the ascent that parachutes always should open with a snap.
>
> "I floated down easily enough, but nearly had heart disease when I discovered that I was keeping along with a railroad train on the Boston & Maine tracks, and seemed to be bound to alight on it. Prof. La Roux had given me instructions about rocking the parachute so as to govern my direction to a degree, but I was 'rattled' for fair over that railroad train.
>
> "Finally I saw that I would miss the train all right, but the top of the depot loomed up. I cut that by a few feet, and as I bumped to the ground that train gave me a quick go-by.
>
> "Sure, I'm going up again. It's great."[54]

Thompson told another reporter that "he enjoyed the trip immensely." But he never did have another go at it.[55]

❧

Near the end of the summer, competition for Wonderland arrived from a completely unexpected source.

Walter Darcy Ryan was born in Nova Scotia in 1870.[56] He trained for a military career but found himself more drawn to science and engineering. He emigrated to the United States in 1892 and went to work for the Thomas-Houston Electric Company in Lynn, Massachusetts. Shortly thereafter, Thomas-Houston merged with the Edison Electric Company of Schenectady, New York, to form General Electric. Ryan, feeling that the science and practice of illumination needed to be put on a more rigorous foundation, asked for funding for a laboratory to study this, and got a $10,000 fund to set up the Illumination Laboratory on January 1, 1899. In 1903, he became General Electric's first illumination engineer. With his engineering approach, he and his laboratory designed electric lighting of all kinds for the new market in electric lights—automobile headlamps, street lighting, building illumination, and others.

It was the time for applied lighting. Electric lights had been showcased in the international exhibitions at Chicago in 1893, Buffalo in 1901, and St. Louis in 1904. The new amusement parks boasted of their lighting, and most featured a Tower of Light as a centerpiece.

It might seem amazing today, but General Electric was not in the forefront of this. They had lost out on the contract for lighting the Chicago Fair to their rival, Westinghouse. Significantly, Wonderland did not go to General Electric to design the lighting but used the services of D. J. Buckley of New York instead.

The next international exposition coming up after the opening of Wonderland was the Jamestown Tercentenary Exposition at Hampton Roads, Virginia, in the summer of 1907, intended to celebrate the three hundredth anniversary of the founding of the first English colony in America. Ryan was determined to win the lighting contract for General Electric. To publicize General Electric and to make a big splash in the media, Ryan decided to literally put on a show.

On the evening of Thursday, July 12, 1906, Ryan gathered his men and equipment in the Relay Yard at Bass Point in Nahant, between the terminating loop of the railroad at the Bass Point Hotel. They erected a peculiar Christmas-tree-like construction of piping, connected to a steam boiler, and nearby set up a platform. On the platform were five searchlights, each mounted on universal joint swivels that allowed them to be pointed in any direction. There was a man at each searchlight. They had rehearsed so that they could move and operate the lights in coordinated, choreographed patterns. Each man had a collection of colored gelatin filters, coated with marine varnish to protect them from water and steam.[57]

A crowd gathered in Nahant, on Revere Beach across Broad Sound, and on boats anchored in Broad Sound, alerted by an advertisement placed two days before in the *Lynn Daily Evening Item*.[58] As darkness fell, Ryan and his crew fired up the boiler, which began emitting steam that rose to a height of forty feet. At 9:30 p.m., the searchlights were turned on, different colored filters placed in front of each, and they were directed through the clouds of steam, where they created trails and streaks of brilliant light, making a huge three-dimensional structure of light in the sky.

The crowd was electrified. Not only were these bars of rainbow color projected into the air, but they began to move in a choreographed fashion to make radiating starbursts and create parallel beams, and to intersect to make weavings of color where they crossed. They made plaid patterns. They duplicated the flags of different nations, something Ryan hoped would be a big hit at the international exhibition.

Using special rotating nozzles, they sprayed the steam into patterns and made colored pinwheels of light and structures given names like "Fighting Serpents" and "Ghosts" The effects were called "Fireless Fireworks." It was the first light show. Directed using hand signals, whistles, and flashlights, the operators could execute any number of moves.

Ryan had hoped that they could carry on the performance for two weeks, if the authorities allowed it. They ended up running it for fifty-four consecutive days in the same spot. People chartered boats from Boston to ride out to Broad Sound to see it. The Boston press representatives "voted it the grandest outdoor attraction they have ever witnessed."[59]

Called the Scintillator, the show's success was demonstrated by its appearance almost immediately in a book, *Looking Forward,* by H. W. Hillman. Hillman was a writer for General Electric, and his book was intended as a sequel to Edward Bellamy's 1888 future utopia novel, *Looking Backward.* Hillman's book purports to be written in the then-far future of 1912, telling of all the marvels achieved by electricity since Bellamy's time and for the six years from its actual writing. It waxes eloquent about the Scintillator:

> "There comes the scintillator," said Ethyl.
>
> Just then the lights were turned low on the pavilion, and a series of five searchlights sent their streams of illumination into view. Steam pipes were located some thirty feet in the air, and as the many jets emitted forth their volumes of steam, the various colors from the scintillator made beautiful clouds of all shades, ever changing as the signals for proper color combinations were given.
>
> The policy of the proprietor of this Mountain House, was to furnish night illumination scenes from the scintillator at least one night each week, and the display apparatus was always on exhibit in connection with holiday festivals.
>
> "I remember," said Tom, "when this scintillator was invented, and commercially introduced. It was only a few years ago. One of the first exhibitions

was given at a seashore resort near Boston, and it was exceedingly popular. Enormous crowds came to the beach on the trolley cars and automobiles, to spend the evening, and witness the beautiful illumination displays. The newspapers commented very favorably upon the invention, and prophesied even at that time that scintillators would be adopted by all up-to-date summer resorts, mountain houses, and wherever the people congregated for an outing, or an evening of pleasure. I remember distinctly, attending the Jamestown Exposition, where 100 searchlights were used in connection with a grand illumination scheme. It was the most marvelous exhibit of illumination which I had ever witnessed."

Tom told the girls all about Prof. W. D'A. Rhine, the inventor of the scintillator, and his wonderful reputation as an illuminating engineer. He said that not more than a year after the first exhibition of the scintillator near Boston, Prof. Rhine's engineering ingenuity had created various schemes representative of the introduction of fireworks displays, and that the next 4th of July he produced the most spectacular exhibit of fireworks by means of the electrical scintillator, without using powder, or any of the ordinary devices which had been common for years in connection with fireworks exhibitions. The results of this wonderful display led electrical papers, and the public press throughout the entire country, to disseminate information about the wonderful illumination scheme, so that the following year, electrical companies in general arranged their plans so that electricity became the agent for 4th of July demonstrations, and the old style fireworks were abandoned in connection with large demonstrations and illumination exhibitions.[60]

Hillman curiously misspells Ryan's last name as "Rhine," as if he had only heard it pronounced, not written down. Nonetheless, Hillman was so taken by the Scintillator that an image of it in use is used as a frontispiece for the book.

Floyd C. Thompson was furious. After all the time and effort taken in constructing and publicizing Wonderland, here was this upstart attraction stealing all the attention to the wrong side of Broad Sound. People who should have been coming to Wonderland, lured by its own searchlights, were heeding the siren song of Ryan's moving rainbow. They were chartering boats to go see the Scintillator, and then they were taking those boats in to the docks at Bass Point and going ashore to the small amusement park there. (There was no dock on Revere Beach, and Wonderland wasn't exactly on the beach, in any case.)

Thompson decided to wage war on Ryan's Scintillator. He directed all the Wonderland searchlights to be pointed at Bass Point in the hopes of drowning it out. But the Scintillator was too far away, and the searchlights gave out before they got there.

Thompson did the only reasonable thing he could do: he bought the Scintillator. Or, rather, he purchased the use of it for the rest of the summer. It was installed on the Wonderland grounds. If people wanted to see the Scintillator, they would have to come to Wonderland to see it. And its colored beams would help pull the paying public in toward his park, rather than those upstarts in Nahant.[61]

The "$40,000 Scintillator," "The Climax of Electrical Invention and Inventive Genius," made its Wonderland Premiere on September 11, 1906, and stayed at the park through the rest of the season.[62] It was a major coup for Wonderland—they got hold of a World's-Fair-class attraction long before any World's Fair did.

∽

For the last weeks of Wonderland's 1906 season, the Ladies Navassar Military Band, headed by Gussia Dial, performed in the park. September 13 was declared "Mayor Day"—Boston Mayor John F. Fitzgerald and other city officials were invited guests.

At 11 p.m. on Sunday, September 16, the gates closed on Wonderland's first season. An estimated 75,000 people were there that day, an unqualified success.[63] The season's headcount was estimated to be 2 million visitors total. Thompson took the leaders of the Navassar band on a victory lap around New England.[64] A week later he received a testimonial from the concessionaires working the midway. Restauranteur Dudley S. McDonald received an engraved cup from the managers of Wonderland for his efforts.[65] Several of the Indians from Kennedy's Wild West show trouped to a Mr. Heally's barber shop in Chelsea, dressed in full regalia, and demanded—using sign language—that they be shaved. No assistant barber was present, so Heally did it all by himself, taking a full hour. Afterward the Indians reportedly said, "Pale face make shave smooth good. Bye bye, see pale face again." Whether the prank was their own idea, or some publicity hound came up with it, it was an atrocious pun.[66]

It had been a good season, and they had every reason to expect the next one would be as good, if not better. But there were unexpected bumps in the road ahead, and it was a much changed Wonderland that opened its gates in 1907.

CHAPTER 5
The Rise and Fall of Floyd C. Thompson

Wonderland company . . . has . . . Floyd C. Thompson of New York City, who, for several years past, has been prominently identified with a number of the big amusement enterprises at Coney Island, for Vice-President and General Manager. . . . For several years past he has been more or less interested in amusement park propositions and theatrical enterprises, latterly in New York City and at Coney Island.

—*Wonderland Souvenir Magazine 1906,* [11]

The description of Floyd C. Thompson given in Wonderland's 1906 souvenir program is not much more informative than the biography he gave to the local newspapers. It tells us about his energy, and how he is a "tireless worker," responsible for every detail of the park, yet not possessed of a "swelled head."[1] But it doesn't tell us who he *was*. Unlike most of the other figures in that booklet, his past experience and background are not given. Where was he from before New York? Which of the Coney Island attractions was he associated with, and in what capacity? How and why was he chosen to be in charge of constructing Wonderland Park? The brief description given isn't revelatory—it's evasive. The Grand Architect of Wonderland really was a cipher.

Was it modesty that made him hide his background? Or was it caution, perhaps fear of revealing that he had little experience in park-building. Or did he, perhaps, have something to hide? That veil he drew across his own past makes us want to tear it aside, both from mere curiosity and from a desire to know what shaped the man who shaped Wonderland.

Floyd Chaddock Thompson was born on April 7, 1871, to Ashley C. Thompson and Helen Chaddock Thompson, originally of Middlebury, New York, a tiny town about midway between Rochester and Buffalo.[2] "Chaddock," his mother's maiden name, a form of "Chadwick," attested to in several places in England, especially Lancashire. Helen Chaddock's grandfather had moved to Linden, New York, in about 1816 and built a log cabin there.[3]

When Floyd came of age he moved to Albany, and about 1890 enrolled in the Albany College of Pharmacy. Pharmacy ran in his family's blood— his father and grandfather had been druggists, and his younger brother, Albert, would also follow that trade. Floyd graduated in 1894, neither a class notable nor a class officer.[4] Within a year he had opened a pharmacy in nearby Catskill, New York. In May 1895, he hired young Florence Lee Burdick of Albany to work in his store.[5] A business romance blossomed, and the two were married on October 15 of that year.[6]

The wedding was held in the home of her parents, Linneus H. and Gertrude A. Burdick of Albany. Presiding was Reverend William Force Whittaker of Albany's First Presbyterian Church. The ceremony was a quiet and a small one, because Floyd's father, Ashley, had just died. After a brief honeymoon, Floyd returned to his pharmacy. Four years later, on July 4, 1899, their only child, Gladys Eulalie Thompson, was born.[7]

In the beginning, Thompson's career was a simple and straightforward one of unassuming, middle-class success. At the age of twenty-nine, he had his own business as a pharmacist in a small town outside the capital of New York State. He had a wife and a new daughter. Nothing in his background or upbringing suggested that he would leave all of this to pursue a career as a builder of amusement parks, a theatrical and booking agent, and a Broadway producer. But that is what he became. The catalyst of this change, diverting his path in life and reshaping his destiny, seems to have been his discovery, around the year 1900, of the power and possibilities of incorporation.

We may never know how he stumbled on the notion, or who may have suggested it to him, but he started modestly enough with his own pharmacy. On October 20, 1900, he incorporated the Westside Pharmacy Company in Albany. The officers besides himself were Thomas E. Ferrier and David M. Post, possibly his employees. His motivation isn't exactly clear, but this choice enabled him to raise money by selling shares and to limit the liability of the pharmacy itself.[8]

He must have liked the way it worked out, because less than two weeks later, on November 1, he formed the Thompson Medical Company of Catskill, New York.[9] The other officers this time were L. H. Burdick (presumably his father-in-law, Linneus H. Burdick), Gaylord Logan, and G. A. Benedick, all of Albany. Exactly what the business of the Thompson Medical Company was isn't clear, but the arrangement had its perks. The June 19, 1901, issue of the *Albany Times* stated that "Floyd C. Thompson has been in this section [of Albany] for a few days with the handsome business automobile of the Thompson Medical Company." If nothing else, Thompson got use of a company car out of the deal.[10]

These two tastes of corporate life seem to have infected Thompson with a desire to expand business beyond his present sphere of pharmaceuticals and the limited world of drugs, notions, and soda fountains. After this point, Thompson began to found, join, or acquire an escalating series of corporations in a variety of interests, getting further and further from his education and his roots.

It started with the Page Book Cover Company of Albany. This company had been established by Nelson H. Clarke and Clara Hawley of Albany, along with Ellsworth M. Page of Buffalo, in July 1897.[11] Its stated purpose was to manufacture, print, and sell book covers, as well as stationery and printing supplies. By 1901, Thompson had acquired it. The directors became Thompson, Frederick H. Gaylord as president, and Thompson's father-in-law, L. H. Burdick, as treasurer and secretary. Their stated purpose was the selling of "self-locking book covers."[12]

Shortly thereafter Thompson moved to New York City, apparently taking his family with him. His motivation seems to have been the pursuit of newer and bigger business enterprises. His address may have been one that he used later—254 Ninth Avenue, between 25th and 26th Streets. There was a drugstore right next door, but it is unclear if Thompson was involved with it or not.[13]

By 1903, he had joined with Albert Scherer to form the Scherer-Thompson Company. In setting up the company headquarters, Thompson started doing something he would continue throughout his career: he picked the most prestigious and conspicuous address he could, undoubtedly to signify that the business was an important and successful one. In this case, the address was 233 Broadway, directly across from City Hall

Park.[14] These were the business offices; the company had a factory at 1252 Willoughby Avenue. If you went in a straight line from the business office across the relatively new Brooklyn Bridge, it took you directly to the factory.

And what did Scherer-Thompson do? Albert G. Scherer was an inventor, with a sheaf of patents, mostly for metal shaping and what we would today call HVAC—heating, ventilation, and air conditioning. Scherer was based in Chicago, so it appears that Thompson agreed to be the business head and manufacturing supervisor for the company in New York.

Their product was clinical thermometers.[15] In their advertisements, Scherer-Thompson claimed to be "the largest manufacturer of High-Grade Clinical Thermometers in the United States," with their goods "in use in the most particular institutions on this continent, among which are over 1500 hospitals."[16] Despite such claims, the only purchasers on record were insane asylums in Ohio and Ontario. Records show the business in operation at least through 1905.

Running such an operation might occupy a gentleman full time, but Floyd Thompson was just getting started. On May 18, 1904, he incorporated the F. C. Thompson Company of New York "for the purpose of manufacturing scientific instruments."[17] His board of directors included a completely new cast of characters—besides Thompson, there was F. M. Ashley and, as secretary, Hattie Dean. Ashley was another inventor, although he lived conveniently close by in New York. Like Scherer, Ashley too had several inventions for piping and plumbing, but he was more eclectic. Several of his patents covered devices for railways, including electric ones. He also had patents for such things as projectiles, violins, and inkstands. Exactly which of these the F. C. Thompson Company was intended to pursue isn't clear. No advertising from the company has been located, and none of Ashley's inventions were assigned to Thompson's company. Why, in fact, would Ashley agree to join a company with another man's name on it? It could very well be because Thompson could by this time show an ability to persuade people to invest in his operations. The F. C. Thompson Company had a capitalization of $25,000, no mean feat.

Ashley already had his name on another company, the Ashley Valve Company of New York, which was incorporated on July 29, 1904. Its purpose was to "manufacture gas valves" and "steam specialties" from Ashley's patents.[18] Ashley was one director, and John J. Rorke of Brooklyn was another, but even more important was another fundraising rainmaker, a man named Max Rosen, who was to become important in Floyd C. Thompson's career.

Ashely and Rosen were two of three directors of still another company, the Leap Frog Railway Company of New York, arguably the most fascinating of all of these corporations. It would change Floyd C. Thompson's life, even though he was not directly involved. The Leap Frog Railway was incorporated in Albany on April 6, 1904, with surprisingly large capitalization of $50,000. Besides Rosen and Ashley, the third director was the inventor of the device, the driving force behind it, Philip K. Stern. The incorporation announcement in the *Middletown [New York] Daily Argus*— usually a dry recitation of facts and figures—bore a tantalizing headline: "What Do You Think It Is?"[19] The *New York Times* for May 8, 1904, gave a vivid description of the device in action at Dreamland: "In the way of a novel switchback [railway] there is the 'leap-frog railway,' which is also over by the sea, starting 500 feet from shore. Two cars running on the same track meet head-on in hair-raising fashion. But instead of telescoping, as they do in railway collisions on land, the cars slide over each other in loop-the-loop style, and continue on their journey. A spill would mean an involuntary ocean bath."[20]

The performance had to be seen to be believed—and we can still see it. Not only have pictures of the construction been preserved, but its actions were filmed and recorded on Mutoscope cards. Videos of the operation can be found easily enough on the internet.[21] It is as startling today as it must have been over a century ago. Each of the railroad cars is identically and weirdly shaped, somewhat like a tank, with ends fore and aft that taper down to the railroad track. Each car bears on its back a section of track as well, so that another car can ride over the top as if riding up and over a small hill. During a ride on the unit at Dreamland Park, a passenger had the opportunity to be in both the bottom car and the top car, being ridden over by the other car in one direction, then reversing and going over the other car in its turn.

It is a completely strange and bizarre thing, and amazing that the peculiarly shaped invention actually works. It is the height of novelty. After seeing this, Floyd Thompson was probably transfixed, experiencing an epiphany: here is what he wanted to do, what he was meant to do—merchandizing novelty to the masses, not drearily compounding and selling drugs over the counter, nor efficiently turning out clinical thermometers for hospitals, nor even inventing scientific apparatus that might see use and utility. He would control companies that presented such exotic and intriguing devices and amusements to the public. Through Frank Ashley he knew Max Rosen, and with Rosen he would rule the entertainment world. Over the next year, Thompson and Rose would incorporate three different companies together.[22]

༄

Their first undertaking was the most ambitious. They gathered together a large consortium of well-to-do investors. Besides Thompson and Rosen, they got Myer Nussbaum, a former state senator; Gates Hamburger, a lawyer; and William Bodge, all of New York. Thompson clearly dug into his past business contacts and lured in John F. Calder and Joseph Coughlin of Albany. On November 30, 1904, they incorporated the Stadium Company of New York "for the purpose of manufacturing and dealing in machinery and apparatus used in the operation of places of public amusement." The capitalization was an astounding $1.5 million.[23] To all appearances, their company was intended to make rides and parts for rides for the amusement parks at Coney Island and the surrounding area. But the real purpose of the corporation was much more than that. For the first time, Thompson engaged in practices he would use in the years to come—he gave his company a deceptive title and published deceptive literature about it.[24]

The stated purpose would have been convincing and lucrative by itself. In 1904, the war between the amusement parks at Coney Island was in full swing. Into the midst of this the Stadium Company appeared, ready to weigh in. But Thompson's group didn't come to sell rides to any of the sides in this competition. Instead, they did something completely unexpected—they acquired the rights to the land Steeplechase Park stood on, along with additional property nearby. Their plan was to tear down Steeplechase Park and erect a completely new amusement park, bigger than Luna Park, bigger than the upstart Dreamland, bigger, in fact, than both combined. It would be called Stadium Park, and it was set to open in May 1905.[25]

They announced their goals in a series of releases in November and December 1904, with one right on Christmas Day. They placed ads in *Billboard* magazine, the news organ of the entertainment industry, announcing that they had "a number of high-class spectacular acts," with "everything new and nothing duplicated." "We are making contracts for the Park right along now," said Myer Nussbaum. "We will have a place as unlike Dreamland or Luna Park as it is possible to put up. None of our shows has been seen outside of the grounds, and nothing outside of the grounds will be found inside of the grounds. Everything is to be patented and copyrighted."

In fact, other sources said that they would be importing some of the big attractions from the recent World's Fairs and exhibitions, but the main point was that their creation would be spectacular and new to Coney Island. It would have five hundred feet of frontage on the ocean. George Tilyou indicated he planned to take the proceeds from his sale and build a new park at Rockaway Beach, and also concentrate on setting up other Steeplechase rides at parks around the country.

Behind the scenes, though, things were not so rosy. As the newspapers observed, there had been at least two months of negotiation by Christmas. Initially, $950,000 had been put up for a contract and lien for the property. In addition, there were to be three payments of $25,000 to Tilyou. The first had been made on October 18. The second was due on December 10, but, despite the awesome assets of the Stadium Company, too much was tied up elsewhere. Thompson and Rosen asked Tilyou for a one-week extension, ostensibly to get the needed documents together, which Tilyou granted. Thompson was able to get the needed $25,000 from John Calder in Albany, keeping the deal alive. And on December 23, the company announced that the final papers had been signed and that workmen would immediately begin the task of tearing down the old buildings.

Tilyou, however, suspicious of the ability of the Stadium Company to make its next payment, announced through a spokesman that the park was still Tilyou's property for now, and that if he did not hear from the Stadium Company within ten days he was going to begin work on his planned improvements of Steeplechase Park for the next season.[26]

By January 15, 1905, Tilyou still hadn't seen his third payment, and Thompson and Rosen put the deal "on hold." Subsequent negotiations failed, the deal fell apart, and the Stadium Company forfeited its first two payments. Stories differed between the two sides on the reasons for the failure. Max Rosen explained that the titles and leases of Tilyou's Steeple-chase Company "were not satisfactory to the financiers of the Stadium Company." Tilyou said that the option had expired after he had agreed to two extensions on the payments and the final payment was clearly not forthcoming. "Some of the other directors of the Stadium Company I believe to be strictly business men," he said, "and my respect for them is of the highest." By implication, his respect for Thompson and Rosen was not. Tilyou immediately set to work on improvements for the summer of 1905, which he continued to run.[27] In 1907, most of Steeplechase Park burned to the ground. Tilyou put up a sign saying they would be back and charged people to look at the ashes. He rebuilt it and ran it until his death in 1914.

Max Rosen, trying to save face, announced that the Stadium Company would nevertheless operate some smaller amusement enterprises at Coney Island the following summer. This wasn't a lie. Even before the fiasco of Stadium Park fully played out, Thompson and Rosen were forming another company. The Consolidated Carousel Company of New York was incorporated on January 7, 1905. Among the directors were Floyd C. Thompson, G. S. Terry, J. F. McMahon, T. F. Murphy, and Max Rosen. Nevertheless, despite this effort, there is no evidence that the Carousel Company was ever able to construct or operate any Coney Island attractions.[28] The failure of both of these organizations to succeed in putting up attractions at Coney Island was public and conspicuous, and it must have rankled deeply. Rosen and Thompson had failed to build what would have been the biggest amusement park in the world, or even to operate in its shadow. Yet both men would continue to press on and pursue this goal, and both would eventually succeed. In the meantime, they did not retreat and lick their wounds, but continued, like determined soldiers, to attack.

It sometimes seems as if Rosen and Thompson were more in the business of establishing companies than in actually doing anything constructive. Even while the Stadium Park business was going on, even when they were starting the Carousel Company, they were working on yet another enterprise—the Bird's Eye View Company was incorporated sometime between August 1904 and February 1905.[29] Among its directors were Rosen as president and Thompson as treasurer. Exactly what they were organized to do isn't clear—the stated purpose of the company was listed simply as "machinery."

Whatever the Bird's Eye View Company was supposed to do, it was having trouble paying its bills. At one point, Max Rosen paid for something with a check for $1,150 drawn on the Cooper Exchange Bank. It was discovered that not only did the company not have enough to cover that amount, but it didn't actually have an account at that bank. Rosen was arrested and taken to court. Thompson, who was not arrested, followed him to court. Gates Hamburger, one of the other directors from the Stadium Company, acted as Rosen's lawyer. He moved for an adjournment and got Rosen released into his custody.[30]

❧

Times were getting hard for both Rosen and Thompson, and the bills were coming due. On September 12, 1905, Thompson was ruled a debtor to his partner Albert Scherer.[31] The next day he was declared a debtor to George W. Cheever and to the Coney Island and Bath Beach Bank.[32] Rosen, whose partnership with one Joseph Prince had gone bankrupt in 1903, was no stranger to the ups and downs of business. In January 1905, the Leap Frog Railway Company was in debt, and by the end of March it had new owners.

As if all of this was not bad enough, it is likely that Thompson was having problems in his personal life as well. Florence came with him to New York, but after this point she seems to disappear from the records. It would not be surprising if the long hours spent on the job estranged them, or that she might have been put off by a man whose life and business had changed so much and so rapidly from the man she had married. Perhaps they divorced at this time or perhaps merely separated. In any event, if Florence and Gladys were not physically with Floyd in Revere, they were evidently in his thoughts. The first song publicizing Wonderland, published in 1906, was dedicated to Gladys Eulalie Thompson. Nonetheless, by 1912, Florence Thompson was living in Grantwood, New Jersey, and Gladys was being raised in Albany by Florence's parents, Gertrude and Linneus. There is nothing to suggest that either of them had any interaction with Floyd after 1906.

❧

For many men, this would be striking bottom. Floyd Thompson's business ventures had failed. He was in debt to numerous people and institutions. He had not only failed to achieve his dream of building the largest amusement park in the world but he had failed in a spectacular and visible fashion. His private life was a shamble.

But it was at this point that he met John J. Higgins, who had just purchased the twenty-five acres between lines of the Boston & Maine Railroad in Revere. Higgins thought it would be a good location for an amusement park, but he didn't know anything about amusement parks, and he needed someone who did. Thompson might not have had capital, but he still knew how to pry it from those who did. And he had a card file full of amusement device makers and novelty acts, left over from the abortive Stadium Company exploit. Together in Boston, far from Thompson's failure and his debtors in New York City, away even from his partner Max Rosen, Higgins and Thompson would incorporate the Wonderland Amusement Company and make history.

Exactly how Higgins and Thompson found each other isn't clear. Did Higgins go seeking knowledgeable people in New York, or did Thompson hear about this opportunity in Boston, possibly through the trade papers and network? Or did they connect by some other process? Whatever the means, Thompson relocated to Boston by the fall of 1905. He and Higgins announced the Wonderland Company in October of that year.

The story of the construction of Wonderland and of the operation of its first season has already been told. At every point, Thompson pushed for the success of the park. This was how he would have run Stadium Park on Coney Island, if he had had the chance, and he wanted to show the world what he could do. But he was also pushing for the success of Floyd C. Thompson. Almost every account of the park in the newspapers carried his name as well. None of the other park directors or officers got such publicity. In the public mind, the two were inseparable, as Thompson wanted them to be. It wasn't J. J. Higgins's Wonderland or Thomas D. Barroll's or Harold Parker's amusement park—it was Floyd C. Thompson's. He saw his own success as linked inextricably with that of Wonderland.[33]

He didn't need to ring his own praises. The newspapers did so on their own, pointing out how the park had been a financial success in its first season. At the end of the season, the proprietors of the midway attractions of Wonderland got together and, through the person of Fred A. Bennett, presented Thompson with a two-hundred-dollar gold watch for his work. This was reported in the newspapers in Boston and New York. This very public recognition of Thompson's accomplishments was undoubtedly the high point of his summer.[34]

It was also, arguably, the pinnacle of his career.

⁓

Point of Pines, five miles north of Wonderland up Revere Beach, had been an amusement area long before most of Revere Beach. It was operating even before Charles Eliot had turned the beach into a park and moved the railroad. The Narrow Gauge had taken people all the way past Revere Beach to that rhomboidal spit of sand, with its grove of pine trees. The enormous Point of Pines Hotel and its restaurant had lured people there. A racetrack was put in nearby, and headline entertainers performed. But it lacked the rides and adrenaline-inducing amusements that had come to characterize the lower portion of Revere Beach. Now someone was trying to change that. There had been an attempt in 1905 by Frank W. Mead and Joseph J. Raymond to establish an amusement park at Point of Pines to be called "Paradise." It did not succeed.[35] But in October 1906, in the same issue of *Billboard* that told of Thompson's gold watch, another piece proclaimed that Thompson had arranged to lease the estate of Thomas J. Baldwin, consisting of fifty-five acres at Point of Pines for the purpose of building a new amusement park. It would be the largest in New England and would be called "White City," following the name given to the influential Chicago amusement park.[36] Many cities and towns had established their own White City amusement parks to try to capture some of the glamor and success of the original. Thompson must have realized that there was no point in trying to be a retread of another park (there was already a "White City" in Worcester), so shortly afterward it was announced that the enterprise was to be called "Vanity Fair."

Vanity Fair would be twice the size of Wonderland, with many of the same attractions and others besides—it would feature some of the ideas that Frank Mead and Joseph Raymond had planned for Paradise. It would have a bathhouse large enough to accommodate 7,500 bathers. It would have a boardwalk half a mile in length. At the center would be the Court of

Honor with an immense lagoon at its center and its own Shoot the Chutes ride larger than the one at Wonderland. There would be a pony track, a circus ring, and fountains. As with most other amusement parks (but not Wonderland), there would be a Tower of Light. The park would boast an open-air theater and a Fighting the Flames attraction even bigger than the one at Wonderland. The park would be built by Aldrich & Shea, the same construction company that had built Wonderland.[37]

The real architect of Vanity Fair was revealed in a series of large advertisements that ran in *Billboard* from October 27 to November 10, 1906, all with eye-catching bold lettering and graphics. The October 27 advertisement was particularly revealing: in large letters it announced that Floyd C. Thompson would be building this new and larger amusement park.

It was as if Thompson did not expect the Wonderland board to read the New York announcement. His own name appeared in huge letters, well before the park was named. His announcement vaingloriously heralded his achievements, which in his account were made *despite* the shortcomings of the Wonderland site—"The Man who made 'Boston Wonderland' the talk of the entire financial and show world on account of its phenomenal success, notwithstanding the fact that it was built in a swamp, with no shade or water frontage." The statement read like a slap in the face to the Wonderland company. It might also have reflected Thompson's annoyance at losing Steeplechase and being saddled with Wonderland, as Steeplechase had immense water frontage and wasn't in a swamp. Whether he intended either of those inferences, there was one he clearly did intend to make to potential investors: if he could make Wonderland a success *despite* these handicaps, imagine what he could do with a location with the advantages of Point of Pines, "the Garden Spot of the Atlantic Coast, the only ideal location, in fact, near Boston for an amusement park."[38]

Thompson again followed his practice of choosing successful locations for his offices. The Paddock Building at 102 Tremont Street was in the heart of Boston, directly across from the historic Granary Burying Ground and a block from the Park Street Church and Boston Common. It became the location for his new corporation, the Point of Pines Attraction Company.

His other ads were similar boasting screeds about the wonders of the location, taking shots at Wonderland and other competitors. His November 3 and November 10 advertisements, as gaudy as their predecessor, announced that "The Garden Spot of the Atlantic Coast can be reached by more people with a FIVE CENT FARE than any other Park in the World, and it has the ONLY PRIVATE BATHING BEACH within fifty miles of BOSTON. It will be of such regal splendor that others will pale into insignificance and comparisons will seem odious." This is the boast of a man who thinks that his position is unassailable. Perhaps he felt that the Wonderland board had no option but to retain him, even as he built its competition. Perhaps he felt that Vanity Fair would be such an overwhelming success that he could utterly ignore Wonderland, as William H. Reynolds had hoped his Dreamland on Coney Island would eclipse Luna Park. Thompson would show Reynolds how to do it right, even if he had missed his chance to do so with Stadium Park.[39]

Construction work began at Point of Pines by January 1907. The boardwalk was installed, and the attractions started to be constructed. The newspapers promoted the new park, just as they had promoted Wonderland only a year earlier.

But Thompson had his own problems. He carried his personal financial burdens from his Stadium Park venture still. On December 9, 1906, he declared bankruptcy.[40] He owed money to John F. Calder, his Albany backer, as well as to the New York Merchants' Exchange Bank, the Royal Bank of New York, and the Coney Island and Bath Beach Bank. He also owed money to the Thompson Scenic Railway Company, which must have been related to his Wonderland enterprise. In addition, he owed money to Andrew J. Kobe and Archibald S. White, both of New York.[41]

Both the Wonderland board and the Vanity Fair organization dismissed Thompson. By January 5, 1907, *Variety* reported that Thompson was "out of the Point of Pines Park."[42] *Billboard* ran an extensive article on Vanity Fair on January 12 but didn't mention Thompson at all. Thompson's Vanity Fair Company was succeeded by the Point of Pines Attraction Company, headed by David H. Posner, a Boston store owner with no previous involvement with amusement parks.[43]

Thompson was devastated. Bankrupt and unattractive to the management at Wonderland who he had abused in print, he needed to find alternative employment. He seems to have begun operating for the New York Vaudeville Contracting Company about this time, possibly from a Boston office not far from his Point of Pines office. On August 3, 1907, the *New York Dramatic Mirror* announced that Floyd C. Thompson, "formerly of Wonderland," would be the manager of the new Eden Musée in Seattle, Washington.[44] The original Eden Musée in New York City was a wax museum that also hosted other attractions and performances. As with Steeplechase, Luna Park, Wonderland, and White City, other cities hoped to capture some of the success of the original by adopting its name. This attraction was completely new. An elevator took patrons directly to the fourth floor, and they descended through the offerings. On the top floor were various concessions. The visitors then descended on the so-called Cascade Stairway, which had steps made of glass, under which water flowed and multicolored lights sparkled, so that constantly changing patterns of light and color were thrown on the walls. Other floors featured an illusion maze, a London ghost show, a "colored stock company," and a motion picture theater featuring color films. It opened in the fall of 1907.[45]

The enterprise had other problems. Because of the rush to get everything open on time, the Eden Musée hired a second designer, and the original, offended that someone else was given authority over the design of the first floor, shot the newcomer with his revolver. The bullet failed to penetrate the victim's coat, so the assailant struck him with the gun, then prepared to shoot him at closer and lethal range. He was prevented from doing this by Thompson, who grabbed a gas pipe and hit the assailant on the head.[46]

Equally serious were charges of corruption and mismanagement. "Eden Musée, which opened with a flurry a few days ago," the *Seattle Republican* reported on October 25, "has gone where the woodbine twineth, and well it may, as it had no sooner thrown open its doors than it began to play a crooked game, so it was reported by some of its employees."[47] Exactly what "idiotic things" were done or by whom was not reported, but by November 23, Thompson had sold his interests in the Seattle Eden Musée and stated that he hoped to open a similar establishment in San Francisco.[48]

Thompson did open such a venue, but not in San Francisco. He went farther south to Los Angeles, where his company bought up the Le Sage building, the former home of the Le Bon Marche department store at 430-432-434 South Broadway, and announced that it would be opening a new Eden Musée there, modeled "in general lines" after the one in New York.[49] Shortly afterward, however, he changed his mind. Significantly, he renamed his one-building amusement center "Wonderland."

The company placed a news story in the *Los Angeles Times* on January 4, 1908, announcing that it would be open in three weeks. "It is our purpose to conduct an enterprise which will not only serve for purposes of recreation, but will have some educational value as well. We will change our bill constantly, and our attractions will be strictly high class," said a spokesman, probably Thompson.[50]

The opening date was set for February 4. News stories days before gave further details of the attractions. Ads appeared almost daily in the newspapers for Wonderland. But, like the Eden Musée in Seattle, Wonderland closed all too soon. It might have been due in part to the economic recession that drained any money for entertainment, or it might have been that the extra funds expended to draw in a jaded public were too much for the new enterprise to handle. Either way, by the beginning of March 1908 Wonderland was bankrupt. An auction was held on March 26 to pay the creditors, selling "furniture, fixtures, and paraphernalia."[51]

Aside from references to his work for New York Vaudeville Company, Thompson appears to have largely dropped out of the historical record for a time.[52] His Albany College of Pharmacy alumni directory gave his address in 1908 as 254 Ninth Avenue in New York, between 25th and 26th Streets, only four blocks from his former offices in the St. James Building, which he might have retained.[53]

～

It is not clear exactly where or when Floyd Thompson made the acquaintance of Bertha "Georgie" Locke. According to her descendants, Bertha Locke was born in Newport, Kentucky, on November 4, 1884.[54] She was the daughter of Minnie Bates Locke and Frank Elmer Locke, an "Eclectic Doctor."[55] Frank Locke had graduated from the Eclectic Medical Institute of Cincinnati in 1882, having written a thesis on external cephalic version births. Eclectic doctors were not recognized MDs and relied on botanical medicines exclusively.[56] Married in January 1884, Minnie and Frank eventually separated, and Frank remarried, to one Elvira "Ella" Cole.[57]

Bertha stayed with her mother, and the two moved frequently, traveling around the country. They lived in Michigan and California, where Minnie died, leaving Bertha virtually an orphan, since she was estranged from her remarried father. She visited with her aunt Edna, staying with her in a Coronado tent city, and later visited her in Los Angeles.[58]

According to her descendants, Bertha met Floyd Thompson when he was working as a manager at Wonderland in California, and newspaper accounts confirm that Bertha was in Los Angeles at about this time.[59] However they met, the two apparently fell in love and were together by 1908. From letters in the possession of their grandson, he was deeply devoted to her. They had two children. Eileen was born in 1909 and Helen Chaddock, named after his mother, was born in 1912, both in Illinois. Floyd doted on them, and their mother prepared them for a life in the entertainment business, giving them dancing lessons. The girls learned to act and to skate as well. Pictures of them with their father show them to be in New York, and they apparently lived in Jackson Heights, Queens. Whether they accompanied Floyd on his other business dealings is unclear.

Thompson appears to still have been associated with the New York Vaudeville agency at this time, and was probably in New York City, since *Billboard* magazine documented his visits to its offices.[60] In the April 6, 1912, issue the paper noted that he had invented (and was presumably promoting) a "novelty" called "The Passing Throng," a carnival show of some kind.[61]

September 1914, however, found him in Michigan City, Indiana, where he incorporated the Jack Rabbit Company. Its business was the manufacturing and marketing of the Jack Rabbit, a children's novelty toy. It had pedals and wheels and apparently was supposed to go very fast. Thompson was still searching for ways to sell amusement novelties to the public.[62]

Things did not go well for the Jack Rabbit Company. On April 1, 1915—April Fool's Day—director Floyd C. Thompson and secretary Ernest H. Baxter of the Hydrocraft Company of 206 North Fifth Avenue, Whiting, Indiana, were arrested on warrants for operating a confidence game.[63] Whiting was literally across the state line from Chicago, virtually within sight of Lake Michigan. As always, Thompson was going for the swankiest address he could manage. The problem was that the pair were purportedly selling a novelty item called the Michigan City Jack Rabbit, but his investors were not seeing any product and wanted their money back. Thompson and Baxter said that they were still waiting for the prototype to come back from the inventor. The pair were arrested on the same charge again two days later.[64]

This might have been the ignominious end of Thompson's career, but he showed again his ability to bounce back and take center stage four years later. Thompson had long been interested in the theater, not only as a manager and agent but also as a participant. He apparently wrote and performed in plays while living in Jackson Heights. (His play *Duty* was performed in 1925.)[65] On October 15, 1919, the mystery-comedy *Where's Your Wife?* opened at the Punch and Judy Theater at 155 West 49th Street in Manhattan. Thompson did not write it—it was the work of Thomas Grant Springer, Fleta Campbell Springer, and Joseph Noel—but he was the producer, and, true to form, his credit is prominently displayed in advertisements. The play got good reviews and was held over after its six-week run.[66] *Billboard* hailed Thompson as a "Theatrical Producer."[67]

It was, however, his last hurrah. Thompson produced no more shows, and further notices of him show a man in decline. In December 1920, *Billboard* said he was working with National Produce and Storage, but the piece doesn't say in what capacity. In February 1921, *Billboard* called him a "former park showman and manager and producer." In June 1921, it briefly said that "F.C. Thompson, formerly an amusement park promoter [stopped at the *Billboard* Offices]. Now in a commercial line. Still gets offers to build parks." Possibly the commercial line was National Produce and Storage, but maybe not. The idea that he "still gets offers to build parks" was surely not serious, but probably a kindness. Still, it must have stung.[68]

On January 28, 1922, *Billboard* noted that Floyd C. Thompson, "former outdoor showman," was "promoting chain stores." But by March he was promoting sodas fountains for movie theaters. In February 1924, he declared bankruptcy once again, in the court at Long Island City, New York. A year later, he had bounced back, and was promoting an electric combined ice cream and water ice machine for boardwalk concessions.[69]

Photographs of Floyd Thompson from this era show him alone on a New York porch or in front of a group of buildings with his daughters, Eileen and Helen.[70] He looks a totally different man from the confident, portly figure that glad-handed Wonderland into existence and who rode a balloon. The later Thompson was thin, white-haired, and fragile, as if the sudden jerk of a balloon takeoff would have torn him in half. The years and the business reverses had taken a heavy toll.

On Friday, June 2, 1925, he was taken to St. John's Hospital, suffering from "heart disease," possibly a heart attack.[71] Floyd Chaddock Thompson died on August 3, 1925, at his home at 138 Nineteenth Street in Jackson Heights at the age of fifty-four. No cause of death was listed, although heart trouble was the likely cause.[72] His body was taken back to West Middlebury, New York, and laid to rest beside that of his father, who had died just before Floyd's first marriage.[73] Reverend Herbert Grant officiated.

૮ઝ

Floyd Thompson was a complex person—clever and inventive, perpetually reinventing himself, bending the rules where he felt it necessary, always trying to produce popular amusements that he thought would sell. He resembled in many ways Cornelius Vanderbilt Wood (or, as he preferred, "C-for-nothing V-for-nothing Wood"), the similarly inventive and unorthodox man who built Disneyland. Like Wood, Thompson moved from job to job, finding himself in the right place at the right time to ultimately step into the role of amusement park fabricator. Both men threw themselves into the role, seeking perfection in the details, and both were relentless self-promoters who did shady things and were ultimately dismissed by the other board members of the park they created. Both then went off to construct other parks and to be involved in other entertainment business activities. And in both cases, this took a toll on their family lives.

CHAPTER 6
Year Two—1907

The owners of Wonderland Park hoped its second year would be a replay of the first successful one, but that was not to be. The first and the biggest change was the shakeup in management. Floyd C. Thompson's betrayal of Wonderland by brazenly trying to construct a bigger and more expensive competitor just up the beach was met with retaliation both from Wonderland and from his anticipated Vanity Fair. The Wonderland board mandated changes before the end of 1906. Thompson was dismissed along with Secretary Horace S. Meese and Assistant Manager John S. Concannon.

It is not hard to see why Meese was sent away—he too was a New Yorker, an outsider no doubt brought in by Thompson, and therefore suspect, although he does not appear to have been directly implicated in the Vanity Fair debacle. It is less obvious why Concannon had to go. Perhaps, the board felt, as assistant general manager, he should have kept the rest of them aware of Thompson's extracurricular activities.

Whatever the reasons, there was a reshuffling of the management at Wonderland Company. John Joseph Higgins, the originator of the project and its treasurer, now found himself thrust into the position of general manager, responsible for the rides and attractions at the park, overseeing staffing and personnel, and making sure that everything ran smoothly. This was a tremendous change for a man who, only three years earlier, had been secretary of a baking powder company and with no obvious experience in the entertainment business. He had seen the operation of the business over the previous year and a half, but now he had to take the reins himself. It would be a baptism by fire.

For his assistant general manager, Higgins promoted the excursion agent, Eugene L. Perry. Here was an opportunity for Perry to shine. The former show producer and performer would have a broader stage on which to showcase his expertise and glad-handing, perhaps making up for Higgins's deficiencies in that area.

To take over the role of treasurer, the company brought in Henry B. Dalton, a Harvard-educated executive who had been president of the Baush Tool Company in Springfield, Massachusetts, until his resignation in the summer of 1906. For publicity, the board reached out to persuade Hugh P. MacNally.[1] He had been on the editorial staff of the *Boston Herald* for twenty years and had been its dramatic editor for the previous six.

Higgins's and Perry's promotions were announced on Christmas Day 1906, possibly in the hopes that it would pass unnoticed.[2] They formally took their positions on New Year's Day 1907. The other positions were filled over the next few months.

There were other personnel changes as well. Fred A. Bennett, the director and ringmaster of the open-air circus, was replaced by Frank Todd. Louis S. Poole and his orchestra were out as the performers at the ballroom; Thomas R. O'Connor took over, leading the Waverly Orchestra.[3]

Exactly why these last two changes were made isn't clear, but it could simply be because contracts ran out. One of the jarring things about Wonderland Park was just how loosely bound the performers and attractions were to the park. It is not surprising that the weekly performers in the Arcus Ring were hired for only temporary gigs and frequently replaced. It is much more surprising to learn that major performers at the park—sometimes involving large and fixed buildings and equipment—were just as ephemeral.

For instance, William H. Kennedy's Wild West Show was apparently not booked for the entire summer of 1906, despite being the second largest human show in the park. Notices in *Billboard* suggest the attraction was renewed on a short-term basis every week for the last month, though it lasted the entire season before immediately going onto performances in the fall in Greenfield, Massachusetts.[4] Still, the show did not return for the 1907 season. Similarly, Princess Trixie found an off-season gig in Massachusetts after Wonderland closed and did not return.[5]

Ferari's Wild Animal Show folded up its baroque-fronted tent and departed as well. So did the Fatal Wedding. The Ryan Scintillator, of course, had moved on. Wonderland did not renew the contract of Hale's Tours (although they effectively still ran one of their shows). Neither

"The South before the War" show nor Gillette's Dog and Monkey Circus returned to the children's theater. You would think that something with a fixed building would remain, but the case of Hale's Tours shows that this was not invariably true. Surprisingly, William Manning and James Armstrong were anticipating, even before Wonderland opened, that their Fire and Flames show would eventually be leaving, despite the immense investment in the construction of the grandstand and the block of to-be-burnt buildings, and the involvement of so many local firemen. They had apparently calculated in advance how many railroad cars would be needed to haul the entire operation to a new site.[6]

Accordingly, Wonderland faced a pretty daunting series of omissions. Probably Thompson had already been preparing to replace some of these and had arranged for some alternate attractions. But others would require constant effort to keep the park running, and there was quite a bit of new construction needed before the park opened for the summer of 1907.

An entirely new ride was set up to the northwest of the Shoot the Chutes and the carousel. It was the Velvet Coaster, which was more of a traditional roller coaster than the Thompson Scenic Railway. Nevertheless, it avoided the big drops and sudden turns that were beginning to come into fashion, making it a much less dramatic ride—hence the "velvet" name. The Velvet Coaster was the invention of William H. Strickler of the Federal Construction Company and had already been installed at other amusement parks.[7]

On the other side of the Shoot the Chutes, the Wild West show was gone. In its place was a pony track, with Shetland ponies drawing two-person carriages around the track that cowboys and Indians had ridden on the previous year.[8] A miniature railway for children went in, with an engine so small that the driver had to straddle it. The train went around a half-mile track that circled inside the fence enclosing the pony track, passing through "Tunnel no. 23" before returning to its starting point.[9]

To replace Ferari's Wild Animal Show they got Blake's Animal Circus, which probably occupied the same space of ground. With Blake's they got an extra—Robert J. Blake had partnered for several years with Charles D. Willard and his Temple of Music, which was also hired for the park (Blake and Willard had performed together at White City Park in Chicago in 1905, among other venues). Willard probably moved into the children's theater, which had the seating arrangements his show required.

Wonderland found another attraction because of a vacation its restauranteur took. D. S. McDonald had gone down to Florida after Wonderland had closed at the end of the 1906 season. While there, he attended a show by Warren Frazee, who went by the name of "Alligator Joe." Frazee was a huge man who claimed to have invented the sport of alligator wrestling.[10] His show boasted a collection of Florida swamp animals, including a large assortment of alligators and a trained manatee. He had plans to franchise his operation and take it on the road, so he came up to Wonderland personally to oversee the operation. His Florida Jungle opened in what had previously been the Beautiful Orient.

In the building formerly occupied by the Fatal Wedding the managers put in a completely new attraction. A large water-filled tank with a heavy glass front on it was placed on the stage, and they called it "Under the Sea." The show featured a variety of underwater attractions and shows.

A new $10,000 bandstand was built near the end of the lagoon, giving an elevated place for Jean Missud and the returning Salem Cadet Band a more impressive place to perform. A museum-like attraction called "Battle Abbey" opened in a brand-new building erected between the photographer's stand and where Ferari's circus had been. In the space where Princess Trixie's tent had stood the company put up a lunch counter.

Finally, the board lined up a host of attention-grabbing performers for limited stints at the park, such as wire-walker James Hardy, "King of the Air"; contortionist Mademoiselle De Loro; the Stubblefield Trio of trapeze artists, and many others. Most of the big attractions from the previous year—the Infant Incubators, the Shoot the Chutes, Hell Gate, the carousel, the Japanese Village, Love's Journey, the Scenic Railway, the Circle Swing, the Palmists, the Third Degree, and the Whirl the Whirl would be there for the new season. Wonderland would have a mix of tried favorites and enticing new attractions, in addition to constantly changing performers in the Arcus Ring and a surprise attraction waiting for later in the season. It promised to be a good season, despite the shakeup in management, which the public probably did not even notice.

∾

Wonderland opened its second season on May 30, 1907. This time, the opening occurred at 10 a.m., rather than at noon, to accommodate the expected crowds. The park personnel had new uniforms resembling sailor's suits, and they increased the sizes of the police and fire departments.[11] A new policy allowed children accompanied by their parents to be admitted free on weekends. In addition, free passes to the park were printed in many Sunday editions of the *Boston Post*. The area around the lagoon was filled with flags of all nations atop staffs, as well as on lines stretching from staff to staff across the lagoon.

Wonderland opened 1907 with a spectacular act too—Lincoln J. Beachey, the aeronaut, who was barely out of his teens. Beachey was born in San Francisco on March 3, 1887. His father, a Civil War veteran, was blind, so Lincoln had to go to work early. He started a bicycle shop at thirteen, and by fifteen was repairing motorcycles and engines.[12]

His older brother Hiram was on the grounds crew for dirigible pilot Thomas Scott Baldwin, and Lincoln joined him. Together they constructed the gasoline engine-driven airship *California Arrow* in June–July 1904, and Lincoln, probably because of his light weight, piloted it on August 3, 1904, at Idora Park in Oakland, California, making the first controlled circular flight in America. The craft later was exhibited at the 1904 St. Louis Exposition, but without Beachey. Later, he produced a new dirigible design, the "Beachey-Baldwin." He traveled with the Baldwin Troupe, exhibiting the *Arrow*.

In 1905, he struck out on his own, traveling to Toledo, Ohio, to get the help of aerialist Roy Knabenshue in constructing his own dirigible. Beachey secured a contract at Luna Park outside Washington, DC, flying his craft as "Lincoln Beachey, the Aerial Wizard." Not content with simply exhibiting at the park, Beachey flew it around the Washington Monument, then landed on the grounds of the White House and asked for an audience with Teddy Roosevelt. The president was not there, but he spoke with Edith Roosevelt and ended up meeting with Speaker of the House "Uncle" Joe Cannon. The incident hit the papers and made Beachey famous. He was just nineteen years old. He appeared later at the Lewis and Clark Exposition in Portland, Washington. His schedule was a full and demanding one, and so when Wonderland solicited him, he was only able to provide a two-week stint at $1,000 a week.[13]

The twenty-year-old aerialist flew his cigar-shaped "rubber cow" made of rubberized silk every day. His most spectacular flight was made on June

6, 1907. He flew from Revere to Boston, swooped over City Hall, up Beacon Street, circled the Congregational Building, over the Union Club, past the Park Street Church, then landed on the Parade Ground at Boston Common.[14]

He had been provided with a message for Massachusetts governor Curtis Guild Jr.—a touch worthy of Floyd Thompson—which he gave to a reporter for the *Boston Post* to be delivered. The governor later congratulated Beachey on his achievement. The whole trip took about forty-five minutes.

He then set off again for Wonderland, circling the State House dome for show, but then ran into difficulties. There was dense fog, which made navigation difficult, and heavy winds. The engine stopped. He was able to get it running again, but he only got as far as Winthrop before it halted again. He landed it on Sunnyside Avenue in Winthrop and was again able to get the engine running with help from some volunteers. He took his dirigible up another time, and again his engine quit. He dipped down below the fog and found himself above Broad Sound, within sight of Revere Beach. There were fishing vessels below, so he dropped down to two hundred feet and asked for help. He brought his ship down to as low as six feet, but he had to throw off ballast and rise again, since the boats did not come quickly enough. Finally, they got a tow line to him and were able to pull him to the beach bath house. From there, human power towed the dirigible back to Wonderland. There was some minor damage getting the balloon into the park, but otherwise all went well.

Since the whole point of an airship is to fly well above the ground, and since Beachey obviously flew well beyond the boundaries of the park, why was Wonderland willing to host Beachey and pay what was, at the time, an exorbitant fee? The chance to see Beachey and his ship on the ground, and to have him and his ground crew answer audience questions.[15]

Beachey only remained at the park for another week after this eventful flight, apparently without further mishap, then went on to other shows.

With the departure of the Fatal Wedding, Wonderland needed a new attraction to put into that building. The idea they hit on was to put in an underwater exhibition. This had been done at Austin and Stone's Dime Museum in Boston and shown itself to be an effective draw. So a large tank was constructed with a heavy sheet of glass on one side, allowing the audience to see into the tank.

The question was what to put into the tank.[16] They used at least three attractions. One was by Fred A. Wallace, who was variously given the titles "Captain" and "Professor." He and his assistants dived in classic rubber suits with hard brass helmets, fed by air pumped in from the surface. Wallace ran the Frederick Wallace Submarine Diving and Wrecking Crew, performing salvage work in Boston waters, clearing wrecks and the like. Performing for audiences at Wonderland in a shallow tank must have been a welcome change of pace. "This promises to be a most novel and educational exhibit," enthused the *Boston Sunday Post*, "and will be made especially interesting by the introduction of considerable comedy business." One published image shows a duel between two suited divers, one holding a knife.

Another exhibit in the Under the Sea tank was with Eugene Fielding of Roxbury, "The Human Fish." Fielding had long been known in Boston despite his youth. In 1902, at the age of fifteen, he had given an exhibition at the Captain's Island Swim Races where he stayed underwater for two minutes and forty seconds.[17] He also "walked" on the bottom and "smoked" cigarettes underwater. At the Orchard Park Water Sports the same year, he stayed under for two minutes and forty-five seconds, and demonstrated eating, drinking, and "smoking" underwater. He also swam for fifty yards underwater. He performed at a water carnival in Boston the same year and engaged in a contest with high diver Charles A. Bigney to swim from the Charlestown Bridge to Boston Light. By 1903, Fielding had bettered his endurance to four minutes underwater. He later performed at Austin and Stone's Museum in their underwater tank, so it was no great stretch to obtain his services for Wonderland.

The third act in the tank was by Bert Letter, "The Handcuff King," whose performance echoed that of Harry Houdini. In Letter's big finish, he was handcuffed and placed in a submerged, iron-barred cell from which he would emerge unscathed.[18]

In mid-July 1907, Wallace finished up his engagement at Under the Sea. His act was replaced by five female "natators" (as well as some male swimmers) who gave "a remarkable exhibition of swimming." They also demonstrated life-saving.[19]

Another change at Wonderland wasn't really all that big. Hale's Tours demanded a royalty payment for the franchise once the theater resembling a railroad car was set up. But motion pictures were readily available, so many franchisees simply obtained the films and showed them in their theaters, neglecting to pay the Hale's Tours organization. In this way, it had actually promoted the development of a motion picture industry in the United States, although that wasn't their intention, and they lost money by it. That may have been the case in Wonderland as well. Wonderland had a contract with Hale's Tours for three years, with an option for Hale's to cut it short, so the decision may have come from that end to dissociate the tours from Wonderland. In any event, after the first season Wonderland no longer advertised Hale's Tours, but it did advertise the *Rocky Mountain Holdup*, which had been filmed as an episode of Hale's Tours.[20]

The film was actually shot in Phoenicia, New York, in the Catskills, rather than the Rocky Mountains. It runs about ten minutes. The bulk of the film is shot, as were most Hale's Tours, from the front of the train, so that the patrons saw a view that an engineer might, looking at the tracks ahead. But twice the camera point of view switches abruptly to the interior of one of the passenger cars, showing the action taking place there. In addition to *Rocky Mountain Holdup,* Wonderland also showed a film of a Mexican bullfight in the theater that summer.

⁓

The name "Battle Abbey" doesn't seem very descriptive. An advertisement placed in the Boston *Post* reported, "In an especially constructed building like some ancient Abbey or giant fortress of old will be found a collection of magnificent paintings by Paul Philippoteaux. They are mainly of battle scenes."[21] The building was apparently completely new, not a repurposed space like the Under the Sea attraction. The building did indeed look like a fortress built of stone, with crenellated towers above. There had been a Battle Abbey at the St. Louis World's Fair in 1904. That one had looked like an immense castle. Inside were six large cycloramas of famous battles in U.S. history, along with smaller paintings and several exhibits of arms. Uniformed attendants explained the details of the images.

The Wonderland Battle Abbey held paintings instead. There was a connection, however. Paul Dominique Philippoteaux was the most famous painter of cycloramas. He painted the still-extant *Battle of Gettysburg* cyclorama, as well as a great many other war paintings. Most visitors would probably have been familiar with the similarly named exhibit at St. Louis, which this tried to copy in miniature. Just as at the World's Fair, the Wonderland incarnation had its curator, Post Commander S. J. Simmons of the Charles Russell Lowell Post of the Grand Army of the Republic, to act as interpreter. The paintings seem to have all been of the Civil War and were insured for $50,000. "Battle Abbey" was set up in the space between the photographer's stand and Ferari's animal show.[22]

Among the paintings exhibited at Battle Abbey were those from Philippoteaux's series chronicling the career of Ulysses S. Grant—*The Battle of Belmont, Missouri; The Capture of Fort Donelson; Shiloh; The Peace Terms at Vicksburg;* and *The Charge at Corinth.*[23]

❦

"Alligator Joe" gave the impression of being a part-Hispanic, part-Indian eccentric alligator catcher and wrestler, a hefty, walrus-mustached raconteur and purveyor of swamp creatures.

In fact, he was Warren Frazee, second son of Randolph and Anna B. Frazee, born March 1, 1873, in the Mayport section of Jacksonville, Florida. His father changed careers many times, working as a farmer in 1880, a steamboat watchman in 1887, and a bartender in 1892. Young Warren was supposed to have acquired both his love of 'gators and his nickname when he visited a "Sub-Tropical Exposition" in Jacksonville that featured a huge alligator named "Alligator Joe." It was kept in the city's Waterworks Park until its death in 1904. Warren was inspired to become a hunter and trapper, and adopted the name "Alligator Joe" himself, along with a fake Seminole accent.

In 1897, he began offering hunting trips to visiting tourists who could afford it. He gathered alligator eggs and shipped them to markets, and brokered deals with the Seminoles for alligator hides. He started gathering together a menagerie of living specimens. In 1900, he opened Alligator Joe's Florida Alligator Farm outside Palm Beach. He gave twice-weekly alligator wrestling performances. Five years later he leased land on the Miami River, west of the city of Miami, and started Alligator Joe's Crocodile and Alligator Farm.

Frazee played the part, dressing in khaki clothing and a broad-brimmed hat and carrying a holstered revolver, which he apparently never used.

"Alligator Joe has never been bitten or wounded, although this has happened to others" said one source.

> He walks about in his alligator coop without fear. He stands and sits upon the largest of them, even rides on them while embracing their chests. The general belief is that he has studied the antics of the beast so well that he is always prepared for the next move. The bite should not be as dangerous as a blow from their powerfully wielded tails.
>
> Joe does not disclose the secret of his art. Many declare that he catches the 'gators by means of a lasso; others believe that he strikes them below the tail with a harpoon. But he is silent as the Sphinx. Among his accomplishments is that of telling tales, as many as one has patience or desire to listen to. One of them, for the veracity of which I cannot vouch, concerns a certain Tom Pucker, who for several years enjoyed most universal respect and envy for gathering more Saurians than all the other nimrods combined. One and all tried hard to explain his unheard-of success, and for a long time endeavored to get on to his tricks. At last a pedlar espied Tom one day on Dunn Creek as he was lying on a huge log which reached out into the stream. One of Tom's legs was hanging into the water. Presently, the pedlar noticed him pulling in his leg, while a large alligator stirred up the mud into a thick cream with mighty thrashing of his tail nearby. Tom's leg was partially concealed in the beast's throat. But this did not seem to cause the bitten one much worry. On the contrary, he drew a large Bowie and drove it into the softer parts of the biter. Then he calmly proceeded to unscrew his leg. He was the proud possessor of a wooden leg, the exterior of which was studded with nails. As soon as the alligator bit into it the nails penetrated the jaw and held him prisoner. Thus the practical Tom served as his own bait. *Si non e vero, e bene trovado.*[24]

Joe clearly was a raconteur as well as an alligator handler. He began touring with his show. In 1903, he shipped two manatees to the New York Zoological Society and appeared himself at the Steel Pier in Atlantic City, New Jersey. On May 9, 1906, he married Della Hamilton of Dade County, Florida, and they honeymooned as Frazee took one of his shows on the road to Kansas City's Electric Park—a working vacation.

So when D. S. McDonald came across Alligator Joe's shows during his vacation between the 1906 and 1907 seasons, it wasn't surprising that Frazee was interested in taking his show personally up to Wonderland in Revere for the summer of 1907.[25] He had his father, Randolph, run the

Electric Park concession in Kansas City while Warren supervised the Wonderland show.

Frazee's Florida Jungle moved into the building that had been the Beautiful Orient the previous year. The overall architecture was left untouched, which meant that those imitation minarets and "onion" domes now ruled over a building housing, it was claimed, two hundred alligators, "albino man-eating crocodiles," and sea cows in "a most picturesque Southern setting with bayous, trees heavily weighted with Spanish moss, with waving palmettos, orange trees in full fruitage, negro warblers, and so on."[26] The *Boston Post* went on to report that "teachers and parents will find this Florida exhibition an immensely valuable object lesson." The signs announcing "Turkish Theater" and "A Congress of Unusual Oriental People" were replaced by paintings of southern swamps and bayous.

One photograph showing the entrance to the Florida Jungle depicts an arched entryway between two huge paintings.[27] Another shows Alligator Joe with one foot on his manatee, and with a turtle balanced atop the manatee.[28] It appears to be in an emptied tank in a lot surrounded by a fence, probably the interior beyond the arch. There were four such compartments for the alligators and one for the manatee. Palm and fruit trees brought from Florida were arrayed around these, with six large paintings showing the Florida landscape.

One tank was devoted to the large alligator "Miami Joe"—"Miami Joe is of the man-eating variety," the *Post* announced sagely, pointing to handler William Salisbury at the show.[29] Salisbury was minus a leg thanks to Miami Joe. He swallowed it, "shoe and all," the article claimed. Salisbury remained, however, to look after the beast.[30]

Once ensconced in his new domain, Alligator Joe began showing the performance that made him a valuable property. "'Alligator Joe', while it seems strange, has a faculty of hypnotizing the animals," reported the *Boston Post*. "He gave a *Post* reporter an exhibition of his skill, and with a weird sound made by the lips, somewhat resembling a mumble and a hiss, he caused several of the large alligators to put their heads out of the water and answer back. Those who were standing in the vicinity gazed in astonishment at this wonderful exhibition, and the girls from the Fire and Flames show pronounced Joe a truly wonderful man."[31]

The manatee arrived on a six-horse caravan, having been shipped from Florida to Boston by boat. It took thirty men to get her from this conveyance into her tank. The manatee was pregnant and due to give birth there at Wonderland. Unfortunately, the mother died giving birth on June 23, as did the four-and-a-half-foot-long baby.[32]

"What Alligator Joe doesn't know about alligators, crocodiles, and sea cows isn't worth knowing," said the *Post*. "He is a most interesting individual to meet, always willing to explain to visitors anything connected with this great Southland exhibition."

☙

When Joseph Ferari left Wonderland, he may have recommended Robert J. Blake as a replacement. Blake had been part of the Ferari-Bostock shows a few years earlier and now had his own animal show. Since he left Ferari, he had been playing at fairs and vaudeville houses. It would have been appropriate to put his show where Ferari's had once been. Unlike the Ferari show, however, Blake's wasn't a display of big cats and fearsome jungle beasts. It was more in the line of the previous summer's Gillett's Dog and Monkey Show.

Robert J. Blake was possibly born in Buchanan, Michigan (where he is buried), but first made a splash in show business in Kokomo, Indiana, where he performed with the George H. Sipe and E. A. Dolman's Peerless Dog and Pony Show. From the start, "Professor" Blake was the animal trainer. One 1895 account called him "probably the most successful trainer of animals in the world."[33] In 1897, the show added monkeys to the act, and the show's title changed to "Sipe, Dolman, and Blake's, America's Greatest Dog, Pony, and Monkey Show." The show featured one hundred dogs, fifty ponies, and twenty-five trained monkeys. The dogs were trained to waltz singly and together, and to somersault forward and backward. They walked a baby carriage and knelt in pews as if in church. The ponies marched in military formation, following verbal marching commands like soldiers. Some performed specialized tricks, including adding and subtracting, like Princess Trixie. The monkeys acted as policemen and criminals, rode the ponies like jockeys, did forward and backward somersaults, rode bicycles, and performed other tricks. The show also had dogs and monkeys walking on tightropes. A tiny pony, "Independence," played leapfrog with a Great Dane.[34]

For some reason, Sipe sold the entire circus in 1899 to Henry B. Gentry of Bloomington, Illinois.[35] In 1900, Blake went his own way, with his own Educated Animals show, which quickly became Blake's Dog, Pony, and Monkey Circus.

For a couple of years, Blake performed on his own at carnivals and fairs around the country. His tricks were the ones he had used in the Sipe-Dolman-Blake Show, with the addition of some new ones—monkeys that rode up in balloons and returned to earth by parachute, like Professor La Roux, and an exhibition of diving dogs. When he visited Baltimore in 1902, the mayor declared it "a clean pretty show, which any man, woman, or child is sure to enjoy. Such marvelous intelligence and training of dumb animals I have never seen. I congratulate Professor Blake on his animals and his truly meritorious entertainment."

Blake must have liked the comic strips of cartoonist Frederick Burr Opper because he began naming his animals after characters in them. Blake's large, bicycle-riding monkey became "Happy Hooligan," named after the hobo whose strip started in 1900. He later acquired a mule who he named Maude, after the Opper strip "And Her Name Was Maude," which featured a mule that kicked people in revenge. Blake's Maude was a sort of "bucking bronco," and Blake offered to pay anyone who could stay on her. Other monkeys received names from other comic strips—"Foxy Grandpa" (from Carl E. Schultze's 1900 strip), "Buster Brown" (from Richard Outcalt's 1902 strip), and "Gloomy Gus" (Happy Hooligan's brother in the Opper strip).[36]

Blake separated from Bostock-Ferari after 1903. Somehow and somewhere he met Charles D. Willard, the musician, and the two hit it off. Together with theatrical promoter George H. Hines, who was manager of a group called the Great Wallace Shows, they formed the Hines-Blake-Willard Syndicate Shows. Later Hines dropped out, and Blake and Willard remained as an entity for many years.

His Wonderland act was undoubtedly similar to his previous shows. Happy Hooligan dressed in human clothes and rode his bicycle. Maude threw any and all comers off her back. The dogs, ponies, and monkeys did their "educated animal" acts, and Happy Hooligan and a pony had a routine in which the pony faked being sick, trying to get out of performing. It took its medicine but wouldn't get up. Happy adopted the dress of a doctor and made as if to "bleed" his patient, at which point the pony immediately got up.

ॐ

Charles D. Willard was born in San Francisco in 1858 to Lucinda J. Willard and a father whose name we don't know. By Willard's own account he started entertaining as a boy of nine, playing guitar and "mouth organ."[37] "I have drifted on and on," he said, "testing the temperament of the music-loving people, and from little weeds I have seen my musical act grow and grow until today I marvel at the strength I have assumed in amusement circles."

It was true, but Willard had followed his crowd-pleasing way into an eccentric branch of music, neither a classical performer nor a traditional popular entertainer. He was irrepressibly creative, seeking out ever newer and stranger and flashier ways of producing the music he loved.[38]

Early on he fell in love with and married a woman of compatible disposition, Ettie, usually called "Kittie." He began his professional career about 1898.[39] In 1900, Charles and Kittie performed at a benefit for the Placerville, California, Methodist Episcopal Church. A newspaper report called them "instrumental marvels."

At about the same time, they joined A. R. Carrington's Greater America Company. Carrington, who performed as "The Drummer Boy of Shiloh," had an entertainment troupe that performed in Los Angeles, Reno, and other venues in that area.[40] The Willards appear to have joined with them in November 1899. They were soon billed as "The Musical Willards," "musical revelators" with their so-called $2,000 act. "The title represents the cost of the finest musical stage setting ever seen in this city," and the new and unusual instruments that Charles and Kittie had acquired and incorporated into their act. According to one source, "They employed instruments rarely ever seen in this country. One of these was the Japanese bamboo calliope, another was the American aluminum chimes. The Turkish mellow pipes and the Guatemala octaphone made up their collection."

Descriptions of the instruments in the Willard collection are frequently misleading. For instance, the "Japanese bamboo calliope," sometimes described as "Japanese bamboo chimes," was likely an Indonesian instrument, the *angklung*. The *angklung* is made of pieces of bamboo put together to form a complex construction for each "note," and a set of these could play a complete set of notes, like a xylophone or marimba. It sounds much like a marimba, but with a more complex waveform. The "American Aluminum Chimes" were probably a variation of these, produced in metal by the musical inventor and innovator John Calhoun Deagan, who patented them in 1900. The Willards would obtain many of their unusual and innovative instruments from Deagan's company over the next twenty-five years. Similarly, the "Turkish mellow pipes" might have been the *miskal*, or Turkish panpipe. The "Guatemalan octaphone" is something of a mystery.

Within a couple of years, the Willards had expanded their collection of instruments to a $20,000 investment. They left Carrington's Greater American Company and established their own troupe, Willard's Temple of Music. They allied themselves briefly with the Gaskill-Mundy-Levitt theatrical organization but shortly took out an advertisement announcing that they were severing ties with that group and setting out on their own. It was about this time that Willard joined with Robert J. Blake and his Dog, Pony, and Monkey Show, and they began traveling together. After playing several venues, they finally hit it big at the White City Amusement Park in Chicago in 1905. Here, they each got their own dedicated, semi-permanent building.

By now they had a great many more instruments, with names like Flukemizer, The Heathen Gods of China, The Bermuda Razzle-Dazzle, and the Scandinavian Harpsichord. They had a special instrument constructed by the W. W. Kimball Company called the Swedish Harmonium at a cost of $4,500. The combined weight of all the instruments was almost two tons, and it made an impressive array when spread out symmetrically in the Temple of Music.

From Chicago they went to Mexico for a time. Subsequently, Willard split his company into three parts. The second company played at Dreamland at Coney Island, while the third went to Palisades Park in New Jersey. But the first company would play at Wonderland Park in Revere.

They occupied the former children's theater, next to the new Under the Sea exhibit. The company consisted of Charles and Kitty Willard, along with four young men and eight young women, all highly skilled musicians, all costumed. (The next year, ads for Willard's show bragged about having "the original Wonderland Ladies.")[41] The show consisted of pieces played on a few traditional instruments, such as an Italian harp, said to be one of the costliest in the world, and unusual ones like the "Japanese Chimes" and the "American Chimes" mentioned above, both of which produced a sound unfamiliar to most people. A lot of the specialized instruments were somewhat like xylophones or marimbas, with a collection of items arranged in different sizes that gave different notes.

A brief description of Willard's act at Wonderland states,

> There are many new attractions this season, among them being Willard's Temple of Music, which is a revelation in the music line. There are wheels revolving within wheels, and emanating from all is sweet music and harmony, while balls of fire are seen dancing, here and there, like little lightning bugs. The many colors resemble a kaleidoscope, and the reflections of thousands of tiny mirrors with revolving jeweled globes that play as they are made to soar through space in the hands of master musicians, an act representing $30,000, is indeed a wonderful attraction.[42]

Electricity continued to be something the Willards injected into their music. Kittie was "The Electrical Lady," using a Tesla-coil-like electrical plate that produced high-frequency, high-voltage electrical "skin effects." Standing on a charged plate, a visitor could apparently shoot sparks from their fingers.[43] But they carried it further. Charles played on a piano keyboard that broadcast the signals wirelessly through Kittie to actuators that controlled the hammers. They had a set of coffee grinders that produced different tones when run and, as an extra effect, were electrified to produce sparks. One of their novelties was the Musical Sawmill, in which different circular saw blades cutting through wood produced different tones, enabling them to play tunes. But they made it even more spectacular by charging the saw blades and having the ladies play them with bows so that the blades gave off sparks every time they were played.

The group had kerosene lamps with special shades that could be played (presumably flickering when the note was sounded), which they later upgraded to electric lights. There was a collection of different-sized heads of Chinese men, each with a braided hair queue that, when pulled, played a note. There were musical flowerpots.

One modern reviewer, looking at the Willards' act, dismissed it as cheap novelty: "The music runs very much to mechanical freak arrangements, oddity of effect being aimed at rather than melody. Several of the instruments employ devices like bamboo chimes, and get their only novelty from the fact that they are worked by three or four players."[44] But this was neither fair nor accurate. In the first place, the Willards, as many contemporary reports make clear, were consummate musicians, artists on "standard" instruments long before they went into novelty ideas. It also ignores the fact that many of those "novelty" instruments were, in fact, just as "real" as more familiar ones, simply less common in the United States. The *angklung*'s novelty derived not from how many people were needed to play it but from the unique sound it generated. The American chimes were Deagan's metal counterpart to the same, again with its unique sound.[45]

Some of the devices were undoubtedly simply excuses for novelty for its own sake, like The Heathen Gods of China. But who could resist the proto-cyberpunk appeal of attractively clad women in welder's goggles playing a rousing tune on rotating, electrified circular saw blades that threw out sparks at every note?

⁓

The Fire and Flames show was almost completely changed for the 1907 season, including most of the cast of firefighters. Gone were Chief F. J. Murphy and Assistant Chief H. Curtis. Replacing Murphy as chief was the one returning member of the fire brigade, James Fitzgerald, who had been the captain of Engine 26 in 1906. At the end of the previous season, twenty-two of the show's twenty-five horses had been auctioned off, many to Boston fire departments.

Stage Manager M. B. Pollock left too, replaced by Frank Robinson, assisted by O. B. Steel. William Snow, who had been a manager of the show, was injured in May 1907 while training a new horse for the show. The horse was pulling the chief's wagon but suddenly bolted at the park entrance.[46] The non-firefighter acting cast seems to have been completely changed from the previous season, with the exception of Lee Piotti and Millie Piotti, who continued to play Ike and Rebecca Cohen, running a pawn shop. The character Sam Wing, a Chinese laundryman, played by A. Frothingham, replaced Sam Wong, who had been played by W. Wentworth. The headings in the cast list differed completely from the previous year's, in agreement with the announcement that there was a new script for 1907. The action took place in McNally's Flats, Sam Wong's Laundry, Pat McCarty's home, Mike Slattery's Rough House, the Salvation Army, and the streetcar. Instead of being harassed by street kids who start the fire, Ike Cohen, "The King of the Jews," is robbed of clothing by a thief.

The 1907 Fire and Flames souvenir book gives a detailed image of the start of the new show:

> When the wide curtains are drawn apart a city square is disclosed. Then follows a scene which, for life-like representation is a triumph of the stage manager's versatile art. Newsboys cry successive editions. Street gamins "shoot craps" till the cry of "Cheese it, de cop!" scatters them. A fruit vender rolls his push-cart along. The blind man is led by the boy fiddler, the man's cane tap-tapping along in pitiful realism. Two men are in a street brawl. One is knocked down and unconscious. The other flees, is grasped by a policeman and struggles all over the square while the ambulance dashes up and bears the victim to the hospital. All is life and animation and the spectators watch with amused and admiring interest.
>
> "Fire! Fire! Fire!!"
>
> The dread cry rises, while the audience gazes in fascination as flames burst from a store adjoining the factory. A policeman pulls in an alarm. The apparatus responds.
>
> Meanwhile the flames have spread to the adjoining building, mounting from floor to floor while the hapless inmates shriek in terror for aid. With terrific explosions the fire speeds on its devouring way, the reports drowning temporarily the screams of the fire-imperilled factory people.
>
> See that fireman scale the walls, swinging from window to window with his hook-billed ladder.
>
> Ah, Heaven! A girl, desperate from fire threatening her from behind, jumps from a fourth-story window to the ground. No, not to the ground. For the life-net had been spread and the girl is safely caught. Perhaps you think that four-story jump was a clever piece of stage mechanism.
>
> The endangered people are all taken from the building. The fire is stubbornly beaten back and down. Of the building a smoke and fire blackened shell remains but no lives have been lost and there is rejoicing among the crowd and applause for the fire ladies.
>
> The curtains are drawn together and a storm of well-earned applause rolls forward from the gratified audience.

Except for the photograph of the new fire chief, all the photographs were reproduced from the previous year's souvenir book. Since the casts had almost completely changed, practically everyone depicted was not actually in the show any longer, but this was evidently not considered important.

The new ringmaster at the open-air circus, replacing the outgoing Fred A. Bennett, was Frank Todd. Todd had spent the previous seven years in theatrical companies, mostly with Marc Klaw and Abraham Lincoln Erlanger's Opera Company, which produced musical comedies. He was notable as a multitalented comic performer. In "A Runaway Girl" in Boston in 1902, "Frank Todd, as a grotesque Scotchman, made a decided hit with his dancing and comic antics."[47] He traveled up and down the East Coast, not only performing but also acting as a stage manager for shows. It was ideal training for running the Arcus Ring at Wonderland.

❧

Besides the aeronaut Lincoln Beachey, the big opening attraction was tightrope walker James E. Hardy, who had performed at Wonderland the previous year.[48] Charles "Sandy" Chapman sang the new march "Take Me Down to Wonderland," while the First Cadet Corps of musicians played in the new band pavilion. "Mlle De Loro will show how gracefully she can bend and twist her lithe body without breaking any bones," observed the *Boston Post*, "and Walter Starr Wentworth, Wonderland's clown, will keep his audience laughing by his antics with his little elephant."[49] The description doesn't do Wentworth full credit. He too had been a contortionist, performing as early as 1864. By 1907, he was seventy-two and still performing as a contortionist. (He added ten years to his age, though, and claimed to be eighty-two.)[50]

Walter Starr Wentworth was born July 22, 1835, in Utica, Michigan.[51] About his upbringing and how he broke into show business we have no record, but he was first recorded as performing in 1864 at age twenty-nine. (It is a sobering thought that when Wentworth was born, James Madison was still alive and Andrew Jackson still had over a year and a half to his tenure as president.) Wentworth traveled around the country, billing himself as "the first contortionist." He called his specialty act the "Packanatomical-ization," in which he fitted his body into a box measuring 23 by 19 by 16 inches. (Fellow performers referred to it as "the box act.")[52] As if that were not enough, he also crammed in six dozen soda water bottles with himself.

Additionally, Wentworth mastered a number of other carnival skills. He was a trapeze artist, worked on the suspended rings, and acted as a ventriloquist.[53] He was a relentless self-promoter and fabulist—you could never be sure which of his stories were true, which were exaggerated, and which were wholly made up. Wentworth was probably the "W. Wentworth" who had played Sam Wong, the Chinese laundryman, in the Fire and Flames show the previous year.

About the length of time he performed, however, there is no doubt as it was preserved in the newspaper record. There are also photographs of him folding himself into that wooden box, bending his body almost double—backward. As he aged, he started tacking on ten years to his age so that he could bill himself as "the oldest contortionist." Another story he made much of was his "selling his body" to science. In one of the first reports of this story, he sold himself to Dr. H. I. Wilder of Cincinnati, on condition that Wilder "wire up" the skeleton after Wentworth had died, showing him in contorted pose.[54] He got a lot of mileage out of telling the story to reporters until Wilder died, which Wentworth felt nullified the contract. In 1902, he told the *Washington [DC] Evening Star* that he sold his body the first time to a Dr. Cowe of Detroit for one hundred dollars. Dr. Cowe died, and so Wentworth felt free to sell himself again to Dr. H. N. Wilder of Kings County Hospital, New York.[55] This Dr. Wilder subsequently died, and so Wentworth was looking for yet another doctor to sell himself to. In a 1902 *New York Herald* interview, he claimed the first doctor was a William Cowe of Utica, Michigan, in 1864 and the second was an H. T. Wilder of Kings County Hospital in Brooklyn. Whatever the truth, it was a good story, and the papers always printed it. Any publicity was good publicity for Wentworth.

He seems to have retired multiple times but returned to show business because he missed it or needed the money. He retired first in 1901, shortly before his son John died, moving in with him to a house in Medford, Massachusetts. Wentworth was still living there, with John's collection of rattlesnakes (which he could take out and display en masse), when he was interviewed by the *New York Herald*.

By 1904, Wentworth was performing again at Hubert's Museum in New York City. He performed a ventriloquist act and billed himself as "the oldest living ventriloquist." He continued working in various venues, including

Wonderland in Revere, then retired again in 1908 to the Actors' Home in West Brighton, Staten Island, where he gave an interview the following year and demonstrated that he could still go through his contortions.

One news account of his Wonderland stint claims he amused the audience by attempting to copy Mademoiselle De Loro's contortionist poses. More than being simply a silly act, clowning with and copying De Loro, he was demonstrating his skills as a contortionist, which may have been better than De Loro's, despite her lesser age. Pretending to not be competent at the art of which he was a master actually required *greater* skill than doing a "straight," noncomedic act.[56]

On July 2, Frank Todd, the stage manager of the open-air circus, complained of stomach pains and was taken to Massachusetts General Hospital in Boston. He died there on July 3 of complications due to "stomach troubles." Funeral services were held a week later at the Church of the Advent in Boston, where he had been a choir boy many years before. The pallbearers were all member of Boston theaters and theatrical companies. Afterward, he was buried in Haverhill, Massachusetts.[57]

No notice of this was made by Wonderland in public, or by the Boston papers, aside from a laconic death notice that did not mention his position with the amusement park. The circus at Wonderland went on without him. No replacement was announced, probably to avoid drawing attention to the fact that he was no longer there. Possibly Assistant Manager Eugene L. Perry took over—he would be visible enough in other roles that summer. Or perhaps wire-walker James Hardy filled in—his contract at Wonderland was extended that summer without explanation. With his waxed moustache, he looked the very image of the circus ringmaster.

In July, the big act was Rose Wentworth the equestrienne. She was well-known to many of the patrons already and appeared with the assistance of Gilbert Eldred and Harry Wentworth. Harry was a son of the contortionist and clown Walter Wentworth, and Rose was Harry's wife.

Harry Wentworth seems to have been born in 1855. He first performed in 1878 as "Master Harry Wentworth, a neat contortionist," like his father. He traveled with the Main and Burdick Circus, appearing in Cincinnati, Hartford, and Baltimore. In Paterson, New Jersey, he was "The Boneless Man." In 1884, he worked with Frank A. Robbins's "Railroad Show" and toured upstate New York, appearing on the same bill as his father in

Camden, Geneva, and Oneida. In these shows he assisted Colonel John Foster, "The Prince of Clowns." Like his father, Harry became a clown.

He joined the Barnum and Bailey Circus for the first time in 1888 with an act of "educated pigs."[58] One played the role of a baby, being fed a bottle, saying "Mama" passably, getting spanked, and then running off. Wentworth trained others to stand on a pedestal. It was while with Barnum and Bailey that he met Rose.

Rose Maude Allington was born in Fall River, Massachusetts, a port town that would later earn notoriety in 1892 because of Lizzie Borden and her supposed axe murders. Rose was a little nebulous about her birthdate, but it appears to have been 1874. Her family was, like Harry's, filled with performers and entertainers.[59] At the age of five, her parents took her to London, where she began to study dancing. She played a page onstage for a production at the Gaiety Theater in London. One day the future King Edward VII attended their rehearsal. He was taken by her long yellow hair, and thinking it a wig, gave it a hard yank. It hurt so much that tears ran down her face. The prince apologized profusely, something Rose never forgot.[60]

After they returned to the United States, Rose started with the Forepaugh-Sells Circus, then joined Barnum and Bailey the next year, going by the name Maude Allington. She stated in later life that she joined Barnum and Bailey at twelve, which would have been 1886. In an 1896 interview for the *Boston Post,* however, she said she joined the circus in 1889, when circus owner James A. Bailey placed an advertisement in the papers looking for dancers and ballet girls for his planned spectacle "Nero." Rose thought her dancer's training would allow her to fit right in. By diligence and hard work, she was brought to Bailey's attention and was soon taught to handle the horses and drive a chariot.[61] Initially, she found the work challenging, telling an interviewer, "Why, those horses almost pulled my arms out!" But she soon learned and began winning chariot races, even against men.

She also learned contortion (despite Walter Wentworth's dictum that contortionists are born, not trained).[62] Bailey, taken by her grace as a dancer and her ability to handle horses, suggested she learn bareback riding. She also studied trapeze, moving from being unable to lift herself with her arms alone to supporting herself by one arm. "From a ballet girl I have advanced until I believe I can take almost any act in the circus," she said.

Allington was always attractive and outgoing, and reporters seemed to gravitate toward her, leaving many glimpses of her training through the years.[63] Furthermore, there was her romance with Harry Wentworth, something the papers found irresistible. It was almost inevitable that reporters drew a parallel between Harry and Rose and the characters Punchinello and Columbine of the *commedia del'arte* Harlequinade: "He is Punchinello still, but sweet Columbine has given up all her past life for love—and Punchinello—and now she is pretty Rose Wentworth, who, in a trig habit, dashes madly around the course in the Madison Square Garden in a jockey race, drives a chariot, swings in a trapeze from a giddy height, or bends her slender body into impossible postures as she slips easily through a small ring," wrote the *New York Times*.[64] "Then the reporter said good-bye, and went away, hoping that Punchinello and his sweet Columbine would live happily ever after."

When they started as a pair, they were listed together as "contortionists," but within a couple of years Rose (now using the last name Wentworth) was getting her own listing, performing as a trapeze artist, bareback rider, and contortionist. In 1897, she was featured in a poster for Barnum and Bailey flipping a somersault on a horse, "The Only Lady Rider Turning Somersaults." It wasn't quite true—she was neither the first nor the only female bareback somersaulter—but they were a rare breed, and the circus can be forgiven for its hyperbole. Another Barnum and Bailey poster from the same year shows Rose and fellow bareback rider Josie Ashton standing confidently atop their galloping horses. She developed an act involving two other girls—an equestrienne trio—that remained a staple of her performances for many years.

The couple mostly remained with Barnum and Bailey through the beginning of the twentieth century but took gigs outside the circus in vaudeville and small venues, especially during the off-season. Shortly after the new century began, however, they began looking for performance places outside the circus.

A picture of Rose appeared in the *Boston Post* on July 21, 1907. "The Wentworths will offer a fascinating equestrian act on the tan bark [that is, on the sawdust]. Miss Rose Wentworth is popular and deservedly known as the 'Queen of the Arena' and is famous for her skill and grace in many lands," enthused the paper. Two days later an article observed, "A big novelty and of particular interest because of picturesqueness, grace, and skill is the equestrian act of Rose Wentworth, for many years with the Barnum and Bailey show. Miss Wentworth is assisted by Gilbert Eldred and Harry Wentworth."

The trio was held over and performed at Wonderland through the week of August 7. They then went across Broad Sound and performed at Bass Point, where the Scintillator had been the previous summer before it was brought to Wonderland.[65]

⁖

Beginning on September 2 and continuing until the closing of the park there would be nightly performances of an "Alice in Wonderland" Parade.[66] The idea seems somewhat obvious for a park called Wonderland, but none of the many other parks of the same name seem to have featured an event or attraction using the Alice in Wonderland theme. The parade was the creation of Eugene L. Perry, the new assistant manager, and the one who would be its chauffer.[67] It fit in with his earlier penchant for productions.

The Alice parade, scheduled for Monday, September 2, had to be postponed because of bad weather. It opened on Tuesday, September 3, to a crowd of fifteen thousand people.[68] Alice arrived at 8:45 in the evening in a "beautifully illuminated up-to-date chariot" driven by Perry. A contingent of Revere police led the way, followed by the Boston Banda Rossa, conducted by Signor d'Avino. They were followed by the Teddy Bear Brigade, led by Hap Ward Jr. Following were the Cheshire Cat, the Mad Hatter, the March Hare, a duck, and other animals. Then the court jester, "Doc" Watson; the court minstrel, Lawrence B. O'Connor (the show's musical director); a troupe of dancing girls; the court dancing master, John L. Coleman (who choreographed dancing events for local groups); and the court of Columbia, led by Helen Norton as Columbia and fifty elves. Louise Osgood of Revere played Alice.[69] The parade concluded with a battle of flowers and confetti, and a tableaux of "Columbia Enlightening the World." The parade was a big hit and repeated nightly.

At about this time, Wonderland announced that it would be closing Fire and Flames for good. There were only a few weeks left in its run, and anyone wanting to see the show before it left should come to Wonderland before the end of the season.

Why close the show after putting it up at such great expense? It is possible that, having saturated its market, the show was seeing a drop-off in patronage, and it was time to replace it with something fresh. The constant use and high temperatures were probably taking a toll on the structures as well. Also, William Manning and James Armstrong had stated at the opening of Wonderland that the show was only a limited engagement.

The London Fire Exhibition that started the craze for these shows had, after all, only lasted a couple of weeks. George C. Hale's recreation at the St. Louis Fair only lasted one summer. The two firefighting shows at Coney Island, at Luna Park and Dreamland, had both closed after only two years of running, so it is not surprising that Wonderland planned to follow their lead. Wonderland announced upcoming auctions for horses and some of the fire equipment after the closing of Wonderland for the season.

Wonderland finally did close at 11 p.m. on Sunday, September 15. The current band, l'Africain's, played "Auld Lang Syne" to mark the end of the season. The park claimed an even higher number of visitors than it had in the first season.[70]

Manning made plans to go to Manchester, England, and set up a Fire and Flames show at the White City there.[71] He also had plans for a new show at Wonderland. J. J. Higgins was asked to join the newly formed Association of Amusement Parks, meeting in New York City. It must have seemed like déjà-vu to him. Once again he found himself a member of the board of a trade organization with its headquarters in New York, for an element of which he had been treasurer.[72]

Things looked bright for the upcoming season. The park had overcome the departure of much of its original staff, including its general manager, and survived the replacement of many of its leading attractions. It had come through beautifully and profitably. It should have been clear sailing after this, but fate leveled two big strikes against Wonderland before the next season. One of these was a massive fire in Chelsea, Massachusetts, that devastated much of downtown. It didn't come close to the amusement park, but it put a damper on the next season.

The other hit was further away but ultimately more devastating. A set of circumstances in 1906, including the San Francisco earthquake, the Bank of London raising its interest rates, and the passage of the Hepburn Act (which gave the Interstate Commerce Commission the ability to set maximum railroad freight rates) all conspired to make the stock market unsteady. Ironically, considering Wonderland was largely financed by money from copper mines, it was speculation in copper that sent the economy over the edge. On October 15, 1907, two speculators, F. Augustus Heinze and Charles W. Morse, tried to corner the stock of United Copper and failed. They suffered huge losses, which translated into huge losses for the banks involved with them, causing a "run" on the banks as depositors tried to save what they could of their funds and redeposit them elsewhere. The Panic of 1907 spread swiftly. Interest rates soared and stock values fell.

J. P. Morgan organized a team of bankers, including John D. Rockefeller, to try to put a stop to the crisis, providing funds to allow banks to pay out the many withdrawals and getting infusions from the U.S. government. Ultimately, a suspension of the Sherman Anti-Trust Act by President Theodore Roosevelt stopped the panic.

The Panic of 1907 was the largest financial upheaval until the Great Depression of 1929, and it had similar effects on most households. Businesses were unable to finance operations or pay their workers. People found themselves with less money to spare for entertainment. Production declined significantly, and unemployment rose from 3 percent in 1907 to 8 percent in 1908. This profoundly affected not only Wonderland but other amusement parks around the country. Many closed down in the wake of the panic, and others were dealt a mortal blow from which they were slow to recover, if they did at all.

But Wonderland had already decided on many of its attractions for the 1908 season, and there wasn't much to do about it. The die had been cast. The 1908 season would arguably have the most impressive shows of any of Wonderland's years.

CHAPTER 7
Year Three—1908

Wonderland's third year started off much as its second had. There was no countdown to opening day in the form of stories about new attractions and changes to the park. Again, newspapers waited until just before opening day to place stories, this time only a week before, although this year the park opened earlier than usual, at 1 p.m. on Saturday, May 23, 1908.[1]

The big attractions remained—the Shoot the Chutes, Hell Gate, the Infant Incubators, the Thompson Scenic Railway, the ballroom and restaurant, and the Velvet Coaster. The Palmistry attraction was still there, although palm readers Estelka Daly and Virginia Knapp had been replaced by one Mademoiselle Ermilla. The Japanese Village remained but was renamed "Land of the Mikado." The bandstand and the open-air circus opened as well. Love's Journey still operated and had added a "Merry Widow" Tunnel for 1908, redecorating one of the ride segments.[2]

But the Fire and Flames show, as promised, was gone. In its place was Pawnee Bill's Wild West Show. The Florida Alligator Jungle had moved on too, and this year the premises, originally those of the Beautiful Orient, were occupied by Darktown, produced by the same William C. Manning who had been responsible for the Fire and Flames show.

In addition, there was a new cement pool for their other big guest of the summer, Annette Kellermann, "The Australian Mermaid." As if to make up for this new water show, Under the Sea appears to have gone, replaced by a new funhouse, Pilgrim's Progress. Willard's Temple of Music had gone from the children's theater, and now that building housed Paradise—The Show Beautiful. Blake's Circus had moved on as well, and its place was taken by Darling's Dog and Pony Circus. But, as if in a bid for continuity,

Darling's also had a recalcitrant, unrideable mule named "Maude."[3] The Rocky Mountain Holdup was gone, replaced by The World in Motion cinema. Finally, Battle Abbey left, and in its place was the Human Laundry. A roller-skating rink was put in the southwest corner under a circus big-top tent, where the Wild West show had been the first year and pony rides the next, with the miniature railroad still circling it. Somewhere in the park was Chiquita the Doll Lady. The open-air circus continued with its rotating acts, but they did not announce a ringmaster for 1908, perhaps superstitiously fearing a repeat of the previous summer's death. This year Stiles's 8th Regiment Band would play the music.

The 1 p.m. opening time became standard for the year. Parking at the Wonderland garage was free.

The Wonderland restaurant was still open and serving its "Shore Dinners," but its manager, Dudley S. McDonald, was not there. In November 1907, he began selling off restaurant fixtures in his Boston establishments, apparently in need of cash.[4] At the end of January 1908, he opened the Holly Club on Hawley Street in Boston, in the heart of the business district. It was a "Bohemian" restaurant, with a fixed *table d'hote* menu. It received excellent reviews and was intended to be a high-class establishment catering to the business community.[5]

Unfortunately, this new venture was set against a background of financial failure.[6] Ten days after the restaurant's opening, creditors filed a petition in U.S. district court to have McDonald's other Boston restaurant declared bankrupt.[7] The establishment, formerly on Tremont Street, had been forced to move because the building was being demolished, and it seems to not have regained its status or its clientele. It owed $2,500 to creditors, including $1,100 to the Boston Ice Company. At the beginning of May, McDonald severed his interests in other restaurants, including Wonderland's, so that he could concentrate on his mainstay, but it was apparently too late. On Saturday, May 16, the R. H. White Company announced that McDonald would henceforth be in charge of its store restaurant. He had taken over operation of the White restaurant as a satellite business in 1903, but now it became his entire business. He dressed in a white linen outfit and oversaw operations as a cook in the kitchen, or from his desk in a corner of the dining room. He put as good a face on the demotion as he could, but it was clearly a decline.[8]

To take his place, Wonderland obtained the services of Charles E. David-son. He knew Charles A. Washburn of the new attraction Paradise, so that might have been how his name came up. Davidson had been running the restaurant at the Hotel Pemberton in Hull, where he had previously been head clerk. He also had run the restaurants at the Princess Anne in Virginia Beach and the restaurant at the Ottawa House Hotel on Cushing's Island off the coast of Maine. He put new signage on the front of Wonderland's restaurant, advertising their shore dinners and cigars.[9]

The Pilgrim's Progress took over the Under the Sea building, with some modifications. The water tank was taken out, as were the audience seats. Across the top was painted a frieze of tall, angular figures, and a banner hung over the entrance reading "Abandon Dull Care Those Who Enter Here," a parody of the Gate of Hell in Dante's *Inferno*: "Abandon All Hope All Ye Who Enter Here." It read as if it was taken from John Bunyan's seventeenth-century literary classic *The Pilgrim's Progress*, the metaphori-cal novel describing the wanderings of the Human Soul in its journey for Heaven and God, trying to avoid temptations such as Vanity Fair. Surely Dull Care was just another such distraction in the book.

Only it wasn't. The true source of the inspiration for this attraction came from much closer to home. The *New York Evening Telegram* on June 26, 1905, began running the comic strip *A Pilgrim's Progress, by Mister Bun-ion*. The title was a very obvious and deliberate pun on the original book (and "Bunion" parodied the name of the author, John Bunyan).

The comic strip was the work of one of the most prolific and influential comic-strip artists of the early twentieth century, Winsor McCay. McCay is better known as the author of the extravagant and gorgeous *Little Nemo in Slumberland* and *Dreams of the Rarebit Fiend*. He also drew and pro-duced some of the earliest animated cartoons, including *Gertie the Dino-saur* and *The Giant Pet*.

McCay's strip *Pilgrim's Progress* featured the tall, thin, angular Mr. Bun-ion, who carried a big, black valise labeled "Dull Care," of which he was always attempting to free himself. That fact alone ought to show where the attraction got its inspiration. The figures in the frieze somewhat resem-bled McCay's drawings but not enough to justify a charge of copyright infringement.

"'Banish Dull Care All Who Enter Here' is written over the portals of 'The Pilgrim's Progress,'" wrote the *Cambridge Chronicle* and *Billboard*, both apparently quoting from the same news release,

> and it is most fittingly descriptive of what one experiences within who once begins and continues a trip through this wonderful mirthland. The journey is a consistent progression, from a gentle smile compelled by the initiatory gentle encounter with the first factor for the merry making to the most hilarious merriment from contact with other mysterious things. Stand in front of this beautifully decorated temple of gayety for a few minutes and listen to the evidences of the royal good time all of the pilgrims are having; watch the crowds as they come out with faces wreathed in smiles and then be advised and follow suit.[10]

How could you turn down an invitation so completely vague? According to one account, Pilgrim's Progress featured moving chairs, tilted rooms, ghosts, dissolving mirages, falling stairways, mysterious passages, and something called the Cantsitonit ("can't sit on it"). According to Gordon Lillie, "Pawnee Bill" himself, Pilgrim's Progress was being managed by James "Jimmie" Callahan, a comedian who used to absent himself from his own show to clown around with Pawnee Bill's Wild West Show.[11]

If the description of Pilgrim's Progress is rather vague, that of Paradise—The Show Beautiful is maddeningly opaque. The show moved into the former Children's Theater, which had been occupied by Willard's Temple of Music the previous season.

Paradise was the creation of Charles A. Washburn. He had had an attraction at Luna Park in Mexico City the previous year, and several years later he promoted a completely different show, but Paradise seems to have only appeared in 1908 in Wonderland.[12] There were many attractions, before and after, that billed themselves as "The Show Beautiful" in their advertisements, but that was only an adjectival flourish attached to the attraction's name to give it some finesse.

The Wonderland show was advertised with pictures of about a dozen well-dressed women seated on a stage designed to look like a prosperous parlor, with a man—presumably Charles A. Washburn—standing to one side. This gave the impression of a beauty pageant, but the descriptions appeared to promise, in addition, something different: "Paradise, The

Show Beautiful, is a temple of female loveliness," wrote *Billboard*. "With fire dances and all sorts of fascinating sights and sounds."[13] Pawnee Bill's column in a later issue of *Billboard* observed that "'Paradise, the Show Beautiful' has been rightly named [as one of the more profitable shows] and from the performances we do not marvel at their large crowds." But he did not go on to describe the performances.[14]

Young women from the show walked through the park and handed out tickets reading:

I AM SINGLE

ARE YOU?

BUT IT MAKES NO DIFFERENCE MARRIED OR SINGLE YOU SHOULD GO TO

PARADISE

THE SHOW BEAUTIFUL

WONDERLAND'S NEW ATTRACTION

IT WILL MAKE YOU

SIT RIGHT UP AND LOOK

With a come-on that provocative, the show undoubtedly got a lot of curious patrons at least coming to look at the outer show. What did they see if they paid the admission?[15]

The closest we get to a description is from advertisements placed by Washburn himself. In an ad in *Billboard* for March 21, 1908, he solicited talent for the show. He was looking for "Eight Serpentine Dancers, A Lady for Poses (Must be Good Form and Good Looking), The Best Fire Dancer in America, The Best Spanish Dancer in America, A Lady for Statue Turning to Life, and Four Handsome Ladies for Ballyhoo (Experience Not

Necessary)."[16] Another ad in *Billboard* the following year, looking for future bookings of the show, stated,

The Handsomest Ballyhoo You Ever Saw

Mr. Manager—Are you looking for something new? Do you want a Real Live One?

PARADISE—The Show Beautiful

162,000 paid admissions at Wonderland last summer. PARADISE is the handsomest, cleanest, most beautiful Electrical and Mechanical Production ever shown for ten cents. Every patron a booster, and catering to the very best. A great show for ladies and children. 21 PEOPLE Show runs about twenty eight minutes.

It is so clean that we were allowed to run Sunday in Wonderland, which is under the supervision of Massachusetts State Police. We will guarantee to beat ANY ten cent show in ADMISSIONS that you have.

Address Charles A. Washburn Care the *Billboard*.[17]

Alas for Charles Washburn, his employees, and our curiosity, Paradise does not appear to have acquired any post-1908 bookings, at least under that name. What the show consisted of we are left only to our own imaginations and speculations. Perhaps the show was like a somewhat later show that ran the circuits in 1913–14, "Caddis: The Show Beautiful," which combined vaudeville with illusions.

As for Wonderland's other funhouse, it underwent some changes too. What had been the Foolish House and the Third Degree was now rechristened The House that Jack Built. The comic Alfred E. Neuman–like figure with the missing toothed idiot grin—evidently now Jack—lost his top hat, monocle, and prospective brides on either side. His hands no longer held bouquets but tools (from building the house, no doubt). And his mouth seemed to have a cigar in it. Possibly the change was necessitated by not having Keystone Amusements, the company that ran the Third Degree funhouses elsewhere in the country in charge of it anymore. The interior apparently did not change.

If any attraction had a right to call itself "clean," it was arguably the Human Laundry. The Human Laundry went up in the building that had been Battle Abbey the previous year, between the photographer's stand and the circus. The attraction was owned and licensed by S. L. Negley and Company of Chicago.[18] It appeared in some parks in 1907 but then showed up simultaneously in a great many more parks in the summer of 1908.

The Wonderland incarnation had a vaguely Chinese shape to it and painted caricatures of two Chinese laundrymen on either side of the entrance arch, one scrubbing laundry in a tub. A photograph of the attraction shows a man in front dressed as a Chinese laundryman, with a long hair queue. Admission was ten cents. The *Cambridge Chronicle* described it this way:

> Perhaps nothing in Wonderland will make you forget the discomforts of a hot afternoon or evening so much as a visit to the Human Laundry where one can get washed, ironed, and well-groomed without mussing, and with heaps of fun. You go in curious, you come out looking spic and span, and greatly refreshed and radiantly happy. Climbing the cool and inviting glass stairway with its cascade of real water, you secure your checks then you pass on to the assorting room where—well, you had better find out what it is all about. Then comes the washtubs, the clothes lines, the wringing machines, the ironing boards, and the re-assembling room where you are put together again and ushered forth into the lights and the merriment of the board-walk. It would be criminal to tell in advance what will happen to you in the Human Laundry.[19]

A much more detailed description of another incarnation of the attraction, with drawings, appeared in the *Baltimore Sun* for May 31, 1908:

> Perhaps this year the human laundry will take the popular fancy, because it is largely nonsense. The processes are numerous and varied.
>
> The visitor is subjected to an imaginary washing in a gigantic tub. He is tossed about in an imaginary sea of suds and thrown headfirst into a meta-phorical rinsing tub. He is rushed through what appears to be gigantic rubber wringers, and just as he feels sure that he is to be squeezed within an inch of his life the giant cylinders pass around him and he is free again.
>
> After that the bluing room, which is simply an apartment with walls of deep cerulean hue. And then a final wringing, and the visitor is run through some marvelous ironing devices and throw[n] down a chute laundered to perfection.
>
> If one goes through all these motions in solitary state it is perhaps not such a screaming farce to be washed, rinsed and ironed, but in company

with half a hundred merry souls, all undergoing the same program, the effect is diverting and picturesque.[20]

෫๑

What had been Hale's Tours for Wonderland's first season became the Rocky Mountain Holdup for the second, dropping the Hale's name but retaining its feature film. For the park's third season there was to be another change—sound. As both the *Boston Post* and the *Globe* announced on May 17, 1908, "The World in Motion," as the attraction was now called, "is an up-to-date scenic temple in which one feature will be the *humanovo* or picture that talks, and another will be illustrated song singing."[21]

Ever since the motion picture had been invented, people had sought to remedy its deficiencies. Film was black and white, and it lacked sound. Overcoming these limitations faced formidable technical hurdles at first. At the time, there were significant technical problems in synchronizing sound with film and amplifying the volume so that everyone in the theater could hear it.

So the announcement that Wonderland would feature Humanovo, billed as "The Picture That Talks," would have aroused a considerable amount of interest. The owners of the process were cagey about not only how it worked but exactly what it was. A newspaper account describing the new addition to the Nickel Theater in Manchester, New Hampshire, for instance, commented, "The Humanovo is a process that renders it possible that vaudeville sketches can be put on stage, whereby comedy of a refined character can be performed. The details of the plan will not be presented here, as the management is desirous that the public tell for itself how the thing is done." This made it all rather mysterious.[22]

The reality was much more pedestrian. It was the brainchild of Adolph Zukor, a fur dealer who got into the motion picture business when making a loan to his cousin, who ran an establishment of Edison kinetoscopes (he would eventually go on to found Paramount Pictures). Wanting to add sound to the projected films he started to show, in 1905 he hit on the simple expedient of having actors reading the lines from behind the screen. He and his chief technician, Will H. Stevens, developed this process to take full advantage of the innovation. Interviewed in 1944, Zukor said that he could not attempt to account for the name, although it is tempting to see in it "Humanovox," dog-Latin for "Human Voice," with the terminal "x" removed.[23] Zukor was not alone in using this technique. Others did so as well, calling it "Actologue" or "Dramagraph" or some equally unrevealing name to cloak it in obscurity and exclusivity.

Not all films were good candidates for the treatment. After all, the makers of silent films produced their dramas and comedies with the understanding that there would not be sound or voices to carry the drama. You could give snippets of dialogue with printed-word intertitles, but these had to be used sparingly. Long dramatic interplay couldn't be used in silent films. Even less could rapid-fire comedy dialogue. Silent film demanded a

Figure 10. The Human Laundry, which had been Battle Abbey the year before. Notice the "Chinese" attendant with cap and long hair queue. The Human Laundry—Souvenir program from Wonderland featuring Pawnee Bill, Revere Beach, Mass., 1908. Courtesy of Historic New England, Boston.

different discipline. Nevertheless, inventors found some films that could be adapted to Humanovo, such as the 1907 film *College Chums*, which actually does have scenes of a man and woman talking, without intertitles. The audience can imagine the dialogue for themselves, having seen the setup for the farce.[24] With Humanovo, they didn't have to. A team of five voice actors filled in the blanks, and people could hear the back and forth as the beau and his righteously indignant fiancée argue.

❧

William C. Manning was in Manchester, England, in the spring of 1908, but he had set up two shows for Wonderland for the 1908 season. One was Pawnee Bill's Wild West Show, which would be taking over the space formerly occupied by Fire and Flames. The other was Darktown, which went in where Alligator Joe's Florida Jungle and the Beautiful Orient had been.[25] The four minarets and domes were still in place above the facade, which gave the attraction an otherworldly appearance.

To modern eyes, over a century later, Darktown looks like an obscene and absurd gathering of racist clichés, just as 1906's "The South before the War" did, only this time in a semi-permanent exhibit. At the time, it was seen as harmless fun, without any malicious intent, and embodying ideas and attitudes that were commonly held, at least among white people. The simple descriptions given in the newspapers are cringe-inducing to modern eyes:

> Manning's Darktown, with its picturesque scenes on the Mississippi levees, in which fifty black, chocolate, brown, and yellow symphonies appear. This aggregation is certain to stir the eye, the ear, and the heart. There are banjo choruses, songs of Dixieland, dancing in the moonlight, alligator hunts, chicken stealing forays, and all sorts of "cut-ups" and revelries. Ole grand daddy is there with his white hair and white whiskers and cane and mule and so is a bunch of little black berries and a pickaninny band. There is a sensational race between the Natchez and the Robert D. [sic] Lee and fire and explosion on board the City of New Orleans. This show is a scream from start to finish, a source of never ending delight and unalloyed merriment.[26]

The write-up undoubtedly came from Wonderland's publicity department, as the park had just opened. Other reports put the number of performers at eighty and called it "one of the most novel plantation shows that has ever been produced in the country." Newspaper accounts likened it to another show that had run in Boston back in 1895—"Black America." However, Manning's show drew from yet another tradition, reflected in its very name, and this one presented a much less positive view of the American Black experience.

The printmaking firm of Nathaniel Currier and James Merritt Ives was active from 1854 to 1907 and is associated in the minds of most people with images of rural simplicity and bucolic splendor. In an era when most prints were black and white, Currier and Ives offered color lithographs, often of striking beauty. Their subjects included natural and humanmade wonders and important news events. But the printers also produced comic series, and among these were the Darktown prints. The Black people depicted were cartoonish, grotesque characters. They were dressed in exaggerated caricatures of normal clothes and were shown as being particularly inept at what they did. In the worst traditions of minstrelsy, the Black characters appeared as clownish versions of human beings, unable to competently perform their tasks. Most offensive, arguably, were the Darktown Fire Brigade images. The Black firemen were shown unable to handle the firewagon, control the hose, or manipulate machinery without breaking it Trying to put out a fire in a decrepit old slave-quarter house, they aim the water into the face of a trapped victim, rather than at the flames; try to catch a person leaping from the building using a woefully inadequate blanket (with holes in it); and carry out a nightgowned victim buttocks first. Trying to use a ladder to rescue people, they swing it away from the building.

The Darktown influence spread well beyond comic prints. Clownish Darktown live performances started to take place, and Darktown Fire Brigades formed. In fact, Darktown competitions sprang up between firefighting companies as a way to show off and perform. Newspapers in the late nineteenth and early twentieth century contained frequent notices of such events.[27] There sprang up a new class of popular music—the Darktown Fire Brigade Marches.

Perhaps this is what suggested the idea of a Darktown company, with fire brigade, to Manning, although he could well have come up with it on his own. Having just managed the Fire and Flames show at Wonderland for two years, it would be a natural leap to a comic Fire Show, and the

Darktown Fire Brigade was a well-established tradition among firefighters. Once that was put into place, the rest of the Darktown performance naturally suggested itself.

The images of the Florida jungles that had been painted over the wording of the Beautiful Orient were once again painted over (or at least, in cases, touched up) to depict southern plantations. Two miniature steamboats were built and put into the lagoon, where they could race and one would have its boiler "explode." A Darktown fire car was built or adapted from a piece of existing fire equipment left over from Fire and Flames. It seems likely that many of the Fire and Flames performers continued on, now performing in blackface beside the real Black people brought in to provide glimpses of antebellum slave life. The images of southern life were, again, idealized idylls from a white perspective, but the fire brigade added insult to that injury.

⌒

Elsewhere in the park was a completely different sort of attraction. Chiquita was billed as "The Doll Lady." Chiquita would, until recent decades, have been called a "midget" because of her proportionate limbs, or more appropriate now a "little person." Perhaps she herself put it best in an advertisement that appeared in 1910, after her stint at Wonderland: "Not classed as a Freak of Nature, but properly termed a Gift of Nature—'Smallest Representative of her Sex'—Twenty Eight Inches in Height, Perfect in Form and Figure." She was witty; spoke Italian, Spanish, and English; and had a collection of miniature presents given to her by potentates and admirers.[28]

But Chiquita wasn't just a trilingual, witty little person. She was a trilingual, witty little person who had been a central figure in a spectacular trial, a *cause célèbre*, six years earlier in Boston. And for a modest fee you could attend her *soirée* and ask her about it.

Chiquita was born Alize Espiriodiona Cenda del Castillo on December 14, 1869. Many sources give her birthplace as Cuba, either in the province of Matanzas or the province of Pinar del Rio, both in the western portion of the island. But it seems more likely that she was born in the Mexican city of Guadalajara. That is where her parents lived, and where she returned at the end of her life. By one account, she attended school in Mexico, was trained to sing and dance, and then her father hired a manager to take her on tours, starting when she was about fifteen. She toured Mexico and Cuba. Her manager rechristened her as a Cuban and brought her to New York, along with her two brothers.

In 1895, Frank Bostock, better known for his wild animal shows, took her contract, stating that it was he who had discovered her living as a peasant in Mexico. Within five years she had become one of his major attractions as his show toured the United States and Europe. Now called Chiquita, she was also skilled in making dresses and in standing on her head, but Bostock was not eager to showcase these abilities. He saw Chiquita as something like P. T. Barnum's Charles Sherwood Stratton, who was exhibited under the name Tom Thumb. Stratton too was a capable performer—an actor, singer, dancer, and comedian who dressed in high fashion and was presented to European royalty. Chiquita owned jewels given to her by Queen Victoria, King Edward VII, and Kaiser Wilhelm II of Germany.[29] Bostock played up Chiquita's entertaining skills while presenting her as a miniature version of the elegant cultured lady. Barnum actually was a distant relative of "Major Tom Thumb" and adopted him. Bostock insisted that Chiquita was practically a member of his family.

Arguably one of Bostock's biggest successes was securing a place for Chiquita at the 1901 Pan-American Exposition in Buffalo. Here her supposed Cuban origin was played up, for President William McKinley, who initiated the Spanish-American War, was the guest of honor. Chiquita had already met the president on February 13, 1901. Carried into his White House office, elegantly dressed, she made a speech thanking him for "all you have done for my people" in defeating Spain and liberating Cuba. McKinley took the pink carnation he was wearing in his label and fastened it to her dress. Surely they would meet again at the exposition, but it was not to be. On September 6, McKinley was shot by Leon Czolgosz at the Temple of Music.

At 1 a.m. on the morning of November 2, 1901, Frank Bostock rushed into police headquarters at the exposition, saying that Chiquita had been kidnaped. She was gone, and he said there was evidence of a struggle.[30] Bostock said that her jewels offered enticing bait to thieves. But the reality was very different.

Anthony Woeckener was a cornet player in a family of musicians whom Bostock had hired to provide music for his show in Atlantic City the previous year and for appearances at the exposition. It was in Atlantic City that Woeckener made Chiquita's acquaintance. "She looked at me and smiled, and I smiled back. . . . I did sing, and that was the beginning of the love affair," he later recalled. They reunited during the Buffalo Exposition, where Woeckener was not only a musician but a "spieler," calling out the attractions to lure in paying customers. He also sold hot sandwiches. Woeckener asked Chiquita to be his sweetheart, and she agreed despite the age gulf between them. He was only seventeen, while she was thirty-two. Nevertheless, they seemed to have real affection for one another. Woeckener would bring over dinner after Chiquita's show. He taught her to write, and she taught him some Mexican Spanish.[31]

Someone saw them at their rendezvous one day and told Bostock about it. He was furious, not only firing Woeckener but boarding up her window and spreading the rumor that Woeckener had broken an expensive calcium light, nearly starting a fire.[32] Woeckener found a job with the Indian Congress on the fairgrounds, however, and was able to stay close until the couple could elope together.

According to the *Buffalo Evening News*, Chiquita was found to be missing at 11 p.m., and the police originally regarded the charge of kidnaping with suspicion, thinking that it might be a press agent dodge to get more publicity. What actually happened was that Woeckener and Chiquita snuck out of her quarters.[33] Woeckener persuaded another employee at the ticket office to leave a hole big enough for her to crawl through that night. They went to the home of Buffalo judge Thomas H. Rochford, arriving around midnight. They were married by the judge, with "Doc" Waddell, a press agent for the Indian Congress, and a man named King, who ran one of the midway games, as witnesses. The couple then went to find a hotel room but were refused at all places they tried because the hotels thought Chiquita was a young girl. As they roamed the streets, they were spotted by one of the clowns from Bostock's show, still wearing his clown makeup. Woeckener told the *Buffalo Evening News* that he pulled a revolver on the pair, threatening, "Give us Chick."

Bostock presented the *Buffalo Courier* with a story that verged on kidnaping, seeing in the elopement a plot to get at Chiquita's supposed $200,000 in her bank account and $35,000 in jewels.[34] He said that Judge Rochford had been in to see him twice, explaining why he agreed to marry an underage boy and "a dwarf of doubtful ability to travel without a guard-ian." As Bostock told the story, Chiquita was beguiled to meet Woeckener that night by a note. When she appeared, he whisked her over a fence and into a waiting carriage, and told her they were going for a supper. There, the boy plied her with wine: "She says that she hardly knew what was going on and did not care very much, as she trusted Tony perfectly." The impli-cation is that Chiquita was effectively tricked into marriage. "Phoebe" the clown—Clyde Powers in real life—was the one who drew the revolver then carried Chiquita back to the show.[35]

Woeckener threatened a habeas corpus proceeding the next day, but Bostock threatened prosecution right back. The article concluded that "Woeckener and Chiquita have had a meeting in Mr. Bostock's presence and admitted the foolishness of their fantastic love."

Another *Courier* story the next day was headlined "Frank C. Bostock Is Suspicious That Union Was Promoted by Others for Motives of Gain—Husband a Poor Boy—Cuban Dwarf, Who Is Worth $250,000, Says She Has Only a Vague Recollection of the Marriage Ceremony."

This may be the way Bostock wanted the story to be perceived. Woeck-ener and Chiquita felt otherwise. Woeckener had Deputy Sheriff Hugh Sloan serve Bostock with habeas corpus papers at his rooms at the Iroquois Hotel. Woeckener then engaged as legal counsel Eugene M. Bartlett of the office of Bartlett and Baker and had Justice Daniel J. Kenefik require Bostock to produce Chiquita in court. Woeckener's father and brother also came up from their home in Erie, Pennsylvania. These were not the actions of a love-smitten boy.

On November 9, 1901, the case was heard by Buffalo justice Henry A. Childs.[36] He dismissed the proceedings against Bostock. The purpose of the habeas corpus procedure was to compel Bostock to produce Chiquita in court so that Woeckener could see and speak with her, but Bostock said that this was impossible—Chiquita had been sent to Canada and was out of the court's jurisdiction. W. E. Creamer, Bostock's attorney, said that Chiquita had gone to Canada with members of Bostock's family and of her own volition. He further stated that Bostock had found Chiquita in Mexico, "illy dressed, uneducated, and living in discomfort." Her mother had died, and Bostock had persuaded her father to let her go with him:

"Mr. Bostock took her to his home. He educated her, gave her horses and carriages and everything else she could wish. He has taken as much care of her as if she had been his own."

Bartlett interrupted to say, "Yes, he has taken as much care of her as he has his elephants. As for the horses and the carriages, they are part of the show, and Bostock claims title to them." He went on to note that the trip to Canada was nothing but a ploy to keep Chiquita out of the court's jurisdiction and away from Woeckener. In answer to the claims that Bostock showed Chiquita great kindness, Bartlett charged that Bostock had knocked her down when he learned of the marriage. As soon as the habeas corpus proceedings were dismissed, as Bostock was leaving the courtroom, Woeckener's attorney served papers on Bostock for a suit for $20,000 damages in separating the couple, and issued an order of arrest for Bostock to ensure his appearance at trial. Bostock met the bail of $1,000, however, and was released.

Bostock's show next appeared at the Cyclorama building in Boston on December 7, 1901.[37] The advertisement for it clearly indicated that Chiquita would be there. Once again, Woeckener's attorney called for a habeas corpus proceeding at the beginning of January so that Chiquita could be produced at the hearing. On January 3, 1902, Tony saw her for the first time since the previous November. Judge James M. Morton heard the case. This time W. H. Baker of Bartlett and Baker was Tony's attorney. "Each took the witness stand. He stood erect and told the circumstances incident to his wedding and the present proceeding. . . . No hero ever proclaimed his love more sincerely or unequivocally than this manly little fellow who asked the venerable justice to restore his wife to him. No heroine ever displayed more concern for husband or lover than this little woman, standing 26 inches in height."

Bostock's attorney asked Woeckener why he had not responded to letters they had sent to him, asking his intentions and whether he would have the marriage annulled. Woeckener answered that he was afraid he might inadvertently sign away his rights. He had sent the letter to his own attorney for advice. He furthermore said that neither he nor his father were aware of Chiquita's financial status and did not want any of her fortune. He affirmed that she had been beaten and abused by Bostock.

Chiquita was called to the stand and was straightforward with her statement, rendered in slightly broken English (her opening statement was
clearly meant to refute claims that she was twenty-three years old):

I am thirty two years old. I want my husband with me. I do as I want to do.
Nobody restrains me. I want to perform my contract. Want Tony to stay
with me, too. If Tony won't stay then I prefer to go with him. I read the contract; know what it contains. Only Mr. Rowley was present when I signed
it. Saw Mr. Bostock just before he left for Europe. He said to me: "Goodbye
and be a good girl." I want to do my contract and to go to Erie after I do
it. Mr. Bostock beat me after I was married. I love my husband most. Don't
want Mr. Bostock or anybody else; just want Tony and I alone.

On January 8, 1902, Chiquita was once again in court. The *Buffalo Evening News* reported condescendingly on her appearance that day:

Chiquita was questioned as to the state of her mind. It appeared her mind
was so small she was still uncertain about its nature, but it was gathered that
she was contented to be with Bostock and did not appear to be pining for
Tony. Accordingly, Judge Morton denied the motion, compelling Tony to
return to Erie, Pa. without his bride.
   In announcing his decision Judge Morton said:
   "I feel that the marriage between this little woman and this 17-year-old
boy should not have taken place under any circumstances. I do not think
the marriage was the offspring of love or affection. There seems to be some
ulterior motive behind this. I think it is our duty to look beyond the mere
surface and ascertain the motive.
   "The wife is not an ordinary person nor of ordinary capacity and intelligence for a woman of her years, yet she understood her contract and the
drift of the examination made here today. I hesitate to give her wishes the
same force and effect that I would give to those of ordinary persons of her
years."[38]

After this, the *Sinclairville [New York] Commercial* reported that Tony,
"unable to learn anything regarding the whereabout or welfare of his wife,
has at last succumbed to the anxiety and worry and yesterday was com-
pelled to quit work, later taking to his bed with a fever."[39]
   If that were the end of the story, it would be a simple tragedy, with the
power of a big businessman and a less-than-tolerant legal authority riding
over the rights and wishes of a young man and his bride, who was treated,

perhaps because of her size, as if she were underage and not competent. But it did not end there. Bostock's circus went next to Glasgow, Scotland. Tony Woeckener wrote to Bostock there, asking if he could at least have the job of cornetist. Bostock had held this out as an offer on the night of the elopement, saying that Woeckener could play in the band and see his bride but not have conjugal rights. Deciding that even this would be preferable to not seeing her at all, Woeckener wrote that he would accept this position. Bostock wrote back that he could have the position and that he should apply to a representative in Boston for a ticket to Scotland.

Woeckener accepted, writing to Bostock and adding a letter to Chiquita. Perhaps Bostock was responding to repeated petitions and possibly an ultimatum from Chiquita herself that precipitated this relenting. Perhaps, he figured, this would soothe Chiquita's tantrums, satisfy the boy, and frustrate any ambitions by the boy's father.[40] Woeckener accompanied Bostock's show afterward on its tour of the United States.

"After that," reported the *Silver Springs [New York] Signal,* "Tony travelled with the show, but only in the unwelcome capacity of husband to the principal attraction." When the show arrived in Lansing, Michigan, "Tony became convinced that it was the intention of the management to rid Chiquita of her husband, at least as an appendage of the show." The landlady of the hotel where they were staying, having quarreled with the matron in charge of Chiquita, confided to Woeckener that Bostock had decided to get rid of him "at any cost." The couple started looking for an escape.[41]

It came when the show was in Elgin, Illinois, in August 1902. The show people were quartered in a hotel called the Cottage Home, with Chiquita and Tony both on the fourth floor. The rooms to either side were occupied by the matron and her husband and another show family "Both were nervous over rumors that they were to be separated," continued the *Silver Springs Signal.* "Their anxiety was heightened by the presence in and about the hotel of several officials of the show, who had no ostensible reason for being there."

Woeckener arranged for the escape, getting the cooperation of a sympathetic policeman to act as watchman. He also engaged a carriage, as at their elopement. Around midnight the policeman signaled that the coast was clear by ostentatiously lighting a cigar. In response, Tony and Chiquita turned out their light. Tony then lowered Chiquita to the ground in a pil-lowcase that Chiquita, the able seamstress, sewed onto a long rope. After she reached the ground, Tony slid down the rope. They climbed over the wall behind the building with the policeman's aid, got into the carriage, and drove off to the local train station.

Tony carried Chiquita aboard in the pillowcase and took an express wagon eastward to Pittsburgh, where they lost no time obtaining a restraining order.[42] Chiquita also sent Bostock a letter reading, "I don't like work, I don't like traveling, and I don't like you, so I'll jump your silly old contract."

Afterward Chiquita toured on her own, accompanied by Tony. She appeared in small venues such as Davenport, Iowa; Astoria, Oregon; Orr-ville, Ohio; Norwalk, Ohio; Quincy, Illinois; and Bradford, Pennsylvania, before securing a full summertime engagement at Wonderland.

A surviving program from a performance by Chiquita from the time she was with Bostock is probably typical of her later performances as well.[43] After a brief piano introduction a lecturer would come out and give a brief presentation regarding Chiquita's physique, history, and character. After this Chiquita herself would be introduced. She would sing in English, Italian, and Spanish such songs as "Won't You Be My Sweetheart," "Pretty as a Picture," "Whisper Your Mother's Name," "La Figlio del Mullenau," "La Mariana," and "La Paloma." Then there would be a promenade and a closing reception, with greetings of the attending crowd.

Outside of aficionados of Wild West culture and residents of Pawnee, Oklahoma, the name of Pawnee Bill is not well known today. His name sounds as if he might have been a Johnny-come-lately imitation of the more famous Buffalo Bill, a cheap imitator stealing the original's act and enriching himself with stolen thunder. But Pawnee Bill was the real thing, a veteran of the Old West and a formidable showman who would before the year 1908 was out rescue Buffalo Bill's own show from financial ruin.

He was born Gordon William Lillie on Valentine's Day 1860 in Bloom-ington, Illinois.[44] At the time the town was on the verge of the frontier, and an Indian reservation existed only twenty miles away. Lillie's father, Newton Wesley Lillie, was a Quebecois of Scottish ancestry who moved from Three Rivers, Quebec, to build a flour mill in Illinois. He married Susan Ann Conant, who came from a Boston banking family, and they had four children—besides Gordon, his younger brother Albert and sisters Effie and Paulina ("Lina").

Gordon was one of those people lucky or unlucky enough to have aspired to and caught their childhood dream. In his case, his dreams came in the form of the frontier adventure stories of William F. Cody, as written up by Edward Zane Carroll Judson Sr. under the pseudonym "Ned Buntline." Buntline claimed that he invented Cody's nickname, "Buffalo Bill," and first wrote of him in the serialized story "Buffalo Bill, the King of the Border Men—The Wildest and Truest Story I Ever Wrote" in the *New York Weekly*, starting in December 1869. Cody and Buntline first met when Buntline was on a temperance lecture tour and saw the attraction of the western life as exemplified by Cody and "Wild Bill" Hickok. Cody was only twenty-three but had enough stories and experiences woven about him to provide lots of material for Buntline. It was the beginning of his rise to fame. Lillie, not yet ten years old, read Buntline's work and was hooked. Buntline, Lillie admitted, was his favorite author, and the young boy yearned to follow Cody out onto the plains and have adventures there.

Lillie got an unexpected glimpse of his hero's life in 1872 when, coming home from school, he saw a crowd outside the St. Nicholas Hotel in downtown Bloomington. They were gathered to see Buffalo Bill, Wild Bill Hickok, and Texas Jack Omohundro, all dressed in show costume as a publicity event for the play *The Scouts of the Plains*. That didn't matter to Lillie, however—he had seen his hero in the flesh.

Gordon got a better chance to approach the cowboy life when his father's mill burned down and the elder Lillie moved his clan to Wellington, Kansas. Gordon visited the camps of the cattle drovers nearby and the Pawnee Indians when they camped nearby. He made the acquaintance of a Pawnee named Blue Hawk, trading his knife for an Indian bow and arrow, which Blue Hawk taught him to shoot and also words and phrases in the Pawnee language.

Shortly after, Lillie met a Texas rider of about his own age, Bob Gray, who had already been up and back the Chisholm Trail twice. Lillie bought a buckskin jacket and other clothes and provisions and a pony, and securing his parents' blessing, went off to try life on the plains. He eventually ended up at the Pawnee reservation in Indian Territory, present-day Oklahoma. Here he was reunited with Blue Hawk and got a construction job, quarrying rocks for the Indian agent's home, working at the government sawmill, and the like. He became a personal friend of Major William Burgess, the first Indian agent of the reservation.

Lillie traveled with the Pawnee on their hunts and learned the language, not only hunting but also fighting with them against their enemies. Chief Spotted Horse of the Pawnee invited Lillie to a meeting, saying that he was growing old and wanted Lillie to become a "white chief" for his people. Seeing the high regard in which the Pawnee held Lillie, a new agent, Major Edward Bowman, made Lillie the official interpreter.

At this time he acquired the nickname by which he would be later known. No one at the Indian Agency called him "Gordon"—he was called "Bill," as many others were. To the agency, he was "Bill Lilly," but the Pawnee found this difficult to pronounce so he became "Pawnee Bill."

In this position Lillie helped oversee the running of the reservation and taught at its school. He also became active in politics, taking the side of the small farmers and "boomers" against large-scale cattle ranchers.

In 1883, Lillie met Charlie Burgess, the son of his former commander, Major William Burgess, who was now working for Buffalo Bill's Wild West Show. Charlie Burgess had been sent to get a contingent of Pawnees for the show. Major Bowman objected to removing any Indians from the reservation without their consent and without the permission of the Indian commissioner in Washington. So Burgess sought out Lillie, who had gained a reputation as someone who could speak the language like a native and was well-respected by the Pawnee. The Indian commissioner eventually gave his consent to removing some Pawnee, provided they were in the charge of someone acceptable to the U.S. government—and Lillie was the ideal choice. He now had the opportunity to work for his boyhood hero—at the hero's own request.

The Pawnees were required to act as if they were holding up stagecoaches, slaughtering whites, and committing other atrocities attributed to the Plains Indians. In fact, the Pawnee never did any of these, having long allied themselves with whites against their traditional Plains adversaries, the Cheyenne and Apache. But a job was a job. For Lillie, his second meeting with Cody was a shock:

I had been carrying around in my mind for a dozen years or more the picture of Buffalo Bill as I had first seen him, well-groomed, with a beautiful buffalo coat.

I never was so disappointed in my life. He had been sleeping on the floor of a tent in some hay, his fur coat was missing, his hair was all matted, and he was drunk.

I found him courteous enough. He was pleased with the Indians and it became my job to assume responsibility for them, to do all the interpreting for them and even to make up as an Indian myself and go on with them.

The show toured throughout the Northeast to general success. When it played in Philadelphia, Lillie saw a young woman come in with an armful of schoolbooks and a smile on her face. Responding to the smile, Pawnee Bill tipped his hat. The woman found this funny—the man with the long hair and fringed buckskin jacket elegantly tipping his hat to her, and she laughed. He afterward saw her at the show and sent her a note saying that he would like to meet her.

She was May Manning, daughter of Dr. William Manning, a prominent physician. May was attending Smith College, working toward a Bachelor of Arts degree. She and her sister let Lillie walk them home and invited him into a house full of guests. Her mother resented the cowboy in the house, although others were intrigued. Lillie unfortunately forgot himself at one point, spitting on the floor.

After that awkward introduction, he started writing to Manning regularly. He insisted that it was love at first sight. Lillie stayed with Cody until 1883, then returned to Kansas and the reservation. He got involved in cattle ranching but found himself with a lull as the cattle fattened on the range, and he rejoined Cody's show for a time. It took them eventually to Philadelphia, where Lillie saw Manning again. At the end of the season, he returned to Kansas. Cody presented him with an inscribed gold medal in appreciation of his services.

Sometime later Pawnee Bill decided to try his own Wild West show, which he took on a tour across country. When Manning graduated from Smith, Lillie courted her, and they were married on August 31, 1886. They went back to Kansas, where May was bored and felt out of place at first. She soon took to ranch life, however, learning to ride and shoot, winning prizes for horseback riding, and becoming a crack shot.

Together the couple launched Pawnee Bill's Historic Wild West, with May as the central attraction, but the show was not a success. Scaled down and retooled as Pawnee Bill's Historical Wild West Indian Museum and Encampment the next year, it was more successful, and the show continued touring for years. In 1908, they sold off many of their cars and settled down to an entire summer in one place, an amusement park outside Boston called Wonderland.[45]

Pawnee Bill arrived early in the spring and stayed with William C. Manning, who would be producing the show for Wonderland. The entire set of Fire and Flames was razed, the false city streets torn up, and the paving hauled away, with only the grandstand left intact. The ground was left as dirt, and a wooden backdrop was erected, with an irregularly edged top that blended into the sky. Upon this was painted scenery—mountains in the distance, with fir trees in front. A huge spreading tree dominated the center of the scene. A log cabin was erected in front with the sign "Taylor's Trading Post." Further to the left was another, smaller cabin labeled "Wells Fargo Express" and "Post Office." To one side was a genuine teepee.[46]

There were nine main members of the cast, including Pawnee Bill and May. There were six bandits (along with their chief, played by Carlos Myles, one of the main actors), six lady riders to follow May Lillie, fourteen main Sioux Indians, fourteen subsidiary Indians ("squaws," "papoose," and assorted "braves"), six Russian Cossacks, and sixteen assorted cowboys.[47]

The show was an extravaganza in fifteen parts entitled "Oklahoma—or—Statehood Day and Pawnee Bill's Buffalo Ranch at Pawnee Oklahoma."[48] While the audience was seated, an opaque curtain separated the audience from the performance ground. When all were seated the curtain was dramatically raised to reveal the recreated Indian and cowboy camp. According to the program, "The scene of this production is laid in Oklahoma, the home of the wily Pawnees, during the early turbulent days before the advent of the railroad and the telegraph. The actors are genuine frontier heroes who have, in many cases, participated in the occurrences which they reproduce with mimic realism." The program described the acts as follows:

1. The opening scene shows Pawnee Bill's Buffalo Ranch at Pawnee, Oklahoma, also the Trading Post, Dance Hall, Post Office and General Store, with Cowboys, Mexicans, Indians, Traders, etc.

II. The Cowboy Quadrille or Mexican Contra Dance led by Pawnee Bill and Miss May Lillie

III. Arrival of the Overland Mail, bringing the usual mixed bunch of passengers, who are heartily received and welcomed by big hearted Zach Taylor and his good wife.

IV. Lariat throwing by Jose Bararo ("Mexican Joe"), the greatest exponent of practical work with the Lasso today in the whole world.

V. On the Round-up—Cowboys from McElroy's (OX) Circle Cross Ranch challenge the boys from the Lazy (≃) Ranch in a contest of riding a wild bucking horse—a western outlaw.

VI. The capture and lynching of Old Antonio—noted Mexican horse thief. In the early days the theft of a horse was considered more criminal than murder.

VII. Arrival of a wagon-train containing a group of Russian emigrants in search of a home in the new country. They turn out to be wonderful riders. (These are genuine Russian Cossacks from Russia, and are here by permission and passport from the Czar of Russia.)

VIII. Chester Byers in trick lassoing and rope spinning, demonstrating the extreme possibilities of the use of the lasso.

IX. The Mohave Cremation, showing the funeral march, death chants, and mode of cremating Indian dead.

X. Old Zach's birthday celebrated at the Ranch by an old time frontier (Break-down) quadrille.

XI. Fancy and trick riding by the Cowboys and Mexicans.

XII. A wonderful and remarkable exhibition of shooting from horseback at targets thrown into the air, by Major Gordon W. Lillie (Pawnee Bill)

XIII. Attack on the Overland Mail by Mexican road agents. They have received information that a large shipment of gold is to be carried. They shoot the Express Messenger, blow the strong box, and pillage the passengers. The arrival of the Cowboys puts to flight the merciless bandits and results in the death of Carlos Myles, their leader.

XIV. Throwing the Boomerang by Australian Cannibal Bushmen—famous black trackers and world renowned Boomerang throwers. They are of the lowest order of the human family, have no marriage ceremony, no religious belief, and do not even bury their dead, yet they possess one secret which baffles the wise men of the earth and defies all laws of gravitation—the art of throwing the Boomerang.

xv. A most realistic reproduction of a sensational midnight attack upon and burning of the Trading Post, in which the ferocity and savagery of the Indian is displayed.

R.W. Scott and George Hammond, Official Announcers

Do Not Leave Your Seats Until the Last Curtain.

The attitudes toward both the American Indians and the Australians aborigines were typical of the time. Having the Native Americans participate in a portrayal of a "savage" attack on traveling whites or on a settlement was pretty much par for the course in Wild West shows. The description of the Australians as "cannibals" is at odds with what is now known and believed about their society, but it was common to describe what was seen as "primitive" societies as cannibalistic as well.

The Indians, all said to be Brulé (today called Sičháŋǧu Oyáte) from the Oglala at the Rosebud Reservation, under the leadership of Chief Henry Iron Shell and Chief Big Turkey, gave riding demonstrations. Between shows, visitors were allowed to see life in the Indian camp. "The Indians are friendly to visitors who call at their tepees, but they are not sociable—Indians never are," reported the *Boston Globe*, which also pointed out that few of them spoke English.[49]

In section 6 of the program, Frank L. Sylvis's specialty was playing the thief Old Antonio, who sneaks up and steals a horse from a group of Mexicans, led by Jose "Mexican Joe" Baroro. They quickly realize that a horse is missing and ride after Old Antonio. He is lassoed and pulled from the stolen horse, then dragged around the set by the rope while being shot at (apparently) by the group. He is then hauled up and "hanged." He kicks several times before going limp. "Sheriff" Pawnee Bill comes and cuts him down. Sylvis went through this grueling routine twice a day.

"I fear every time I feel that lasso around me and am jerked off my feet that it may be my last hanging," said Sylvis, clearly playing up the risk for the newspapers. "I've been in the circus business for eight years and have performed all manner of so-called death-defying exploits, but my present job beats them all for taking chances."[50]

Figure 11. One of E. E. Smith's photographs of Pawnee Bill's Wild West Show at Wonderland. Cowboys and Sioux ride on the stagecoach in front of the log cabin containing Taylor's Trading Post. *Performers with stage coach in Pawnee Bill's Wild West Show*, gelatin dry plate negative. Courtesy of the Erwin E. Smith Collection of the Library of Congress on Deposit at the Amon Carter Museum of American Art © Erwin E. Smith Foundation, LC.S6.337.

The cowboys would let the horses run free over the marsh just north of Wonderland to eat grass in the morning, then gather them back in the afternoon, giving what was essentially a free show. It was also good publicity.

One thing they hadn't counted on was that over a dozen of their horses, freshly brought from Oklahoma, had the equine disease glanders at the start of the season. The disease was highly contagious, and as soon as it was discovered, the animals were segregated and put down to prevent its spread. The first nine to have the disease were immediately killed, just before the park opened, and the remaining fifty-two tested by veterinarians of the Massachusetts State Cattle Bureau. Fourteen more were killed later. All of the stricken horses were promptly replaced. Glanders was a particular problem around this time, afflicting Buffalo Bill's show as well and adding to his financial woes.[51]

The cowboys got a chance to do some real-life scouting for criminals in mid-August, when two criminals shot a police officer in Lynn, just north of Revere, and were thought to have taken refuge along the unsettled portions of the Saugus River. Pawnee Bill asked for volunteers to search the area. All his men were said to have volunteered, but he selected fifteen to search Oak Island and the banks of the Saugus. They spent four hours but did not find anyone.[52]

At the end of August the Catholic Church of the Immaculate Conception in Revere celebrated its fiftieth anniversary, and did so at a special service attended by fifty members of the Wild West show—cowboys, Indians, Mexicans, and Cossacks—all in their show costumes.[53]

∽

Pawnee Bill and his Wild West Show occupied the large arena with a large company, but the other big attraction for that summer was a single individual: the world-famous and slightly notorious swimmer and diver Annette Kellermann.

Annette Marie Sarah Kellermann was born on July 6, 1886, in the Darlinghurst section of Sydney, Australia. Her father and mother were both accomplished musicians. Frederick Kellermann was a violinist well known in music circles in Australia. Her mother, Alice Charbonnet Kellermann, was born in Cincinnati, Ohio, to an American mother and French father. She had studied at the Conservatoire de Paris and was an accomplished pianist and composer. She had been sent by the French government to the International Exhibition in Melbourne to show off Pleyel and Erard pianos, but when the exhibition ended, she stayed with Frederick. They married and opened the Conservatoire de Musique in Sydney. Among Alice's students was Helen Porter Mitchell, an opera singer whom Alice taught the piano. Mitchell was better known by her stage name, Nellie Melba, and became a musical superstar, the first noted musical performer from Australia.[54]

The Kellermanns had four children—Maurice, Annette, Marcelle, and Fred. Annette was physical and precocious, trying to walk very early but not succeeding. By the time she was two, she still could not remain upright, and the doctors told her that she had rickets, which causes the leg bones to bow outward.

Today, rickets is known to be caused by the lack of calcium and the vitamin D needed to metabolize it and incorporate it into the bones.[55] It was known that the bones could be encouraged to grow by exposing the patient to plenty of sunshine and to give them doses of cod-liver oil. To straighten Annette's already bent leg bones, she had to wear heavy iron braces that pulled her bones in the proper direction and encouraged them to grow straight. Annette had to wear the braces until she was seven years old. She felt isolated from the other children by this treatment and withdrew.

After the braces were removed, her legs were still weak. Her doctor prescribed a regimen of swimming to help build up her legs, and her parents found a teacher in Sydney near the site of the present-day Opera House. Little Annette hated the lessons. "I loathed it," she later said. "They had to drag me kicking and screaming to the lessons."

But within two years she had added bone and muscle, and her legs were straight. And Annette found that she liked swimming and was increasingly good at it. At Cavill's Baths, a section of Sydney's harbor protected by anti-shark netting, she competed against and learned swimming and diving from the best swimmers in Australia. By fourteen she was the best of the female swimmers and was even beating the boys. The Australian swimming competitors convinced her that she would be able to do what no woman had yet done—swim the English Channel. Annette sailed for England in 1904 with her father.

They had little money when they arrived and were devastated to find that the British saw swimming and diving as strictly amateur pursuits. She could not raise any money giving exhibitions, as she had hoped. The British disapproved of professional athletes. Frederick Kellermann finally hit on a scheme to generate publicity—Annette would swim down the Thames. The course they chose was from Putney to Blackwall, a distance of twenty-six miles. It was a grueling effort, since she had, because of their financial straits, not been eating well, and the Thames was not as clean as it has become today. But her feat made the front pages. She was given offers to swim off the coast and to give exhibitions of swimming and diving.

She was invited to swim at the exclusive Bath Club, where she would be seen by the Duke and Duchess of Connaught. A representative from the club informed her that she could not perform, as she had been doing, in a men's suit with her legs showing. She decided to add stockings to cover her legs. To prevent a gap between the stockings and the pants of the suit, she had them sewn together, thus creating the prototype of the one-piece coverall suit that would eventually be known as the "Annette Kellermann."[56]

But her purpose in England was to swim the English Channel. At the time, the only successful crossing by a swimmer had been by Captain Matthew Webb in August 1875, some thirty years before. The *Daily Mirror* sponsored the Webb Memorial Channel Race on August 24, 1905, the thirtieth anniversary of Webb's success. There were five contestants, with Annette the only woman. She wore her usual swim clothing (although the men competed naked, covered in grease) and with swimming goggles attached. None of the competitors succeeded. Annette had to cede defeat because of sea sickness. She tried two more times to do the channel without success. Still, it was a magnificent effort, for all that—in 1905 she was within sight of the French coast before being forced out.

She participated in races in France and on the Danube, and for the first time performed on the vaudeville stage at the Hippodrome in London, swimming and diving in a large tank on stage. Her signature action was to yell the traditional Australian call "Coo-ee!" before diving. She then crossed the Atlantic to perform at the White City Amusement Park outside Chicago. In 1908, she agreed to join the show at Wonderland for the entire summer.

Kellermann was hardly unknown when she got to Wonderland. Her Channel-swimming feat had made the American papers, and her biography (with a drawing of her) had appeared in the *Revere Journal* the year before.[57]

Kellermann performed in a special cement pool and enclosure built specifically for her, allowing her to demonstrate dives and swimming. It measured twenty-five feet long and fifteen feet wide and generally six feet deep, although there was likely a deeper point to allow Kellermann to perform high dives. It was fed with local artesian well water. Exactly where it was, and what it looked like, is not recorded.[58] An image of her in the 1908 souvenir book shows her sitting on part of what might have been her enclosure, which appears to have been a raised wooden platform standing in front of trees and grassland. Perhaps her tank was built in the northeast portion of the park, beyond the grandstand that showcased Pawnee Bill's

Wild West Show. There would have been wooded space near there, and few other areas in the park would have been appropriate.

Based on descriptions of her shows elsewhere, Kellermann probably came out, gave a small speech, then demonstrated several dives (one report said that she demonstrated eighteen different types of dives), followed by several different swimming strokes. She might have given a brief lecture—her favorite causes were more sensible bathing costumes for women, the health benefits of swimming, and healthy eating. She said that if she had her way, swimming would be a compulsory exercise—it was the ideal way to work out, and she never found a boy or girl who could walk that could not be taught to swim. After that she might have gone on to give a demonstration of a different kind. She advocated the game of "Diabolo Tennis," in which two players lobbed a wool ball with a specially fitted "pulley on a spring" toward each other across a net on a sort of miniature tennis court. She liked the game because it was more taxing and strenuous than regular tennis.[59] Her performance lasted half an hour.

Kellermann did not restrict her activities to Wonderland Park but did intend to compete in swimming challenges, as the newspapers had originally reported about her. It was her intention to make the ten-mile swim from Charlestown to Boston Light.

Annette Kellermann's intended big feat for the summer was to swim from Charlestown Bridge, near Rowe's Wharf, to Boston Light, a swim of about ten miles (she estimated it to be twelve). She practiced every day, swimming in the ocean in addition to her usual shows at Wonderland. On Saturday, July 25, 1908, she swam across Broad Sound from Bass Point Nahant to Crescent Beach in Revere, a distance of five miles. She made it in "record time"—two hours and eight minutes. A crowd of more than two hundred greeted her when she came ashore, "fresh as a daisy" at 6:05 p.m.[60]

She had twice been over her intended course in a light boat, looking for problems and things to watch out for, and she was convinced that there were no unexpected problems. At 12:55 p.m. on Thursday, July 30, she dove off the bow of the press boat, the *Marion*, just at Charlestown Bridge. She swam for six hours and twenty minutes and was heartbreakingly close when the turn of the tide made it "inadvisable to continue." She had just pulled abreast of Black Rock Beacon, beyond Bug Light, and the turning of the tide made further progress virtually impossible. The *Boston Post* observed that she "showed no signs of exhaustion at the end of her long swim." The previous year forty men had tried the same course, none of them getting as far as she had. Fifty boats followed her on her course, shouting encouragement, and there was an estimated crowd of ten thousand watching from shore. She finally consented to be brought aboard the press boat, where she was rubbed down and drank beef tea before a short rest under covers. Half an hour later she came up and attacked the ham and chicken sandwiches provided for her.[61]

A month later she was invited to a special ceremony by the management of Wonderland. A new special platform was erected at the eastern end of the lagoon for the "Alice in Wonderland" show. It was more clearly boat-shaped than the previous year's, and workers at Wonderland had painted "Annette Kellermann" on the "prow." At 8:30 in the evening of August 31, Annette climbed up to the "bow" and broke a bottle of champagne over it, saying, "I wish thee luck and christen thee the Annette Kellermann."[62]

There is an almost ubiquitous story that when Kellermann first went out to practice her swim on Revere Beach, dressed in her abbreviated, form-fitting bathing suit, she was immediately arrested for indecent exposure because of the inadequacy of the suit. This case went to trial, where she skillfully argued her case, saying that it was outrageous to expect a woman to do competitive swimming while weighted down with all the extraneous frippery that was typical of American bathing suits. The judge saw the wisdom of her arguments and allowed her to continue swimming in her outfit. The case made headlines across the United States and around the world and brought her much publicity.

The story is everywhere and has been—almost—universally accepted. Different reports of the incident place the year variously between 1907 and 1913. Examination of the newspapers of Revere, Boston, and the surrounding towns, however, reveal no stories whatsoever about the incident for any of these years. Nor did it appear in newspapers elsewhere in the United States. In 1975, a *Boston Globe* reporter went in search of the police report of the incident and could find no record of it.

If Kellermann had really been arrested for indecent exposure, especially in 1908, it could not have failed to make the newspapers. They were full of stories about her as it was, and if the star swimmer had been arrested because of her bathing suit, that would have been an irresistible story. One cannot blame the silence on a desire to "hush up" arrests for skimpy bathing suits—there are newspaper accounts of those on Revere Beach, even for the year 1908.[63] Nor can it be attributed to a respect for Kellermann's privacy—when she was arrested some years later for speeding in her automobile, it made the papers in several places across the country.[64] The only possible conclusion is that the incident never actually happened.

The story made its first appearance in 1925 in a piece in the *Los Angeles Times*. She related much the same story in her unpublished autobiographical notes, "My Story," now in the Mitchell Library of the State Library of New South Wales.[65] These notes were used in the writing of the script for a biographical movie, *Million Dollar Mermaid*, and Kellerman herself, doing publicity tours to promote the film in 1952, repeated the story again to newspapers. So clearly the ultimate source of the story was Kellermann herself. But why tell this story? Perhaps to draw attention away from another scandal.[66]

In a strange twist of fate, when Kellermann came to Boston she was introduced to Herbert H. and Maybelle Pattee, the inventor of Wonderland's Love's Journey and the woman he wooed on it and married. Kellermann rented a suite of three rooms at their house on Revere Beach for twenty-five dollars a week. The Pattees' son Herbert Eldrige had been born the previous year. Herbert Pattee Sr. had stayed on in Revere, first to supervise his ride, then to pursue other amusement park aims. He later put together a swimming and diving show, initially for Wonderland and later took it on tour, and it may have been this common connection of exhibition swimming that brought he and Kellermann together. Helena Higgins, the wife of John J. Higgins, the general manager of Wonderland, introduced them.

It was a crowded house. Not only did the Pattees live there with their infant son, but Pattee's mother was with them as well. In addition, Annette's aunt Josephine had come with her from the White City park in Chicago as chaperone.

It seemed a convenient and happy situation. At first, Kellermann said, Mrs. Pattee was friendly toward her and she rarely saw Mr. Pattee. When not swimming or performing, she exercised in the house and practiced the Diabolo Tennis.

But after three weeks she sensed that Maybelle Pattee did not care for her, and the Pattees were constantly squabbling. So Kellermann moved out and obtained alternate lodgings, thinking nothing more of it until the following March, when she was hit with a bombshell.

Maybelle Pattee was suing Herbert for a divorce—so much for happy endings—and named Kellermann as the cause of the trouble.[67] The case was taken to Judge Frederick Lawton. Maybelle's description of married life with Herbert sounded horrible from the first.[68]

She said that Herbert struck her and never gave them more than six dollars, refusing even to give little Herbert a teddy bear. She said that he furnished a flat for himself and his mother, and when she demanded that he support her and the baby, he agreed on the condition that "Miss Kellermann will live in the flat, too, understand?"[69]

The last straw according to Maybelle was that Herbert spent hours in the kitchen with Annette Kellermann, drinking beer and eating cheese and crackers. This was particularly galling, since Maybelle felt that, miserable as their life together might be, he should be spending his time with her, not carousing with a house guest.[70]

Kellermann was performing in Philadelphia at the time, and she gave her response to the press.[71] She said that she hardly knew Mr. Pattee, even as a passing acquaintance. She certainly never drank beer with him. "I could not do it and keep up my work," she insisted.

It was true. Kellermann swore she hadn't touched alcohol since coming to the United States. She was a health food aficionado who advocated eating steamed celery, then drinking the water used to steam it. She lived largely on fruits and vegetables, and shunned red meat and carbohydrates. It is a toss-up whether she saw as the most unlikely and objectional behavior charged to her the implied hanky-panky with Herbert Pattee, the beer drinking, or the eating of cheese and crackers.

Actually, Maybelle Pattee never made any charge of sexual infidelity, regardless of what the public thought. Herbert Pattee denied it as well, so Kellermann found herself at the center of a scandal in which everyone involved denied she was at fault. (Certainly it would have been difficult, with Pattee's mother and Josephine Kellermann acting as chaperones in the house.) But she still did not like being associated with what appeared to be a trumped-up charge to allow Maybelle Pattee to obtain a divorce.

Herbert Pattee issued three statements—one for the press, one to his wife, and one to Annette Kellermann.[72] He denied any wrongdoing with Kellermann (although he did say that she did occasionally eat crackers). He also denied Maybelle's accusations of his cruel treatment. He went on to say that she would not come with him when his business took him to Providence, Rhode Island, and that she had deserted him three times saying that he was "too old—the she was fickle and should never have married." Herbert was, at forty, more than twice Maybelle's age when they married. "I forgive her," wrote Pattee. "I gave it to Father Time and his rough road of experience to teach her that which she finds it so difficult to learn."

He wrote a letter to Maybelle, saying that their life had once been a happy one but that he recognized that it had changed, and that he would not stand in the way of a divorce. He wrote an equally eloquent letter to Kellermann, apologizing for what she had been brought into and wishing her success.[73]

Maybelle Pattee was granted her divorce on March 15, 1909.[74]

Despite what Pattee had written to Kellermann, the story of the divorce and the accusations of night-time carousing over beer and crackers were all too juicy and irresistible for the papers, and this story, unlike the alleged one of her arrest for indecent exposure, made the newspapers across the country and beyond. Kellermann downplayed it as much as possible, and it soon died away.

Is it possible that Kellermann told and repeated the spurious story of her arrest for indecency on Revere Beach as camouflage, a way of drawing attention away from the lascivious story of the divorce? "Oh, yes," that story in effect says, "Annette *was* at the center of a storm of stories, but it was because of her bathing suit. It was a scandal, but surely you can see that she was in the right." Kellermann was by no means a naive youngster by this point. She had had to deal with gaining good publicity and deflecting stories that did not redound to her good qualities. She had picked her fights with care, and this would be another case of that. It worked. In 1925 and again with the release of *Million Dollar Mermaid*, she drove the arrest story home, and today it is still told on the internet—sometimes about the only thing people know about Kellermann—while the scandal of being at the center of a divorce—even an unjust one—has been completely forgotten.

ℰↄ

Behind the scenes, the first rehearsals for that year's performance of "Alice in Wonderland" were held.[75] Advertisements in the newspapers using the Tenniel illustrations from the *Alice in Wonderland* books readied the public for the show.

It was first performed on August 31, 1908, coinciding with the Beach Festival on Revere Beach. Annette Kellermann christened the stage/boat bearing her name, and Alice, played by Louise Osgood, appeared in a rickshaw drawn by boys from the Japanese Village. There was a procession of the characters around the lagoon before they arrived at the stage. Probably because of Kellermann's presence at the park, the parade had a nautical theme to it, with many characters dressed as sea creatures.

Eugene L. Perry, the Wonderland assistant manager, once again acted as the director and master of ceremonies. Many fairies flitted about, and costumed actors played a bear, a rabbit, and a large-eyed cat (presumably the Cheshire Cat, although from his photo his grin was not his outstanding feature).[76] There was much singing and dancing, and for one week Ethel Wright of Melrose performed cornet solos. John J. Coleman was again the dancing master, and Lawrence B. O'Connor was once again in charge of the music.

Figure 12. The end of the lagoon and the midway at Wonderland from the 1908 souvenir book. The sign reading "Annette Kellermann" might be the pool where she performed, or it might be "The Good Ship Annette Kellermann" where the "Alice in Wonderland" show was performed. Band Stand and Section of Board Walk at Wonderland—Souvenir program from Wonderland featuring Pawnee Bill, Revere Beach, Mass., 1908. Courtesy of Historic New England, Boston.

The *Revere Journal* described the show:

Alice, in the person of little Louise Osgood of Lynn, will arrive at the administration building in Wonderland at 8:30 o'clock every evening, seated in a magnificently decorated Jinrikisha drawn by tiny Japanese lads, at her side will sit the famous hatter. She will make a circle of the Lagoon on the broad board walk. She will be escorted by a glittering procession headed by a platoon of police and the Waltham watch factory band. Then will come a bevy of dancing mermaids, a group of sea shell dancers, a platoon of dancing sea shells, anemones, and miniature lobsters; then will follow a company of tiny sailor lads and lasses and a battalion of teddy bears, Cheshire cats, March hares, and a giant giraffe. The gorgeous pageant of one hundred characters will pass along to the center arena where a stately ship has been constructed. Captain R. W. Watson will be on the bridge with his gallant crew. The final[e] will be a superb tableau of marvelous beauty with the manning of the ship's yards and a battle of roses and confetti.

Elsewhere, on the ship *Annette Kellermann,* "here upon its deck will be given a long programme of fascinating dances with solos by Miss Mabel Crane; 'The Two Little Sugar Plums' specialty by the brunette octette of eight young and pretty girls, choruses and marches and after a unique lobster dance by Louise Osgood, who is the Alice, she will take her place at the wheel of the goodly vessel. There will be nothing left undone to make this spectacle one of superb, captivating beauty."

The Alice show that year opened with a very non-Alice in Wonderland song, "My Dream of the U.S.A.," written by Charles Roth and Ted Snyder.[77] Snyder was one of the most prolific music publishers in New York. He gave Irving Berlin his break in music and would in 1923 compose the music to the song "Who's Sorry Now." The audience was invited to sing the chorus of "My Dream of the U.S.A."—it was printed on postcards and distributed:

> I saw Washington cross the Delaware
> I saw Stark mid mountains green
> I saw Warren fight at Bunker Hill
> Andrew Jackson at New Orleans
> I saw Davy Crockett at the Alamo
> Taylor fight at Monterey
> And they all fought for our liberty
> In my dream of the U.S.A.

Eugene Perry actually didn't quite make it to the end of the season at
Wonderland and the end of the "Alice in Wonderland" run. He left the
park before the official end of the season. He was so well-liked by the Wonderland employees that on September 10 he was given a sendoff, with gifts
of a diamond stick pin and a seal.[78] In the future, he would receive similar
gifts when he left one post for another. It was said at the time that he was
going on to New York City to become manager of the People's Vaudeville
Company, although *Variety* said his next post was managing the Bijou in
Fall River, Massachusetts, beginning September 17.[79]

Just before the park closed, John J. Higgins returned from an extended
trip to the West, where he inspected other amusement parks near New
York, Cleveland, Philadelphia, and Chicago and pursued new acts and
attractions for the next season.[80]

September 20 saw the last performance of "Alice in Wonderland," of
Annette Kellerman's diving act, of Pawnee Bill's Wild West Show, of Chiquita's soirees, and of all of the park rides and attractions. The park closed
out what was arguably its most impressive season at 11 o'clock that night.

The good times did not last long. Cold reality closed in soon after the
end of the season. On October 2, 1908, Beatrice Shaw Perry filed a suit for
divorce from Eugene Perry, accusing him of cruel and abusive treatment.
This, she asserted, had begun a year before, after their move to Revere. The
couple had been living separately since September 1908. Beatrice requested
custody of their ten-year-old son, Harold.[81]

A much more serious problem for Wonderland than the loss of Perry
appeared the next week. It turned out that Wonderland had failed to meet
its expenses for the 1908 season and had been operating at a loss. The attendance in 1908 was smaller than in previous years, despite the increase in
attractions. People did not spend as much money as they had previously.

Newspapers gave many reasons for this. First among these was the poor
economy overall in the wake of the Panic of 1907. People simply had less
money, wages were down, and people were less ready to part with their
dwindling funds in the name of entertainment.[82] In addition, some attractions were privately owned, like Louis Bopp's Carousel and his Whirl the
Whirl, which effectively siphoned money out of the park. Some of the
larger attractions—the Chutes, the scenic railway, the Hell Gate, the Circle Swing, and the Love's Journey—were now in their third year and had

lost the glow of novelty. Finally, the park itself was not on the beach and lost the immediacy that attractions right on Revere Beach Boulevard had.

Interest coupons had been paid through July 1908, but there was no money to continue payments. Wonderland was, in effect, broke. The park was still privately owned, with no obligations outside its bond- and stock-holders, but they still needed to be paid. The stockholders' meeting was to be held on October 14, and that would decide the fate of the park. It was possible the park would be sold, either in one lot or broken up as separate real estate parcels. The season that had opened with high hopes and expectations ended in what was essentially bankruptcy, with the future of the park uncertain.[83]

CHAPTER 8
Year Four—1909

FOR SALE

A GREAT AMUSEMENT PARK

WONDERLAND

REVERE BEACH————————MASS.

This magnificent property is in the best of condition.
It includes about 25 acres of land on which Wonderland is
built, as well as buildings and devices owned by the company,
representing a total expenditure of over $500,000.
Property can be inspected at any time.
Full particulars upon request.

J. J. HIGGINS

Secy. Bondholders' Committee

53 STATE STREET   BOSTON, MASS.

This was the large advertisement that appeared in the January 16, 1909, issue of *Billboard*.[1] The park had failed to turn a profit the previous year and now was in debt to its many suppliers. The debt would have to be satisfied by the sale of the park. In November the committee appointed to consider the future of Wonderland had made a trip to New York and to parks in the West to see if they could find a buyer, apparently without success. The *New York Clipper* observed in their February 6 issue that "Wonderland Park, Revere Beach, Mass., will be sold at auction early in March, the landholders having foreclosed the mortgages. The past season was not a success. One of the faults of the park from a business point of view has been that as it did not extend to the beach boulevard, many smaller attractions took away the trade."[2]

The *Boston Globe* for January 30, 1909, announced that "the bondholders and the stockholders, who are one and the same . . . got together recently and after a committee report it was decided to dispose of the property in order to satisfy the creditors. The American Trust Company is trustee for the mortgage. Many reasons are ascribed for the failure of the big amusement resort, but last season's hard times had much to do with it." Others gave as a reason that too many attractions were not owned by the park and were siphoning money away from it.[3]

The auction was held on Monday, March 8, 1909, with Walter S. Fox as auctioneer. The park, valued previously at half a million dollars, sold for one tenth of that. The purchaser was General Manager J. J. Higgins. Higgins, Eugene V. R. Thayer, and John T. Burnett of the reorganization committee paid $50,000.[4] Higgins did not say if the park would be reopened in the summer. Ten days later, the Walnut Avenue Company was certified in Boston and became the official owner of the Wonderland property.[5] Nine days after that the Suffolk Leasehold Company was certified, with Wonderland president Harold E. Parker as the head.[6]

Over the next year, Suffolk Leasehold, which owned the land on which Wonderland sat, allowed Walnut Avenue Company, the owners of the park and buildings, to operate on its land.[7] The Wonderland debt holders had to be satisfied with their proportionate payouts from the $50,000 paid for the park. By a bit of legal and financial legerdemain worthy of a Wonderland magician, the stakeholders of the original Wonderland Company, now with Suffolk Leasehold and Walnut Avenue Companies, got to retain control of the park and its profits while slipping out of its crushing debt.

As it turned out, Wonderland did reopen that summer of 1909, but with significant changes. They could no longer afford the kind of extravagances that had marked the previous season, and austerity and belt-tightening were the strategies to follow. Closures were not announced, of course, and press releases are always relentlessly upbeat and forward-looking, but probable changes can be identified from the absence of reporting about them in the press or advertisements.

No big show took the place of the old Fire and Flames and the Wild West show. In all likelihood the entire grandstand and arena was cordoned off. For the first time, there appears to have been no circus taking the place that had been occupied by Ferari's, Blake's, and Darling's establishments. The Human Laundry, the Pilgrim's Progress, and the Third Degree were no longer mentioned in press materials. The same was true for Darktown and the Palmistry and Astrology house. Paradise—The Show Beautiful was significant in its absence. All of these may not have closed, but it is likely that most of them did. W. C. Manning, who had managed Fire and Flames for two years and then both the Wild West show and Darktown, had gone to manage the Scenic Theater in New York in November, and after that was bound for England to oversee his Fire and Flames show there. He would not be organizing any new shows for Wonderland this year.[8]

What was left? The big rides continued. They had already been paid for, and they brought in steady cash. The Shoot the Chutes, the Thompson Scenic Railway, Hell Gate, Love's Journey, the Velvet Coaster, and the motion pictures (formerly Hale's Tours, then Rocky Mountain Holdup, then The World in Motion) were all open. One would have expected the Circle Swing to remain open, but it isn't mentioned in any newspaper accounts or advertisements.

The Bopp Carousel and the Whirl the Whirl were no longer listed and were almost certainly gone. The Infant Incubators, too, were closed, and the interior of that pseudo-Elizabethan structure given over to Funny Mirrors. They probably placed the mirrors that had been in The Foolish House/The Third Degree/The House That Jack Built there, since that funhouse was evidently closed. The restaurant and ballroom remained. A new carousel, suited to children's sizes, was opened in the northeast corner of the park.[9] But the Japanese Village was no longer mentioned. The contract for the village only extended for three years, with Wonderland having an option to refuse for 1909. It is likely the operators did, and the Japanese Village was shuttered.

In place of the open-air circus they had an open-air vaudeville. Circus acts, those death-defying thrill acts, were expensive. Comedy and singing were cheap. Wonderland's free offerings for 1909 included a lot of vaudeville.

One of the big cultural movements of 1909 in Boston was a look forward to the year 1915 and the wonderful things the future would bring, when the country and the city had advanced beyond the privations result-ing from the Panic of 1907. Why exactly a date six years in the future was picked isn't clear. Perhaps it was because 1915 was a nice "round" number, divisible by five, and much closer than 1920. A series of exhibitions was planned to tout the glories to come in 1915. In the fall, for instance, an exposition was planned for the former space of the Museum of Fine Arts in Copley Square from November 1–27. There would be 39,000 square feet of exhibitions, including scale models of the city, models of good versus bad tenements, an underground view of New York, a model of Philadelphia, a Curtiss Aeroplane and other airships, a talking arc light, and motion pictures. There would be marionettes and the "Boston's 1915 Woman's Orchestra," but the major feature was on civic improvement.

This exposition had a direct connection to Wonderland. J. J. Higgins was one of the organizers of Boston 1915, and the Higginses were also season ticketholders. The exhibition featured models of several airplanes, as well as the Wittemann glider that had flown in Franklin Park. All of these would be featured at Wonderland in the 1910 season.[10] In addition, Wonderland decided to fit into the forward-looking theme with its own "1915" shows for the 1909 season, including the "1915 Minstrels" and "1915 Vaudeville."[11]

It wasn't all shuttering; there were some additions. Besides the new car-ousel, the Suffolk Company ordered two new McCahill Iceless Soda Foun-tains for the park, one sixty feet long (the counter, presumably) and one twelve feet long.[12] And they had a new musical spectacular to take the place of "Alice in Wonderland."

There was, as in the previous two years, little advance publicity for the coming season. On May 22, 1909, the *Boston Globe* announced that the park would be opening the following Saturday, May 29, at 1 p.m., and the *Boston Post* made the same announcement a day later.[13] These items both stated that the full program of attractions for the season wasn't fully decided yet but would include the major rides, along with Henry's Min-strels, motion pictures with illustrated songs, Brenck's Golden Graces, an Illusion Palace, and performances by Teel's Band.

There was to be a new admission policy for 1909—once you paid your admission to the park, almost all of the attractions inside would not cost anything extra. It was not only a way to lure people in but it meant a sav-ings in ticket sellers and ticket takers.

Despite the changes in the park's official ownership, it was announced that management would remain essentially unchanged. There was, however, one necessary change. With Eugene L. Perry gone, the park was shy an assistant general manager, not to mention a director for any musical extravaganza.

They found their new assistant manager in the person of Nicholas J. Lawler of Greenfield, Massachusetts.[14] Lawler wasn't new to Wonderland. In fact, he had been with the park almost since the beginning, but he had spent the first three years working not in Revere but at the Wonderland office in the Boston Stock Exchange building.

Lawler was born on April 7, 1865, in South Deerfield, Massachusetts. When he was seven his family moved to Leicester and again to Greenfield when he was sixteen. He worked at a number of businesses—silver-plating and shoemaking—before settling down with his brother in a real estate and insurance business at the age of twenty-three. He also later served as a deputy internal revenue collector. At some point, like many of the others who ended up at Wonderland, he got involved in the theater and entertainment business. He served as manager of the Holyoke Opera House and became a director of the Eastern Theater Manager's Association.[15]

In 1908, he had been in charge of the Excursion Department, just as Perry had been before becoming assistant general manager. When Perry left it was only natural for Lawler to take his place. "He has brought ripened experience and good judgment to his present position and is getting excellent results all along the line," enthused the *Greenfield Recorder*, his hometown newspaper.[16]

There was one other important change: Major Thomas J. Barroll, formerly the managing director of the Wonderland Company, was now the treasurer of the Walnut Avenue Company.[17]

Wonderland opened as planned on May 29. The new park hours were 1 o'clock until 11 p.m. The day was described as "gloomy," but the park itself was hung with bunting and fresh flowers, streamers, and flags in an effort to make it appear bright. On Monday the park opened two hours earlier because of the Memorial Day holiday.[18]

The open-air vaudeville featured the Yankee Comedy Four, Louis Chevalier, and company in a comedy sketch entitled "The Lucky Liar." This had been a big success for Chevalier's company the previous year, and they continued to perform it for almost a decade afterward. One paper called it a "condensed comedy," implying it was shorter than a proper theater show, rather like a longish skit. Another newspaper called it "a winner that drew lots of laughter and applause." It was just the right thing, and the right length, for a Wonderland show, which would require a brisk turnover. The plot was described as "a succession of funny situations and incidental comedy that culminates in one final large laugh, when [Chevalier's] wife discovers that the chorus girl with whom she has discovered her better half, in her own parlor, is her long-lost sister from Squeedunk."[19]

Another act was "Sam Gordon and Emma Shakan, eccentric singers and dancers." The *Buffalo Courier* declared that their act was "the best seen at the Park this season."[20]

Brengk's Golden Graces was an interesting and quite different show. "Professor" Ernest Brengk presented a series of tableaux in which a live model, dressed in stiff clothing and covered with bronze dust so that she appeared to be a golden statue, posed in the shape of a famous work of art. The *Oakland California Tribune* described one such show in 1907:

> The Four Golden Graces are beautiful. They display the effects of skillful training as models. They pose as "Venus After the Bath", "Venus' Dream", as Psyche, and as other figures, all in a fashion designed to delight the great plain people who have a spectacle just for the spectacle's sake.
>
> The four Golden Graces appear on the stage covered with gold, apparently their limbs encased in a glittering substance, their lithe forms posed to represent Venus or such other characters as they may be imitating, and when the mellow radiance of the electric lights fall upon the picture they make, there are "Oh's" and "Ah's" from the delighted crowds.[21]

Mr. and Mrs. Harry Thorne performed with their troupe the farce "An Uptown Flat," which had a long history. The Thornes had been performing it all over the country for more than a decade, at least twice in Boston.[22]

Another vaudeville act was William "Willie" Sisto, who appeared as "The Italian Statesman" in a routine entitled "His First Speech." It purported to be the first public address to his constituents by a newly minted American politician of Italian ancestry, whose speech was a collection of misplaced and mispronounced words and malapropisms: "He makes a political speech in broken Italian and, of course, always gets the cart before the horse," reported the *Bluefield [West Virginia] Daily Telegraph* of a later performance.[23] As if this were not enough, he played the "common mouth harp." In fact, he played six of them in rotation, juggling them continually. He played them "with cleverness and ease." The line "His act is a scream from start to finish" appears in so many descriptions of his act that it must have come from his press release.

The week of June 13 saw many changes. One was the introduction of a play, *The Princess and the Prophet*, which told the story of King Herod, John the Baptist, and Salome. It had a cast of a dozen people and was performed in the six-hundred-seat theater that had originally been the children's theater. It was performed "with appropriate scenery and costumes and with incidental dances." The play ran twenty minutes, three of them occupied by Salome's dance.[24]

か

This time also saw the arrival of the big musical productions of the summer. Normally, the major production came a month later, but this year, in the absence of any big spectacles or summer-long acts to draw in the crowds, the Wonderland management obviously felt it was necessary to push the musical production forward, to give the public something to see. That something was a musical production of *Cinderella*.[25]

They no longer had Eugene L. Perry to act as both assistant manager and musical director. Nicholas Lawler was a competent manager, but even being a theater owner doesn't prepare you to direct performers. Wonderland needed a musical director.

They found one in the person of James Gilbert. Born in 1849, Gilbert was sixty years old in 1909, but he was still performing on stage, acting, singing, and dancing. He had been a member of various Boston light opera companies, performing in Gilbert and Sullivan operettas (he had taken the role of Dick Deadeye in more than one production of *H.M.S. Pinafore*), and directing and producing them as well.[26] His wife, Florence A. P. Gilbert, was both a performer and director too.

In addition to his work in Boston, James Gilbert produced and directed summer shows at the Lakeview Theater in Lowell, Massachusetts. "There is no stage director in the country more skillful or better versed in this line of work than James Gilbert," enthused the *Lowell Sun* in 1903. "A comedian and singer himself, of national reputation, who has been associated with many of the leading comic opera organizations, Mr. Gilbert may be depended upon for some delightful weeks of comic opera during the coming summer months."[27]

Possibly even more important than these qualities, however, was Gilbert's reputation for working with amateur companies that had to mount productions with limited time and resources. He had helped Harvard's Hasty Pudding Club put on its yearly shows. As the *Boston Sunday Post* remarked of the 1900 Hasty Pudding production, "The fact that *Wytche Hazelle* has been in rehearsal ever since February, and that it is produced under the stage direction of James Gilbert, so well and popularly known as manager of these amateur theatricals at Harvard University, are sufficient guarantee of the smoothness and excellence of a first night's performance."[28]

Wonderland had been cagey about its production, not naming it until shortly before the first performance. An initial inkling was an announcement on July 18 that James Gilbert would be producing it and giving the names of the four lead actresses—Irene Martin as Cinderella, Blanche Benton and Margaret Meredith as the stepsisters, and Martha Hale as the Prince of Salerno. For some reason, Hale did not work out, and three days later it was announced that Lulu Strater would be taking over as the Prince. The change of cast might be seen as an indication of things to come—Gilbert did not let the show remain static but constantly changed things.[29] The show as seen in August would be very different from the show that premiered in July.

The show opened on Monday, July 12, 1909, at 8:30 p.m. Like the "Alice in Wonderland" show, it began with a grand procession of the actors and characters around the lagoon, the Prince and Cinderella drawn in a floral-decorated carriage. The company arrived at a new stage built on the boardwalk. This was apparently not the good ship *Annette Kellermann* of the previous year but a new stage, possibly built along the midway, between what had been the plot of land used by the animal shows and the grandstand used for Fire and Flames and the Wild West show.

Gilbert was aided in his work by the dancing master, Walter Kee, who was also well known for training dancers and ballet girls.[30] One of Kee's charges would later be selected by Maurice Ravel for his ballets.[31]

Several of the performers already had experience in the theater. Irene Martin, described as "dainty and petite," had been with the Castle Square

Theater Company, which operated in the enormous Castle Square Theater on Tremont Street in Boston. She was said to play "the title role with
charm." Another review stated that she "plays the title role in a decidedly
winsome way." Lulu Strater, the new Prince, had been with John "Hap"
Ward's vaudeville company, Ward and Vokes. She had also appeared in
Broadway musicals. Reviews declared that she "makes a real swagger Prince
Charming."[32]

Blanche Benton and Margaret Meredith played the evil stepsisters, here
named Spitefulella and Vixenella.[33] One review said they "created many a
hearty laugh by the 'business' they introduced." Another noted that they
"make big hits at every performance by their clever character work." The
roles apparently called for much makeup, because another review praised
their willingness to "sacrifice their good looks to make character hits."
Moreover, they were said to "introduce a most artistic dancing duet."[34]

In addition, Etta Payser, Mabel Peirce, Cecelia Fitzgerald, and Gertrude
Fitzgerald were pages; Anna Kiley, Vera Dwyer, Rena Dwyer, Bessie Boyle,
and Helen O'Neil were fairies; and about fifty other young girls participated in singing, dances, marches, and tableaux. All parts were performed
by girls and young women, pages and prince included. Teel's Band provided the music.[35]

Reviewers praised the production for its artistry and delicacy and its
wonderful electrical and lighting effects: "While the greater part of the
production has been planned to please the adults, there is much in the
unfolding of the story and in the introduction of the characters that is sure
to delight and mystify the children." Another review observed that "in
every detail of youthful, feminine loveliness and cleverness; of handsome
costuming; of bewildering dances and marches; of novel color effects and
pretty, well sung choruses, 'Cinderella' is indeed a captivating summer's
night entertainment." It is hard to believe that the entire show (without
the parade) was said to occupy only half an hour.[36]

It was only a little over a week after the show opened that Gilbert began
to introduce changes. The show appears to have been loosely constructed,
with no fixed score or scenes. As long as the story was told, other acts
or songs could be "dropped into place" in the production, regardless of
whether it had anything to do with the story of Cinderella. By July 19,
Lottie Lesley, who had been with the company of the musical farce *The*

Broken Idol, was singing "You Can't Stop Me from Loving You" in the show "in a way which wins her enthusiastic applause."[37]

By July 24, the show had expanded to two shows per day, one at 3:30 p.m. and one at 8:30 p.m., although only the later one had a parade. New dances were added that incorporated the skipping of floral decorated ropes. Lulu Strater, the Prince, now sang "Eliza" with a chorus backing her up, and Lesley's song was changed to "Sadie Salome (Go Home)"—an interesting choice, given the presence of the play "The Princess and the Prophet" elsewhere in the park. Cinderella and her stepsisters got a new dance together.[38]

"It is the Great Spectacular Production of the season," bragged an advertisement in the *Boston Post*. "The Most Brilliant Fairy Extravaganza Ever Produced in any Amusement Park in America."[39]

Through the weeks at the end of July and the beginning of August, Gilbert was swapping the performers, putting them in different roles. By August 7, the newspapers were acknowledging that "changes are made from week to week in the singing, dancing, and other numbers."[40] Gilbert took to advertising in the newspapers for new cast members. On August 9, they introduced the "Florodora" sextet dance. "Florodora" had been an immensely popular musical first performed in London in 1899 and shortly after in New York. The highlight of the show was a "double sextette" dance, where six elegantly dressed women met up with six equally elegantly dressed men for a coordinated dance. The "Florodora Girls" who performed in it became immensely popular. In the Wonderland production, with its all-female cast, the dance would have had to be altered or perhaps women took the male roles.

In addition, there were new solos, duets, chorus numbers, and a new skipping rope dance. The advertisements began to "sell" the production as a "Beauty Show."[41]

August 21 saw several big changes. Rena Dwyer, who had been playing a fairy the previous month, was now promoted to the lead. She also got a solo rope skipping dance. Estelle Tearle, still playing the Prince, got new solos. But the biggest change was the addition of two new songs. They seemed to be even less appropriate for the show than many of the others that had preceded them, but they had several things in common, chief among which was their extraordinary popularity.[42]

The songs were "My Wife's Gone to the Country, Hurray!" and "My Pony Boy." Despite their popularity, *Collier's Magazine* was not impressed:

> Popular Songs! Can they sink lower, or has the bottom been reached? The absurdity lies not in the fact that they are un-lyric and vulgar as in vapidity. . . . For your chastisement, take this:
>
> > *Pony boy, pony boy, won't you be my Tony Boy?*
> > *Don't say no, here we go off across the plains;*
> > *Marry me, marry me right away with you.*
> > *Giddy up, giddy up, giddy up, whoa! My pony boy*
>
> The music, to conceal the quality of these, must in truth work hard.

The vast public didn't care. Both songs were sung at the 1909 Pharmacist Convention. They were written up in the popular *Green Book Magazine* in an article entitled "Making the Song That Makes the Play." The article noted, "Such successes as 'I Wish I Had a Girl' and 'My Pony Boy' were written by hitherto unknown writers. A man who a year ago was a waiter in a restaurant is one of the authors of 'My Wife's Gone to the Country.'"

That waiter-turned-songwriter was a twenty-one-year-old man named Israel Beilin, who had just changed his name to Irving Berlin and would one day become arguably the most successful American songwriter. His compositions eventually included "Alexander's Ragtime Band," "Easter Parade," "White Christmas," "Puttin' on the Ritz," and "There's No Business Like Show Business." "My Wife's Gone to the Country, Hooray!" was, by his own admission, his "first big hit":

> I got the idea of that from a Chicago fellow. He and I were having a little drink and chat near dinner time and noting the clock I said to him 'Almost supper time. Suppose you've got to be beating it home?' He said 'Oh, no! My wife's not in the city.' Now you'll probably laugh, but right then it occurred to me that 'My Wife's Gone to the Country' would be a capital name for a popular song. The music buzzed in my head. I got somebody to write [the music] and there it was." But it still wasn't a success. It was that "Hooray!" by way of punctuation that "made" the song. "That lone word gave the whole idea of the song in one quick wallop. It gave the singer a chance to hoot with sheer joy. It *invited* the roomful to join in the hilarious shout."[43]

And shout they did. It is probable that, as with Bertha Ring's songs discussed in chapter 4, the audience would join in on the chorus, shouting a joyous, carefree, cathartic "Hooray!" at the end. The singing of this song was specifically referred to in the ads for Cinderella, and it continued to be popular for decades.

Lottie Lesley's song "Sadie Salome" was also written by Irving Berlin. He was supposed to have urged the song on a down-on-her-luck showgirl who had just been thrown out of George M. Cohan's show *The Talk of the Town* for being unable to dance. (Some sources claim he actually wrote the song for the girl.) Knowing her to be a talented comedienne, he pointed out that the song had to be sung in a Yiddish accent. Even though she spoke no Yiddish (or Hebrew, despite being Jewish herself), she did so, and the song became a hit for young Fania Borach, who had taken the stage name Fanny Brice.

The song is sung from the point of view of Sadie's boyfriend Moses, who is aghast to see her performing in as risqué a piece as Richard Strauss's *Salome* doing the "Dance of the Seven Veils." It was while performing this song that Florenz Ziegfeld saw Brice and hired her for his "Follies," and her rise to stardom began. Brice's schtick was "The Yiddish (whatever)," performing as an Indian or a cowboy or other part with a heavy accent. Hopefully Lottie Lesley was able to put on a convincing accent as well.[44]

"My Pony Boy" was similarly a big hit with the public. In this case, though, the songwriters—lyricist Bobby Heath and composer Charley O'Donnell—did not achieve the stratospheric heights of Irving Berlin. But they achieved a modest degree of fame. The song first gained recognition through its use in the Broadway show *Miss Innocence*. The song became popular as background music for Westerns, and when sound movies came around, it ended up being used for a dozen movies. It became a Western cliché, and from there it became a folksong and lullaby, so that eventually it became a piece of nostalgia. It was undoubtedly in that spirit that Bruce Springsteen covered the song, supposedly for his son Evan, in 1992 on his album *Human Touch*.

"Pony Boy" too was featured in the newspaper advertisements for *Cinderella*. Wonderland needed to catch a break after all its bad luck. It got two, in the forms of these unexpected hit songs, and James Gilbert's ability to use them for the success of the park.

About this time the park introduced electrical effects.[45] The rope-skipping for *Cinderella* included electrical ropes, evidently holding rows of tiny lights, possibly colored, danced by five fairies. They had trained under Vera Faust, "the premiere danseuse of the Augustin Daly musical comedy company." The Cinderella parade, probably in part due to the earlier setting sun, became an electrical parade, festooned with possibly colored lights, anticipating by many decades the Disneyland Main Street Electrical Parade. Nearly seventy-five people appeared in the procession. At intervals, they unfurled banners spelling out "W—O—N—D—E—R—L—A—N—D" in golden letters. There was also a serpentine dance by May Campbell.

The *Cinderella* show produced one of the few non-paper souvenirs from Wonderland, a pot-metal slipper, 4-1/8" long, painted gold outside, and with a hole at the ball of the foot where it might have been once mounted to a base. On the sole is written "Compliments of Wonderland."

The *Boston Sunday Post* for August 29 observed, "This 'Cinderella' show is the great carnival hit of the season at Wonderland, and by many considered the greatest free spectacle ever presented at any park in America, yet it only runs for one-half hour; but 15 singing, dancing, and marching numbers are crowded into those 30 minutes, making a performance distinguished for its brightness and celerity." The *Boston Globe* on the same day repeated the above word-for-word, and added, "Director James Gilbert is constantly introducing new musical and dancing numbers into the big brilliant success 'Cinderella,' which is presented every afternoon and evening. The novelty incidental for the week will be 'The Brinkley Girl,' sung and danced by about 20 of the pretty chorus girls."[46]

That same week, Gertrude Fitzgerald—who had played a page in the first few weeks of the show and now was the Royal Songbird of the Court—got a solo, "The Songs My Mother Used to Sing." This was probably the 1879 song by J. P. Skelly. (The more familiar "Those Songs My Mother Used to Sing" by H. Wakefield Smith was not written until 1914.) Her performance was considered such a selling point that it was listed in the newspaper ads for the show.[47] Ida Halverson was now the Chief Page.

At the beginning of September the producers added "Tipperary" as a singing and dancing number, for which they included Irish jigs by twenty of the girls.[48] All of the elements from the previous week were so popular that they were held over. This very full schedule seems to have held until the show ended at the last week of Wonderland's season.

e/o

The end of August saw a new production at the park, a blackface show entitled "In a Medical College" by Dick Plunkett's company, starring Plunkett, Ben Walker, and the team of Alfred M. Frothingham and Bessie Denham.[49] Plunkett himself made a specialty of blackface and minstrel shows. He had appeared in Boston area theaters since at least 1903 and was fifty-two years old. He lived in Everett.

"In a Medical College" was by no means new—it had been published in 1877 and doubtless used for many years before being published for the play services. It was the work of Frank Dumont, a white minstrel performer who started his own company of Dumont's Minstrels about 1895 at the Eleventh Street Opera House in Philadelphia.[50]

The description of his skit in the catalog reads:

One Night in a Medical College

Ethiopian Sketch in One Scene, by Frank Dumont

Characters, seven male, one female
Plays twenty minutes. Scene, a dark dissecting room in a college. Unusually funny, with a trifle of terror.
Price, 15 cents

The sketch was originally performed by Dupree and Benedict's Minstrels in Gloucester, Massachusetts, on April 5, 1876. Rather surprisingly, the script is not filled with transcribed dialect and does not read like the expected blackface jargon and pronunciation. Presumably the script gave the dialogue "straight," and the performers were expected to render it in the appropriate blackface style.

The play hits several of the stereotypical characteristics of Blacks as portrayed in minstrel shows—fear of lightning and thunder, pretentious names, fear of ghosts, and exaggerated actions and properties.

e/o

The park closed at 11 p.m. on September 12, 1909.[51]

It had been a difficult summer, but the efforts had paid off. Without the extravagances, closing down the more expensive-to-run attractions, and possibly because James Gilbert's constantly changing show encouraged repeat viewings, it was reported on October 20 that, far from being in the red, Wonderland had realized a dividend of 2 percent.[52]

Gilbert, having been such a success, was asked to stay on for the next year as assistant manager.[53] Wonderland would go on for at least another year. There was an ominous sign, however. The *Revere Journal*, Wonderland's hometown paper, wrote about the park in its August 14, 1909, issue: "One of the most notable improvements in amusement places at the Beach within the past decade was that extensive and architecturally wonderful creation known as Wonderland. It arose, like an Aladdin creation on a marsh that to some extent disfigured the background of the Beach water front, and had a great run of popularity, attracting by its novelty at first people from far and near."[54]

It was a bad sign that the park still had a month in its 1909 run when this was written, and still had the 1910 season ahead of it, yet the piece spoke about the park only in the past tense.

CHAPTER 9
Finale—1910

Despite the profits made the previous summer, Wonderland's run was nearing its end. There were no notices or stories about the park in any newspapers in the spring, which was by this time usual. But there were still no stories through the month of May, and it became clear that Wonderland would not open at the traditional start of summer as it always had, on Memorial Day. June came, and there were still no announcements. Would Wonderland open at all?

Finally on June 11, 1910, the *Boston Globe* announced that Wonderland would be opening for the season on June 17, the latest it had ever opened.[1] That was Bunker Hill Day, celebrating the Battle of Bunker Hill in 1775. It gave some slim justification for the park's late opening.

If "austerity" had been the watchword the previous season, this one was "austerity squared." The rundown of the park's attractions is more remarkable for what was absent than for what would be there. As with the previous year, there was no mention of the Circle Swing, the Whirl the Whirl, the funhouses, the Palmist, or the Japanese Village. There was no mention of the Miniature Railroad. There was a motion picture theater, but it was not touted as a major attraction. The Shoot the Chutes, Hell Gate, Love's Journey (still with the Honeymoon Tunnel), Thompson Scenic Railway, and Velvet Coaster were still there. Resurrected, surprisingly, were the Infant Incubators, after a year's absence. The Funhouse Mirrors that had displaced them were moved to one of the other buildings.

The ballroom was still there and probably the restaurant. Teel's Band continued to perform the music in the park, with two parades daily. But the papers no longer announced the weekly roster of vaudeville performers,

if there was a changing roster. And there was also no big musical production as in previous years.

There were some new additions, but they were few in number and very
low-key. One of the biggest changes was that admission to the park itself
was completely free, a policy written in letters over the Walnut Avenue
entrance.[2] A late postcard of the entrance shows the sign in place. The eagle
appears to be gone from the entrance, and off to one side is a sign advertising the soft drink Moxie.

Taking over the domed and minareted building beside the lagoon that
had originally housed the Beautiful Orient, then the Florida Alligator Jungle, then Darktown, was the Wonder Wander, an attraction mainly for
toddlers. One report noted, "It contains a fascinating array of tilts, teeter
boards, swings, self-propelling whirls, and other mechanical contrivances
for giving the boys and girls a succession of rides, on which they work their
own passage and continue the trips as long as they please. When the rides
wear out, there is a rattling Punch and Judy show on the side, which no
child could leave till the last act."[3]

The name of the attraction came from a well-known poem, "The Dinkey
Bird" by Eugene Field, a writer of childhood verse best known for "Wyn-
ken, Blynken, and Nod." The 1898 poem opens,

> In an ocean, 'way out yonder,
> (As all sapient people know)
> Is the land of Wonder-Wander,
> Whither children love to go,
> It's their playing, romping, swinging
> That give great joy to me
> While the Dinkey-Bird goes singing
> In the amfalula tree!

The big attraction for the summer was the Captive Balloon. Unlike the
La Roux balloon from Wonderland's first year, this one was tethered to a
long coil of rope, had a basket, and would take paying customers aloft.
Wilbur Davis was the balloonist and navigator. This attraction remained
in place the entire season. The balloon was christened the "Wonderland,"
as La Roux's had been. It was located in the southwest corner of the park,
where the Kennedy Wild West show had originally been. The amusement

also contained several scale models of airplanes and a full-sized Wittemann glider. Among the models were one of Santos Dumont's miniature monoplane "Demoiselle," a Bleriot airplane, and a Glenn Curtiss model. These had been featured at the "Boston 1915" Exhibition the previous fall, and it was probably the connection that the Higginses had with that affair that allowed them to obtain the models for Wonderland. The timing was good because the first American Air Meet had occurred in January 1910 in Los Angeles, and the second meet would be at Squantum in Boston Harbor in September. The Wright brothers and Glenn Curtiss would be there. Because of the upcoming air meet, the *Boston Sunday Globe* on August 14 published a long and illustrated article on many of the same planes that happened to be represented at Wonderland in miniature.[4]

The balloon held 100,000 cubic feet of hydrogen and would take two people aloft on every trip to a height of 900 feet. The price was an exorbitant one dollar apiece, at a time when the average workingman's wage was twenty-two cents an hour. On busy days, the round trip took nine minutes.[5] The first passenger was Lucy Smith of Lynn.[6] An account of a trip taken in the Wonderland balloon that summer written by Harry V. Lawrence was printed in the local newspapers. He later gathered them together in a privately printed volume in 1914 entitled *Little Stories*.[7] One of these stories appeared in the *Exeter [New Hampshire] News Letter*, presumably in 1910:

Night Trip in a Captive Balloon

On a recent night I made an ascension in a captive balloon located at "Wonderland," Revere Beach, Mass. Mr. James L. Leavitt, a former resident of Exeter, accompanied me and to say that it was a beautiful night is putting it mildly.

At about 9:45 p.m. we climbed into the basket after "jollying" the attendants about the chances of the rope breaking and letting us drift away. The men removed the bags of sand from the sides of the basket and we slowly went up into the sky. We had left our straw hats on the ground and when we reached our highest point, 800 feet, the easterly breeze had taken us out over the end of "Wonderland."

The only noise we could hear was the flapping of the American flag on the side of the balloon and the straining of the rope that held the basket. Far below the lights of "Wonderland" looked as though the ground was studded with diamonds and we could also see the long line of lights leading from the city of Lynn out to Bass Point. The houses below us in the town of Revere looked like dry goods boxes and we could also see the lights of Boston, Winthrop, Chelsea, Malden, Medford, Somerville, and Everett, and altogether it was the finest night scene I ever witnessed.

When we reached our highest point the basket leaned slightly, as we were not directly over the spot we had started from and the strain on the rope caused this condition. In a short time we were pulled down by a powerful motor located near the ascension point.

This balloon was made by Leo Stevens, the celebrated air pilot, and seemed to be perfectly safe. I can strongly recommend one to try a trip of this kind if he wishes to see a beautiful panorama at night.

Another summer-long attraction was a performance of the "Garden Scene" from *Faust*. This seems like an odd choice for a summer entertainment. Presumably derived from Goethe's version of the story, which appeared as a play in 1808 (and was revised twenty years later), it contains a scene in the garden of Marthe, the neighbor of Gretchen, whom Faust is pursuing as a love interest. Faust and Mephistopheles, the Devil to whom Faust has pledged his soul, enter Marthe's garden to testify to her husband's death. Mephistopheles and Marthe discuss the difficulties of a wandering, single life. In the meantime, Faust and Gretchen talk quietly together, Faust praising her and Gretchen saying she is unworthy of such praise, being a peasant girl with rough hands. Faust returns that no learning or beauty could compare with her loving nature and humility. Gretchen tells of her sad and lonely life, and picks a daisy and begins to play the game of "He Loves Me, He Loves Me Not" (the first appearance of this in a popular play). It ends with "He Loves Me," which makes Faust elated. Gretchen runs off, and the sky darkens. Mephistopheles tells Faust ominously that it is time for them to go.

This basic story must have been stripped to the bone. A Wonderland ad called it "Faust without the Frills."[8]

es

One of the main attractions for 1910 was something completely unlike any of Wonderland's other shows. It was a lecture and presentation on a piece of then-recent history.

Matthew Alexander Henson was born in Nanjemoy, Maryland, forty-five miles south of Washington, DC, along the Potomac River, in 1866.

His parents were free-born Black sharecroppers. They moved to Washington, DC, when Matt was very young, and he grew up in the city. His mother died when he was seven, and an uncle raised, him, sending him to school in Washington for over six years. Afterward, Henson went to Baltimore, where he found a ship that would take him as a cabin boy. He became an able-bodied seaman and spent the next four years traveling to China, Japan, Manila, North Africa, Spain, France, and through the Black Sea to southern Russia.

At the age of twenty-one he was back in Washington, DC, working as a clerk in a store selling hats and furs. It was here that he met Lieutenant Robert Peary, then a civil engineer with the U.S. Navy. Peary was getting outfitted for a trip to Nicaragua, where he was to be part of the team surveying an alternate route across Central America through Nicaragua to place an interocean canal. Learning that Henson was a seaman, he invited Henson to join him as his manservant. Henson accepted and remained with Peary as he rose to become the engineer in charge of the project.

Peary had already decided that he would be the first man to the North Pole and had made one trek across Greenland, accompanied only by a Danish officer. On every subsequent expedition north, Henson would accompany him. In 1891–92, 1898–1902, and 1905–6 they made other expeditions, pushing further northward each time.

Henson learned to speak Inuit, to build igloos and other shelters, to build a cookstove, and to drive a dog sled. He developed great stamina. He became as essential man in the party and was an obvious choice when Peary made his final attack on the pole in 1908. They sailed, as in the previous expedition, on the ship *Roosevelt* under the command of Captain Robert Bartlett and a team of twenty-four. For the final stage only six pushed forward—Peary, Henson, and four Inuit, named Ootah, Egigingwah, Seegloo, and Ooqueah. On April 6, 1909, they established their farthest northern camp, named Camp Morris K. Jesup.[9] Peary unrolled a special thin, silk U.S. flag he had saved for the occasion. It was, based on their observations, within five miles of the pole.

Peary's feet were frostbitten, and he had to ride much of the way on the sledge. Henson was sent ahead to the estimated location of the pole to assert their claim, followed forty-five minutes later by Peary. Together, they planted a flag to mark the spot.

Upon their return, however, things changed. Dr. Frederick A. Cook, who had been a surgeon on one of the previous expeditions, claimed to have reached the pole before Peary. The tired and frostbitten Peary found himself plunged into a seemingly never-ending series of controversies. But it was more than that. As Henson put it, "The Commodore was never a well man from the minute after he'd finished taking those observations at the Pole. It seemed to be an effort for him to speak. All his strength had been concentrated on getting to the Pole. Once he got there his strength gave out."

For Henson, there was more to it than Peary's taciturnity. As Henson explained later in an interview, "After we returned to the United States I only saw him twice. . . . I had no money. I was broke. You know, we got no pay on those expeditions. . . . I had to do something when I got back to support myself and my wife. And I was all in too—too weak, too sickly to work at a job."

What he did was to contact William Aloysius Brady, the New York producer of shows and manager of star properties. Brady saw in Henson such a property and offered to set up a series of lecture dates for him across the country. Astonishingly, Peary forbade Henson from lecturing, but Brady booked him anyway. In the end, it hardly mattered. After giving one lecture in New York and several in the Midwest, Peary, his wife, and Captain Bartlett sailed for England to deliver lectures there and on the continent, leaving the American lecture circuit open for Henson.

Henson asked Brady what he wanted for setting up the lectures, and at first Brady refused any fee. When pressed, he agreed to take twenty-five dollars "for cigar money" (Brady loved his cigars). In return, he looked after Henson. After several lectures, Henson said he was too sick to continue and would have to stop. Brady took the train out to see Henson, agreed that he wasn't well, and sent him back to New York to recuperate before continuing. Somehow, he rearranged the schedule for Henson's appearances.

Matthew Henson arrived at Wonderland on July 2, 1910. There was a stark and simple advertisement in the *Boston Post* the day before:

WONDERLAND
Tomorrow
MATT HENSON

Who was with Peary in his
Dash to the Pole,
Daily, 1 to 11, Admission Free[10]

Elsewhere was a fuller explanation: "The Management of this popular resort are alert to give the public the best of everything. The latest engagement made is that of Matt Henson, commencing July 2. The story of the frozen north and the land of the midnight sun will be fully related by pictures and stories, and also his actual experiences in his many expeditions in quest of the North Pole with Commodore Peary."

The day after his appearance, the *Boston Globe* elaborated: "Matt Henson, the principal attraction at Wonderland, prefers to tell a simple story of his part in the dash to the north pole rather than to discourse on the scientific significance of the greatest achievement of the centuries. The dogs and Arctic sledge laden with stores and equipment as seen in Arctic exploration appear on the Boardwalk." Henson would appear for the rest of the 1910 season at Wonderland.[11]

If his appearance was like his earlier ones, it probably consisted of him wearing his polar outfits and telling about the several trips to the Arctic in pursuit of the pole, illustrated with films and slides.[12]

On stage, Henson showed no ill-will toward Peary, but interviewed backstage in Syracuse, New York, in March 1910, he did express disappointment that he had not heard from Peary since their return—except to not carry on a lecture tour. He was also disappointed that Peary had not paid him for the many photographs that Henson had taken and that Peary had acquired for his own use:

> I built the sledges, I had charge of the packing of them and I looked after the equipment. . . . On one of our expeditions in 1895, as we were crossing Independence Bay, Peary called for volunteers to accompany him. Who do you suppose stuck to him? There were just two of us, Hugh Lee and Myself. He treated Lee in much the same manner as he has treated me after we came back from that trip, and on Peary's last expedition to the Pole Lee would not accompany him.
>
> On one occasion, when Peary was in danger of meeting death from an infuriated musk ox, I saved his life, and another time, when his feet were frozen, I took care of him. These are not the only occasions on which I saved Peary's life, but he isn't a man to remember such things after the danger passed.[13]

Later accounts said that in some of his lectures Henson was treated badly and hooted off stage, but there is no indication of that happening at Wonderland. He received solid tributes in the New York papers on his return, and many statements of confidence in him and his abilities from other Arctic explorers.

In the first four years of Wonderland, the accomplishments and character of African Americans had been represented almost exclusively by the images associated with minstrelsy—"The South before the War," Darktown and its outrageous Darktown Fire Brigade, several blackface acts and minstrel shows, and Plunkett's "In a Medical College." One of the booths featured the infamous "African Dodger." There was something redeeming that the feature show of the final year highlighted an amazingly positive figure from Black history, the first man to reach the North Pole.

↝

Another Wonderland show wasn't so historic, but it was entertaining, and no doubt inexpensive for the park. William Watson King was an up-and-coming billiards player in the 1890s and an expert at the game of "fifteen ball." He married Martha May Davis of Syracuse, New York, but their home in the Montgomery Flats area was devastated by fire, and they lost everything. They hit the road, with King playing tournaments and giving exhibitions while his wife watched, living in Los Angeles and later Chicago.[14]

Eventually Martha asked W. W. to teach her how to play the game, and she practiced assiduously, making her amateur debut in 1903. She "defeated all comers" except her husband, who was by now the recognized champion of the Pacific Coast. Both of them gave lessons while in Chicago, then started to hit the road together giving demonstrations as "The Kings of Billiards."[15]

After appearing in several cities, including Washington, DC, the Kings came to Wonderland to give exhibitions, demonstrating straight, fancy, and trick shots. Undoubtedly, they finished up with what became a staple, a game of fifteen ball between the two of them. The Kings appeared at Wonderland in July.[16]

Like Annette Kellermann before her, Martha May King was an advocate for physical exercise and held that billiards was good exercise. Eventually, in 1912, she opened up a billiard hall for women only in Kansas City. It had fifteen tables and female attendants, so that women could come without feeling as if they were invading a male domain.[17]

While Henson and the Kings provided regular shows, the reinstalled incubators also drew crowds. Diversity of babies was one feature this last summer. At the beginning of the year the incubators held one Black baby, and near the end of the summer an Indian baby, "the object of much curiosity on the part of the ladies," also arrived.[18]

At the other end of the park, in the cement diving and swimming tank once used by Annette Kellermann, a show featured six female swimmers and divers, organized by Herbert H. Pattee, the designer of Love's Journey.[19] This swimming show too remained the entire summer.

One of the stranger acts in the pool was Mother Berlo's Drowning Act. The Berlo family was to swimming what the Von Trapp family later would be to Austrian singing. Elizabeth and Anthony Berlo had ten children, and all of them were expert swimmers, except for Anthony, who couldn't swim a stroke.[20] The Berlos followed Kellermann's dictum of swimming as the best exercise and believed that everyone should swim, including little Barbara, who was six that summer. Three of the Berlo girls were in Pattee's Diving Venuses, which is undoubtedly how their mother got pulled into the act. The Venuses were presumably a comedy act, since no one would be entertained by a realistic portrayal of an old woman drowning (Elizabeth was sixty-three that year). Perhaps she gave an exaggerated "going down for the third time," or turned the tables and rescued a would-be rescuer. Whatever she did, Elizabeth was in good shape for it. Two years later, she and her then eighteen-year-old daughter Kitty swam four and a half miles across and up the Hudson River, from Edgewater, New Jersey, to the foot of 152nd Street in Manhattan, arriving in this unusual fashion at the Washington Club. It took them forty-five minutes. According to newspaper accounts, Elizabeth Berlo had to be forcibly restrained from swimming back the same way.[21]

Sometime during the summer, probably in July, a quiet business deal took place, without any public announcement. The Wonderland grounds were sold to one Solomon Sirk, a businessman who wanted to establish an artificial ice plant in Revere. His plan was to use spring water pumped from the grounds and modern refrigeration plants to produce ice on the spot, evidently saving on both water and transportation costs.[22] In the past, ice had been sawn from the frozen lakes of Fresh Pond in Cambridge and Chebacco Lake in Hamilton and stored in sawdust-insulated ice houses. These were supplanted by ice houses making their own ice when refrigeration became available. There were plenty of established ice houses in the area at the time, so Sirk was evidently hoping that the slight edge given by proximity and readily available water would allow him to compete.

As some critics had observed, a large part of the problem with Wonderland was its off-the-beach location. "One of the faults of the Park from a business point of view has been that it did not extend to the beach boulevard," said the *New York Clipper* on February 6, 1909. "Many smaller attractions took away the trade."[23] This did not seem to be a significant problem on first sight. The park itself was within easy walking distance of the beach. Indeed, on its opening day, the beach entrance was the most heavily used. It was located not far from a present-day pedestrian bridge from Revere Beach Boulevard to a subway stop and about as long. The walk is not long or hard, but it was apparently inconvenient enough to discourage business. In the first place, there was no railway stop at that time at the bridge, and the walk from the nearest station to either the Walnut Avenue entrance or the beach-side Beaver Street entrance was about the same distance. Patrons, though, had plenty of amusements directly on the boulevard, so why wouldn't they simply stay there, rather than making the extra effort?

The original conceptual art for Wonderland showed what was obviously a new train stop on the Boston & Maine Railroad right at Wonderland. Had the Wonderland management been able to persuade the B&M to construct a stop either along its main line or on the curving spur that defined the edge of the park, things might have been different, but as it was, there was no method to directly spirit patrons to the gates of the park.

There had been the Panic of 1907 to explain the prodigious drop in attendance for 1908, but the park had rebounded in 1909 and might have in 1910 as well. Certainly the hard times had retreated enough that people were going to the beach again—but they were going to the boulevard, not to Wonderland. It was somewhat tragic to see that many of the people whose attractions had appeared in Wonderland itself now put up attractions directly on Revere Beach Boulevard, or would in the near future.

Louis Bopp had started before Wonderland, with his Hippodrome and other carousels. Even as Wonderland was operating he opened new attractions along the boulevard and expanded the ones he had. Charles Willard put up a new Temple of Music on the boulevard, and with his frequent partner Robert Blake opened another enterprise on the boulevard as well. H. H. Pattee, the inventor of Love's Journey, started working the new Luna Park on Revere Beach. More Thompson Scenic Railways went up on Revere Beach and at Bass Point across Broad Sound. This, of course, was in addition to the establishments by other dynasties along the beach, such as Ridgway's Nautical House/The Pit and the various dance halls. It is telling that when a consortium bought the Monitor and the Merrimac, the big diorama show that was the centerpiece of the 1907 Jamestown Exposition (the same one that Walter Darcy Ryan built his Scintillator for) and had spent the two previous summers at Coney Island, they brought it to a newly built building along the boulevard. In previous years, it would have come to Wonderland.[24]

Wonderland was caught on the horns of a dilemma. In order to bring in the crowds, they needed shows sufficiently spectacular to encourage people to make the extra effort to come in from the boulevard. But those shows were expensive, and if the park operated them, it would lose money. The key to success, as George Tilyou showed with his Steeplechase Park, the oldest existing amusement park on Coney Island (and which would continue for half a century after his death), was to keep expenses down, not squandering money on "name" acts and big shows but relying instead on established attractions to draw in the crowds, producing revenue with little outlay. But Tilyou's Steeplechase Park was right there on the bowery at Coney Island Beach. If Wonderland simply tried to rely on its existing big attractions to bring in patrons and money, relying on Shoot the Chutes, the Thompson Scenic Railway, and the Velvet Coaster, they would lose out. Bigger and better and newer rides were going up along the boulevard. The few new attractions for 1910—Matt Henson, the Kings, the Diving Girls, and Teel's Band, didn't provide enough interest to keep the park going.

When the Irish League from Lowell made their annual trip to Revere Beach, it was reported that "in former years the party went to Wonderland, but this year they will patronize the attractions on the boulevard and particularly the Battle of the Monitor and the Merrimack. . . . The production is better than the Johnstown Flood or Fire and Flames."[25]

The newspapers gave a countdown until the closing of the park, warning visitors that they only had so many days before the park closed to enjoy the thrills of the scenic railway and Hell Gate. Whether the public was generally aware of it or not, certainly the park personnel knew that it was not merely a few days until the season closing, but until the closing of the park itself forever. "Only a few days more if you want to Ride on the Scenic Railway, Circulate in Hell Gate, and Gesticulate on the Velvet Coaster," proclaimed an ad in the *Boston Post* for September 3. The park would close on Labor Day, Monday, September 5.[26]

On Sunday, September 4, the *Post* proclaimed, "Today and Monday only remain of the season at Wonderland, for on Monday at 11 p.m. a final blast on the big horn will have ushered into history one of Wonderland's most successful seasons." Perhaps it was successful by some measure, but certainly it was not as profitable as the first two seasons. The *Globe* for the same day proclaimed that "at 11 o'clock Monday evening the final whistle will be blown, and, as its note dies away, one of the most successful summers in the history of the amusement park will terminate. There will be a parade of people in fancy costumes, confetti will be showered and a good time generally at the closing ceremonies."[27]

The weather on Labor Day was predicted to be "fair." The September 4 *Globe* stated that "the celebration of Labor Day this year promises to eclipse anything of a similar kind which the friends of Boston's toilers have witnessed in recent years."[28] But the next day it looked less inviting. "Unsettled weather with showers and moderate winds, mostly southerly, is the Labor Day forecast given out at the local weather bureau last night," the *Boston Globe* reported in its September 5 edition. "It will probably be suitable outing weather and if the showers are not too frequent or too heavy the numerous sporting events scheduled for the holiday may not be seriously interfered with."[29]

How it played out in Revere is not reported, nor was anything significant reported about the last day.

☙

The owners lost no time in starting to sell off the park assets. On September 11, advertisements appeared offering to sell GE Alternating current motors, steam boilers, a gramophone with seventeen records, a tent, a Gould's Pump, and ticket choppers from Wonderland. An advertisement selling off the captive balloon that had been used that season, as well as the full-size glider, was printed in the September 4 *Boston Sunday Post*, before the park even closed. In October an advertisement for rolltop desks from Wonderland appeared, and at the end of the month another one announced,

FOR SALE
The Property Known as
WONDERLAND
REVERE BEACH
Comprising about 25 acres of land,
many buildings, devices, and
equipment. Full particulars and
description of property can be
obtained from
WALNUT AVENUE COMPANY
Room 306, 53 State St., Boston[30]

But the land had been sold to Solomon Sirk, hadn't it? Even before the park closed, things had gone wrong. Wonderland had a swift and final closing, but the final disposition would not turn out to be so clean and simple.

CHAPTER 10
After the Ball Was Over—1911 and Beyond

After the Ball is Over
After the Break of Morn . . .
After the Dancers' Leaving
After the Stars have Gone
Many a Heart is Aching
If you could Read them All
Many the Hopes that have Vanished
After the Ball

—Charles K. Harris, "After the Ball" (1891)

Wonderland was closed, but it still existed legally for several years, hiring new personnel and engaging in business dealings—and problems.[1] Its first order of business was to have the park dismantled and sold off before it could deteriorate or be vandalized, so that as much of the property's value as possible could be reclaimed. Even before the park closed, an advertisement appeared selling the captive balloon and the full-size glider. The very next week, advertisements for miscellaneous bits and pieces appeared in the papers. And these were only the ads with "Wonderland" as the point of contact. No doubt much else was sold through other locations, and a great deal was surely sold through direct contacts rather than through advertisements. The park's generators, transformers, and miles of copper wiring, not to mention its many electric lights, would all bring a tidy sum once disposed of. The great Morandi-Proctor cooking ovens at the restaurant and the McCahill Iceless Soda Fountains could be sold to other food venues.[2]

Probably many of the rides that could be broken down and shipped elsewhere were sold to other amusement parks, just at the St. Louis Shoot the Chutes had been sold to Wonderland. If so, no records of the sales have survived. The incubators could be sold to other parks, as could the funhouse mirrors and motion picture projectors. The rails and the cars from the Thompson Scenic Railway could be moved elsewhere, but it wasn't practical to move the tracks and their platforms. Hell Gate was built into the park and not moveable, and most of the buildings would probably simply have been dismantled.

By May the wooden tracks of the scenic railway were being dismantled. As the *Boston Sunday Post* for May 7, 1911, observed, "Over in Wonderland, yesterday, all was as hushed and deserted as Boston's City Hall on a Circus Day. The only sound from the big Scenic Railways was the deep, resounding baritone tones of a carpenter's voice as he smashed his thumb with a hammer."[3]

The contract for tearing down the wooden structures went to Robert R. McNutt, Inc., who was still selling lumber from Wonderland twenty years later.[4] He offered planks of various sizes, sheathing boards, windows, and hard pine floor timbers. In 1914, a writer for the *Boston Post* observed that pieces from the old Wonderland buildings had been used in the building of several summer homes along the beach.[5] The 1914 Bromley Fire Insurance Map of Wonderland shows only the administration building still standing, along with a new large building at the center of the park labeled "Ernest A. Kimball." In October 1917, a piece in "The Observant Citizen" in the *Boston Post* commented that the only reminder of Wonderland was one brick building.[6]

In 1911, Everett N. Curtis, who had graduated from MIT and Boston Law School, was hired as receiver for the Wonderland Company for its business dealings. In that year Harold Parker and the Wonderland board petitioned the Middlesex County Commissioners for a reduction in the tax rate for the still unpaid taxes for Wonderland from past years, claiming that the park was no longer a paying proposition and could not afford to pay. This was granted in July 1911, reducing the Wonderland tax bill from $350,000 to $150,000.[7]

The case of Solomon Sirk, prospective ice dealer and the purported purchaser of Wonderland for ice houses, came to court in August 1911. The cause of contention was that Sirk said that he had been promised that the ten artesian wells on the land would provide five hundred gallons of fresh water per minute. In reality, he could pump no more than seventy gallons per minute. Sirk wanted to be let out of his contract to purchase the land.

The court found in September that John J. Higgins had not fraudulently misrepresented the capability of the wells but honestly believed it to be true. The judge ruled that no damages were due, but that Sirk's rescission was limited to repayment of the $5,000 he had put down as a deposit on the land.[8]

Higgins turned around and immediately sold the land again, this time to John E. V. Hayden and James F. Briggs on October 14, 1911. These were two Revere and Chelsea developers who hoped to develop the property as had originally been intended, as building lots for residences. The final papers were passed in February 1912. They announced that the lots would be available within weeks.[9] But nothing of the sort happened. The lots sat undeveloped. Maybe it was thought to be too difficult to guarantee that the lots would not flood. In February 1918, part of what had been Wonderland flooded at an exceptionally high tide. Had the park still been in operation, there would likely have been some damage.

Nonetheless, another plan to develop the land appeared in July 1919 under the name "Wonderland Park." The streets were laid out and plans for sewerage, water supply, and electricity were set out. The developers planned to plant a thousand rock maple and silver poplar trees along the laid-out streets, but, again, none of this took place.[10]

The Wonderland grounds were still occasionally used for viewing fireworks, but the undismantled portions could be dangerous. In August 1914, six-year-old Salvo Di Lio of Revere was playing with some friends in the remains of Wonderland. He stopped to peer over into the pit that had once been the Hell Gate ride and fell in, hitting his head on a board and falling unconscious. There was two and a half feet of water in the pit, and the boy drowned. Police pulled him out, and Dr. Fred F. Andrews performed artificial respiration, but he was unable to revive the child.[11]

In 1919, bicycling promoter Nat Butler set up a six-lap track on the site of the old track in the southwest corner of the park, with a grandstand for ten thousand people.[12] The cycling races continued there for many years.

In October 1917, North Shore Road opened, cutting across Wonderland and separating what had been the northwest section of the park from the rest, passing through where the original carousel and Hell Gate had been.[13] The road still exists as Route 1A in Revere, otherwise known as the Veterans of Foreign Wars Parkway. The traffic circle ("rotary" in Massachusetts jargon) called Butler Circle is just about at the edge of Wonderland.

On May 22, 1921, the visitor total at Revere Beach topped 250,000 people. For the first time, the crowd at Revere exceeded that on opening day at Wonderland.[14]

In the 1920s, part of the Wonderland grounds was used as a miniature golf course.

On June 12, 1935, a new greyhound racetrack opened up, employing the oval that had been used for bicycle racing. The new facility was dubbed Wonderland Racing Park, and it would stay open until August 19, 2010.[15]

A new Wonderland ballroom opened near the entrance to the race park in the 1940s.

In January 1954, Boston's Blue Line subway opened its furthest station near the race park and ballroom. Appropriately dubbed Wonderland Station, it is credited with helping to keep alive the amusements along Revere Beach that had begun to suffer decline when the Narrow Gauge railway ceased operation in 1940.[16] For the people of Boston, the Wonderland Amusement Park was now forgotten. The name "Wonderland" was attached to the subway stop, the ballroom, and the raceway, and for most people never signified anything else.

Constructions and store locations are ephemeral, but as things stand at present, most of what had been Wonderland was located in the property currently occupied by the Wonderland Marketplace Shopping Center, located between Kimball Avenue in Revere and Route 1A. The curve at the back of the mall to the southeast still has the form of the Boston & Maine Railroad spur. The property line behind what is at this writing the Laundromax laundry and Shanghai Gardens restaurant on the other side of 1A follows the curve of the Wonderland property line, and the property map tracks the two peculiar jogs the property line showed in 1906. The line of wooded land to the east of the Laundromax building matches the property line of Wonderland.

The front of what is now Big Lots sits precisely where the southern canal next to the lagoon was and runs parallel to it. Walnut Avenue doesn't go into the road behind the mall, but there is a pedestrian walkway that is about where the entrance ramp once bridged the B&M track. The administration building and the succession of Wonderland buildings going east from it—the nursery/hospital, Fatal Wedding, children's theater, Hale's Tours, the Japanese Village, the Palmistry and Astrology building, the Third Degree, Princess Trixie, and the photography studio—occupy much the same ground that the Wonderland mall buildings do today. Possibly the mall was built there to take advantage of the pilings driven in to support the Wonderland buildings in the marshy ground.

Ferari's tent would be in the parking lot, as would the Fighting the Flames grandstand and stage, the station of the scenic railway, Beautiful Orient, and the front portion of the ballroom/restaurant. The rest of that building stretched at an angle across what is now route 1A and onto the former Wonderland racetrack grounds. The 1906 Wonderland ballroom was about a thousand feet to the west and a little south of where the present-day Wonderland ballroom stands.

The Kennedy Wild West Show grounds extended from what is now the 99 Restaurant across 1A onto the racetrack grounds. The scenic railway entrance building was located about where the St. Jean Credit Union building (erected in 2019) now sits. The tracks went across the current 1A, bending at a right angle just about at the edge of Butler Circle and proceeding west-northwest until it reached the dog track, which is where the scenic building of the railroad was. The dog track itself stood wholly on Wonderland property, as did most of its own grandstand. The beach entrance to Wonderland was south of where the present Massachusetts Bay Transportation Authority (MBTA, colloquially known as the "T") pedestrian bridge stands. It was located where the first pedestrian pathway sits to the south of the T bridge and passed through what is presently the Water's Edge apartment building.

✌

And what of the people involved in Wonderland? Some were only peripherally involved in the park, or only appeared there briefly, while others were integral to the park's construction and development. The ones in show business often appeared for years afterward in the entertainment trade papers. Some simply faded away with time. Of those not involved in the entertainment business, most disappeared from the stage of history after they played their brief parts.

John Joseph Higgins disappeared after his involvement in the disposition of the property Wonderland had occupied. During the last year of Wonderland's operation, he tried to branch out into other businesses. In 1910, he founded J. J. Higgins and Company. It distributed the Vohr Ozone Maker (breathing ozone was seen as a healthy experience, its toxic effects not yet appreciated).[17] It also sold business books and books on running a farm.[18] But the advertisements for J. J. Higgins and Company ceased after 1911. After tying up the affairs of Wonderland, Higgins seems to have vanished from the Boston area. He was later recorded as living in Jacksonville, Florida.[19] He died in 1942 and was buried in the Catholic Cemetery in his native Savannah, Georgia.[20]

☙

Harold Parker continued his work on the Massachusetts Highway Commission. When Chairman William E. McClintock resigned in June 1908, Parker took his place, while still president of Wonderland. He continued in that role, attending an international roads conference in France to represent Massachusetts. He retired from the position in 1911 and promptly went into the paving business. In 1913–14, he was appointed an advisor to roads for the state of New York by Governor John Alden Dix. He died on November 29, 1916. In his memory, a state forest was named after him in North Reading, Massachusetts.[21]

☙

Thomas D. Barroll continued in the Massachusetts National Guard, becoming a member of the Draft Board during World War I. At the age of fifty-eight he married. He and his wife moved to Miami in the mid-1930s, and he was still alive in 1945.[22]

☙

James Walker Jr., Wonderland's assistant treasurer, who was divorced from superstar Blanche Ring, appears to have stayed out of the limelight in later years. He ran for some local offices, and in 1920, as color sergeant of Boston Light Infantry (Tigers) Veterans Association, was appropriately elected paymaster. He died in 1931 and is buried in Mount Auburn Cemetery in Cambridge, Massachusetts.[23]

๛

Eugene L. Perry, the onetime excursion and advertising agent turned assistant general manager under J. J. Higgins, continued on in show business. He had retired from Wonderland well-liked by his employees, but it had taken a toll on his marriage, and he was divorced immediately afterward. In 1909, he served as manager of Steeplechase Pier in Atlantic City, one of George Tilyou's ventures. In October of that year, only a year after divorcing Beatrice Shaw Perry, he remarried to Margaret J. Roche, also from Boston. Significantly, they were married at his booking agent's office in Philadelphia.[24]

He was manager of the Schubert Auditorium for one month in 1911 before being transferred to other duties. In 1912, he became manager of the Broad Street Theater in New York, and on February 3, 1917, of Keith's Riverside Theater in New York City, "a much coveted position." He left in August 1917 to become a special representative for the Fox Film Corporation, supervising operations in California, Oregon, Washington, Idaho, Montana, Arizona, New Mexico, and part of Mexico. Before he left New York, the employees at the Riverside Theater gave him a grateful sendoff at which he received two pipes—one for morning and one for evening—a box of tobacco, a box of cigars, and a fountain pen, all this after only seven months in office. Perry certainly inspired affection among his employees. He died in 1947.[25]

๛

Atillio Pusterla, the designer and inventor of the Hell Gate ride, was just getting started. The ride that was to be installed as Love's Rough Journey in Wonderland, then as Razzle Dazzle, ultimately was used in Chicago's Riverside Park as the Aquarousel, where it remained in place for several decades. Pusterla was hired by the New York State Supreme Court to paint the mural *Law through the Ages* in the foyer of the New York County Courthouse as part of a Works Project Administration piece, and it is still there today. He patented a flying machine in 1911. He painted the murals for the Parliament building in Ottawa, Canada, and the tower of the Lewis and Clark monument in Astoria, Oregon. His *sgraffito* technique was not well-suited for an outdoor monument, so this last piece deteriorated badly over the years. The Lewis and Clark memorial was restored to its original beauty in 1995. Pusterla died of a heart attack in 1941 at his home in Wood-cliff, New Jersey.[26]

∽

D. S. McDonald, the original Wonderland restauranteur, went bankrupt in 1908. He went to work in the R. H. White restaurant, which he had in former days managed as a sideline. He was still there at the beginning of 1910, but by the end of May he was running the Hotel Lucerne. He died in 1916 of a cerebral hemorrhage at the age of sixty-six and is buried in Mount Auburn Cemetery in Cambridge, Massachusetts.[27]

∽

Louis Bopp, who had several interests outside Wonderland on Revere Beach and who owned the Wonderland carousel and Whirl the Whirl, continued to run his other Revere Beach interests long after Wonderland closed. He committed suicide in St. Petersburg, Florida, on March 19, 1923, shooting himself in the head. It was thought that he killed himself out of despondency, having never gotten over the death of his son, Louis Jr., during the influenza epidemic five years earlier. He is buried in Royal Palm South Cemetery in St. Petersburg.[28]

∽

Herbert H. Pattee, after struggling along financially following his initial triumph with Love's Journey, finally achieved lasting success. In 1908, he became manager of the Winter Garden Theater in Boston. Two of his acts in the fall were Willard's Temple of Music and Oscar Babcock's Daredevil Bicycle Stunts (which had been featured at Wonderland). Pattee became the manager of Revere Beach's own Luna Park in 1909. He started com-petitive swimming contests there, weeding out potential swimming per-formers. He became known for "the water game" (swimming and diving girl shows), general theatricals, and by 1920 directing motion pictures. This must have been relatively easy for the former Broadway actor. *Variety* listed "Pattee's Mermaids" among the 1913 shows.[29] In fact, he wrote a musical comedy about diving girls in 1914—"Bunkum's Diving Girls." Pattee seems to have been active with shows and patents until the 1920s.[30] He remarried on September 10, 1914, to Helena Louise Gandrean of Lynn and had two children with her.[31] But they divorced sometime in the 1920s, and Helena remarried. By 1921, Herbert was managing another Luna Park in Miami, Florida.[32] He died on June 18, 1936, in Manhattan, and was buried in Mount Hope Cemetery in Westchester, New York.[33]

❧

Harry Guy Traver was just at the beginning of a long career when he sold the Circle Swing to Wonderland. He likewise sold that ride to parks all over the country. He founded the Raver Circle Swing Company in New York City in 1904, then used the profits to set up Traver Engineering Company in Beaver Falls, Pennsylvania, in 1919. At the Traver Engineering Company he designed more rides, many of them classics of the American amusement park, such as the Caterpillar and the Tumble Bug.[34]

But he was most famous for his roller coasters, in particular four that he built in the 1920s. His "Terrible Trio" consisted of the Cyclone in Crystal Beach Ontario; the Cyclone at Palisades Park, New Jersey; and the Lightning at Revere Beach. A fourth, the Zips at Oak Amusement Park in Portland, Oregon, completed the set. The Lightning was built in 1927. It was made of steel, not wood, and its only level section of track was where the passengers boarded. The only reason it wasn't called the Cyclone like the others was that a Cyclone roller coaster already existed at Revere Beach—built in 1924 by Traver, although not designed by him. The steel construction allowed for steep curves and sudden changes in direction. The ride was incredibly dangerous (one person was killed on the second day of operation), yet immensely popular. Lightning operated until 1933 and is still regarded as one of the most extreme and brutal of roller coasters.

Traver designed nine coasters in his life and constructed thirteen, in addition to all the smaller rides. He died in 1961 in New Rochelle, New York, running a small amusement park.

❧

Joseph Ferari, who ran Ferari's Wild Animals in Wonderland's first year, joined up with Dreamland at Coney Island in 1911. He retired from the act in 1918. His brother Francis died in 1914, but Joseph survived until 1953.[35]

⁊⁊

William C. Manning went on to a long career as a manager after Wonderland closed. By then he had already set up another Fire and Flames show in Manchester, England. In 1912, he organized a carnival and midway at Revere Beach. It featured a big plantation show, a girl show, pit shows, and a pony track. He started organizing a "mammoth scenic spectacle" traveling under a "Wild West Tent" with multiple train cars to carry it and its concessions, intended to travel from city to city. He was still working on this project in 1918. That year he was managing Pawnee Bill's show, the Monitor and Merrimac exhibit that had been at Jamestown and later Revere Beach, and a revamped Darktown Fire Brigade. The next summer he opened a permanent version of Darktown at Victory Park, Buckroe Beach, in Virginia. He advertised for "High-Class Colored Comedians, Sketch Teams, Musical Artists, and a 13-piece Colored Band." In 1921, he managed the Hurley Big Monkey Speedway on Revere Beach, "one of the big money getters on the beach," according to *Billboard*. He also managed a diving girl act that summer. In October of that year, Manning suffered for several hours with what he thought was a bilious attack before he called his doctor. It turned out to be a perforated appendix, and his doctor rushed him to Frost Hospital and operated. Manning spent a couple of weeks recuperating and announced that next season he would have something new for the entertainment world.[36] Unfortunately, we will never know what it was. The 1930 census reported him still living in Revere at 12 Everett Street, just a stone's throw from where Wonderland had been. He had disappeared from the entertainment news. The census gives his occupation as "painter" in an auto-body shop.[37]

Manning's senior partner, James J. Armstrong, continued to be the oldest and longest-running theatrical agent, and one well-liked in the business, until his death from pneumonia on February 4, 1918, at his home in Jersey City. *Billboard* called him the "Dean of all Vaudeville Agents," and reported that he "was always quick to respond to those who were needy. His good deeds are numbered into the thousands."[38]

❧

William H. "Bill" Kennedy continued to play the entertainment circuits, doing "Coney Island" amusement parks in Cincinnati, Ohio, in 1907 and Baltimore in 1908.[39] His appearances started to slow down after seven years, and in 1914 the entertainment paper the *New York Clipper* could ask, "Wm. (Wild Bill) Kennedy—Where are you and your Wild West? Have not heard from you for lo these many moons. A word, 'Wild Bill.'"[40] He, his wife, and many of the Wild West performers were with the Tom Atkinson Circus in Arizona in 1925.[41] Kennedy died on August 4, 1952, at the age of eighty-two of a heart ailment. His wife, Betsy, survived him. He is buried in Rose Hill Cemetery in Oklahoma City.[42]

❧

Robert J. Blake continued with his dog and pony show and in his association with Charles Willard for many years. They had a combined show in Canada in 1908 and opened a place on the boulevard in Revere Beach in 1909. According to a news story in the *Kokomo [Indiana] Daily Tribune*, both Blake and one of his horses, Bonita, were afflicted with apoplexy (a vague term that could mean internal bleeding but which more commonly meant what is now called a stroke, where a blood clot restricts blood flow to part of the brain) on the same day, June 16, 1916.[43] He was taken to the hospital and died the following night, as did the horse. Blake had returned to Kokomo two or three years previously. He was fifty-one years old.

❧

Charles D. Willard himself was extremely busy, with three separate Temple of Music/Trip to Harmonia companies, as well as his collaborations with Blake. Willard was performing until at least 1922, had visited Europe, set up a long-lasting Trip to Melodia at Luna Park in Coney Island, and finally settled into a semi-permanent location in Venice, California.[44] A young assistant who joined Willard's show in Venice was Kenneth Strickfaden, an excellent fit because he was fascinated by and talented in working with electrical devices. Strickfaden ended up acquiring many of Willard's electrical apparatus after Willard eventually retired and used them to create electrical effects for the movies. Strickfaden is most famous for building the devices used in the 1931 Universal film *Frankenstein* and its many sequels. He continued to work in film and in putting on electrical demonstrations for decades afterward, and provided the apparatus for Mel Brooks's film *Young Frankenstein* in 1975.[45] Ettie Scott (Kitty) Willard died in 1924 at sixty-one, but Charles was exceptionally long-lived, dying at ninety-eight in 1957. They are buried side by side in Cottonwood Cemetery in Cottonwood, Arizona.

❧

Warren Frazee, aka "Alligator Joe," had married Della Hamilton of Dade County, Florida, just before leaving for Wonderland in May 1906. The marriage lasted less than three years. He was performing at the Kansas City Electric Park Fair in 1909 and there met and married Cleopatra Croft of Kansas. They moved into his house in Palm Beach along with her mother, Carlotta, and his father and mother, Randolph and Anna.

He lost the lease to his alligator farm in 1911, when Miami wanted to gentrify its image. Alligator Joe moved elsewhere. He was in demand for the 1915 Panama-Pacific Exposition in San Francisco, and he shipped 4,500 alligators and crocodiles there, along with other assorted Florida swamp life—a manatee, pelicans, and blue heron. He became ill and was admitted to San Francisco's German Hospital on May 27, 1915; he died there four days later at the age of forty-three. An autopsy revealed that he suffered from pleurisy, pneumonia, tonsillitis, and fatty degeneration of the heart. His body was cremated. His Florida Alligator Jungle went on to a last—presumably precontracted—stop at San Diego and was then sold, its value estimated at $5,295.[46] His Florida property was bought by Paris Singer, son of sewing machine inventor and proprietor Isaac Singer, who built a home for disabled World War I veterans, the Touchstone Convalescent Home, which was later converted to a country club.

❧

Lincoln Beachey, the young dirigible aeronaut, continued his flights until about 1910, after which he obtained and flew an airplane. He showed the same sort of imagination and daring with heavier-than-air craft as with the dirigible. Wilbur Wright called him one of the best pilots. He was immortalized in verse by Carl Sandburg in 1912 in the poem "To Beachey." Sadly, he crashed into San Francisco Bay during an exhibition at the 1915

Panama-Pacific Exposition and was killed. For years later, his death was commemorated in an odd way by another poem—a jumping-rope rhyme:

> Lincoln Beachey thought it was a dream
> To go up to Heaven in a flying machine.
> The machine broke down and down he fell.
> Instead of going to Heaven he went to . . .[47]

☙

Contortionist and clown Walter Wentworth seems to have retired multiple times but returned to show business because he missed it—or needed the money.[48]

In December 1913, according to one account, he entered the Massachusetts State Infirmary in Tewksbury, Massachusetts, which was then functioning as a poor house, suggesting the old performer was broke. He died on February 6, 1916, having finally achieved the age of eighty that he had claimed for the previous ten years. He is buried in Glenwood Cemetery in Everett, Massachusetts.[49]

☙

The story of bareback rider Rose Wentworth and clown and rider Harry Wentworth went on for a surprisingly long time after their days at Wonderland. After playing Bass Point, the Wentworths joined the Pubillone Circus in Havana, which then went to Mexico, playing in Merida and Mexico City. Harry returned to New York City in February 1908 without Rose to arrange to send more acts for the circus to Mexico City. Something evidently happened while on the road because it appears they separated, both socially and professionally. Each went on performing but without the other. Harry was in Buffalo, New York, in July and August 1909. In interviews she gave later in life, Rose said that Harry died in 1909 but did not say where or under which circumstances.

Rose kept reinventing herself, performing new acts. Her official retirement notice appeared in *Billboard* for April 25, 1914.[50] Rose came out for one last performance to raise money and spirits for the war cause in 1915.

After that, she returned to her home in Willow Grove, Pennsylvania, on the death of her mother, taking care of her aging father by 1925. She started a boardinghouse for animals, typically keeping thirty dogs, ten cats, and assorted other animals, including an aged parrot.[51]

An interview in *Billboard* in 1945 observed that she was past seventy. She couldn't do the somersaults any longer, she said, but she could still keep on a horse. "She retired thirty years ago and hasn't been to a circus in twenty years," said the paper commented. She repeated her story about marrying Harry at fourteen and his death in 1909.[52]

Rose was still listed in a Circus Who's Who in 1954.

And what of Harry? Did he really die in 1909? And of what? He was still performing in July 1909.[53] An article on clowns of the past that appeared in *Billboard* on December 19, 1914, mentioned him among those that had passed away.

But then a news item, datelined Chicago, appeared in the *Urbana [Illinois] Courier-Herald* for Friday, October 10, 1913:

Clown Tells of Shattered Romance

Chicago, Oct. 10—The story of a shattered romance of a former circus clown was related to the police by Harry Wentworth, who is fifty eight years old. He asked to be sent to the bridewell. He said his wife, once a bareback rider, deserted him in Jenkinstown PA, taking $23,000 from the bank.[54]

Was this for real? The facts it relates all fit—Harry would have been fifty-eight in 1913. He was last seen in Chicago. Rose was, of course, a famous bareback rider. And Willow Grove is only five miles from Jenkintown, both districts in Philadelphia. Rose, in fact, gave an interview to the Jenkintown newspaper. If the man was an imposter, he was well-versed in Harry's history.

One can imagine other scenarios—a destitute Harry, or one suffering from blood poisoning from a broken foot not quite in his right mind, blaming Rose for his downfall and absconding with his money. Or maybe she really did run off with it, using it to finance her show. The story of the Harlequinade said that Punchinello and Columbine overcame many obstacles before they were finally married. But it doesn't say what happened afterward.

❧

Annette Kellermann, although world famous by now, was just at the beginning of her career. She continued performing for large crowds in major cities. In 1912, she finally married her manager and partner, Jimmy Sullivan, in Danbury, Connecticut.[55] They remained married for sixty years, until Sullivan's death. Kellermann made twelve movies between 1907 and 1924, in addition to several nonfiction films, utilizing much underwater photography. One of the films, the 1916 *Daughter of the Gods*, contained a nude scene. Only the last of her films, *Venus of the South Seas*, exists in its entirety, but portions of some of the others remain.

She lectured women's groups on diet and exercise, advocating for form-fitting bathing suits. She wrote *How to Swim* in 1918 and *Physical Beauty: How to Keep It* in 1919 to spread her philosophy. She maintained that she didn't have facial prettiness but said that anyone, with effort, diet, and exercise, could have a good body. She opened a health-food store in Los Angeles.

Always wanting to keep her act fresh, she learned tightrope walking and performed a cross-dress musical act on stage. The couple lived in California and Florida for a time but later returned to Australia. Kellermann lived to see the bikini bathing suit become a hit, but she deplored it, despite her stand on practical swimwear, saying that most women didn't have the body for it.[56] She continued to swim daily herself into her old age. She outlived Sullivan by two years, dying in 1975 at the age of eighty-eight.[57]

❧

Gordon William Lillie "Pawnee Bill" joined up with Buffalo Bill after the 1908 season at Wonderland, and they toured as "The Two Bills." May Lillie, who disapproved of the merger, returned to manage the couple's buffalo ranch in Pawnee, Oklahoma. The Two Bills show only lasted two years, then went bankrupt itself, and was foreclosed on in Denver. Afterward, Bill Lillie busied himself with the ranch and other business and banking activities. The couple celebrated their fiftieth wedding anniversary in 1936 in Taos, New Mexico. In September of that year, returning by car from a celebration in Tulsa, Bill lost control of the car and crashed. May died of her injuries. He survived, though injured physically and morally, and died six years later at the age of eighty-one.[58]

❧

Alize Espiridiona Cenda del Castillo, "Chiquita, the Doll Lady," continued to travel and perform, accompanied by her husband, Anthony Woeckener, playing Buffalo again in 1907 to general acclaim. Despite rumors of her death or of a divorce, they continued in their careers and marriage for many years. Despite Frank Bostock's fears and predictions, and against the odds, the Woeckener's marriage seems to have been a long-lasting and happy one.

Near the end of her life, the couple returned to Guadalajara, Mexico, the probable place of her birth, and she lived out the rest of her life there, dying in 1928. A notice in *Billboard* on August 6, 1932, notes, "Anthony C. Woeckener, former husband of the late well-known midget, Chiquita, after four years off the road is again touring. He is with Bahnaen's Circus Side Show with J.C. Weer Shows."[59]

In 1913, a piece of music was copyrighted by one Anthony C. Woeckener and published by Willis Music of Cincinnati, Ohio. Although possibly written by someone else, as a cornetist from a musical family, Woeckener was likely enough to have written and published music. The title of this piece was "May Your Heart with Mine Forever Rest," which is perhaps the best summation of the story of Tony and Chiquita.[60]

❦

Matthew Henson, the polar explorer, wrote a book about his experiences but it did not sell well.[61] His original tour of lectures was satisfactory, but there was little to follow it up, and he needed a living. He was fortunate to get a commission from President William Howard Taft at the office of the Collector of Customs in New York. It was not an interesting or well-paying job, but it kept Henson employed. He received a small pension from the armed forces, but, as he did not complete a full twenty-five years, he was unable to get a full pension, and the retirement rules kept him from working longer. His wife's job at a bank helped with the budget. And he still occasionally lectured.

Some people tried to draw attention to his situation, like journalist Lowell Thomas, who wrote a piece on Henson in 1939.[62] He was made a member of the Explorers Club in New York in 1937. Near the end of his life he received more recognition. A new biography of him appeared in 1947, and he was invited to meet Harry Truman and later Dwight Eisenhower at the White House in 1954.[63] He died in the Bronx in 1955 and was buried in Woodlawn Cemetery there, as was his wife in 1968.[64] In 1988, they were reinterred at Arlington National Cemetery, where in addition to the memorial stone there is a large bronze plaque devoted to him.

ფ

The people in this history, even those who were premature infants in the
Infant Incubator exhibit, are all dead now. Wonderland closed in 1910, and
the gulf separating that from today is at the outer extent of a human lifetime. A quotation from Stanley Kubrick's *Barry Lyndon*, suitably adapted
for our own age and situation, seems an appropriate way to conclude:

> It was during the administrations of Theodore Roosevelt and William How-
> ard Taft that the aforesaid personages lived and quarreled. Good or Bad,
> Handsome or Ugly, Rich or Poor, they are all equal now.

NOTES

Chapter 1: Opening Day and Background

1. The barkers' cries were reported in Rollin Lynde Hartt, "The Amusement Park," *Atlantic Monthly*, May 1907, 667–77, reprinted in Rollin Lynde Hartt, *The People at Play: Excursions in the Humor and Philosophy of Popular Entertainments* (Boston: Houghton Mifflin, 1909), 56, and *Boston Morning Journal*, July 14, 1906, 9.

2. *Boston Morning Journal*, August 11, 1906, 9.

3. *Boston Sunday Post*, April 1, 1906, 23.

4. *Boston Globe*, May 31, 1906, 4.

5. The ecology of Oak Island, when it still existed as a separate entity, was documented in Herbert Andrew Young, *A Catalogue of the Flora of Oak Island, Revere, Massachusetts, with Notes* (Salem, MA: Peabody Academy of Science, 1883).

6. Lieberman, *The Train on the Beach*.

7. Collen Sullivan, *Captain Paul Boyton—"Roughing It in Rubber": The True Adventure Story of One Man's 25,000 Miles in a Vulcanized Rubber Suit* (Seattle, WA: Booksurge, 2006); Paul Boyton, *The Story of Paul Boyton* (Milwaukee: Riverside, 1892).

8. *Revere Journal*, August 3, 1889, 4.

9. *Pittsburgh's Illustrated Society and Club Paper*, April 15, 1905, 30; Peter Tonge, "Jousting with the Lachine Rapids—Montreal's Latest Attraction," *Christian Science Monitor*, March 9, 1984, www.csmonitor.com.

10. "Shoot the Chute," Wikipedia, https://en.wikipedia.org; Spacemtfan, "Shoot the Chutes: A Look at the Original Water Ride and Intamin Contributions," ParkVault, February 28, 2015, https://parkvault.net; J. J. Newburgh, "Coaster," U.S. Patent no. 411,255, September 17, 1889, http://patft.uspto.gov.

11. Paul Boyton, "Amusement Device," U.S. Patent no. 849,970, April 9, 1907; "Heart of Coney Island," www.heartofconeyisland.com; Michael Immerso, *Coney Island: The People's Playground* (New Brunswick, NJ: Rutgers University Press, 2002), 60–86; Stephen M. Silverman, *The Amusement Park: 900 Years of Thrills and Spills and the Dreamers and Schemers Who Built Them* (New York: Black Dog and Leventhal, 2019), 129–30, 153–55.

12. Roltair is one of the generally underappreciated geniuses of the amusement park world; see Joseph Nickell, *Secrets of the Sideshows* (Lexington: University Press of Kentucky, 2008).

13. Immerso, *Coney Island*, 53–56; Silverman, *The Amusement Park*, 156–60, 177–78, 189–95; "Heart of Coney Island."

Chapter 2: The Boulanger of Wonderland

1. On the Great Baking Powder War, see Civitello, *Baking Powder Wars*; Abraham Cressy Morrison, *The Baking Powder Controversy* (New York: American Baking Powder Association, 1907), 1:126–45; and *Report of the Industrial Commission on Trusts and Industrial Combinations* (Washington, DC: Government Printing Office, 1901), 12:364.

2. Basic biographical material on Higgins can be found in *Wonderland Souvenir Magazine 1906*, [15].

3. "John Joseph Higgins," Find a Grave, www.findagrave.com.

4. Higgins was co-incorporator with A. W. Morehouse. *Thomasville [GA] Daily Times Enterprise*, July 19, 1895, 4; *Atlanta Constitution*, April 26, 1903, 3; *Thomasville Times Enterprise*, February 19, 1904, 12.

5. *New York Times*, June 5, 1900, 6.

6. *Boston Post*, November 29, 1906, 12. The marriage is also recorded in "Higgins Wedding," Marriages, 1841–1915, vol. 563, p. 704, entry 813, Massachusetts Vital Archives, www.sec.state.ma.us.

7. John Henry Huddleston, *Harvard College Class of 1886 Secretary's Report* (New York: De Vinne Press, 1907), 230.

8. *Lowell [MA] Sun*, October 25, 1905, 12.

9. *Billboard*, June 9, 1906, 8.

10. Besides the biography of Parker published in the *Wonderland Souvenir Magazine 1906*, there are obituaries describing his life in the *Journal of the Boston Society of Civil Engineers* 4 (December 1917): 443–44; *Good Roads: A Weekly Journal of Road and Street Engineering and Contracting* 50, no. 24 (December 9, 1916): 242; *Proceedings of the American Society of Civil Engineers* 43 (1917): 1891–92; and *Historic Homes and Institutions and Genealogical and Personal Memoirs of Worcester County Massachusetts with a History of Worcester Society of Antiquity*, ed. Ellery Bicknell Crane (New York: Lewis, 1907), 1:218.

11. *Wonderland Souvenir Magazine 1906*; *Boston Sunday Post*, April 15, 1906, 10.

12. *Boston Globe*, November 18, 1905, 10.

13. Cornelia Barroll died in 1885 at the age of thirty after only four years of marriage.

14. Barroll's supposed association with the B&O also appears in a story about Wonderland in the *Boston Sunday Post*, April 15, 1906, 10.

15. Report of the Railroad Commissioners, December 1893, in *Kentucky Public Documents* (Frankfort, KY: E. Polk Johnson, 1893), 2:171–72; *Poor's Directory of Railway Officials* (New York: American Bank Note Company, 1892), 478; *Report of the Eastern Kentucky Railway Company to the Railway Commissioners of Kentucky for the Year 1890* (Frankfort, KY: E. Polk Johnson, 1891), 166. Barroll is also listed in the reports for 1892, 1894, and 1896.

16. *American Mining and Metallurgical Manual* (Chicago: Mining Manual Company, 1920), 210.

17. "Modern Financial Institutions and Their Equipment: The Merchants National Bank of Boston," *Bankers Magazine,* July 1915, 73–78.

18. *Wonderland Souvenir Magazine 1906,* [7]; *American Mining and Metallurgical Manual,* 206–9, 211; "Note and Comment: The Case of Bigelow v. Calumet and Thecla Mining Company et al.," *Michigan Law Review* 6 (1907–8): 480–87.

19. Many of the members knew each other socially as well as through business. Besides Thomas Barroll's connections mentioned above, at least three of the members of Wonderland's board were members of Lancaster's First Church and later in the Lancastriana Club. Helen Maurer Lennon, *Lancaster Revisited* (Charleston, SC: Arcadia Books, 2005), 11.

20. *Annual Report of the Public Schools of Harrisburg, Pennsylvania with Manual for the Year Ending the First Monday in June, 1904* (Harrisburg, PA: Star-Independent, 1904), 58.

21. *Wonderland Souvenir Magazine 1906.*

22. *Boston Sunday Globe,* December 17, 1893, 26; *Boston Post,* April 25, 1891, 4; *Boston Sunday Post,* January 13, 1895, 16.

23. *Boston Globe,* May 24, 1896, 31; *Boston Globe,* June 4, 1896, 2; *Boston Globe,* May 17, 1896, 29.

24. *Boston Sunday Post,* August 21, 1904, 12.

25. The song actually had been performed on the vaudeville stage before *The Defender* opened and recorded onto cylinders. "In the Good Old Summertime," Secondhand Songs, https://secondhandsongs.com. But publishers were wary of printing seasonal music. The reception of Ring's version convinced them otherwise, the sheet music became a bestseller, and the song something of a classic that is still remembered today.

26. *Boston Sunday Post,* August 21, 1904, 12.

27. *Boston Sunday Post,* August 21, 1904, 12; *Boston Sunday Post,* December 4, 1904, 16; *New York Herald,* August 18, 1904, 18.

28. *New York Times,* August 18, 1904, 7; *New York Herald,* August 18, 1904, 18; *New York Press,* August 18, 1904, 10.

29. *New York Morning Telegraph,* August 18, 1904, 10.

30. *Boston Globe,* August 18, 1904, 11.

31. *Boston Post,* December 1, 1904, 5; *Boston Globe,* November 30, 1904, 8; *New York Dramatic Mirror,* December 17, 1904, 10.

32. *Cambridge [MA] Chronicle,* August 18, 1899, 6.

33. *New York Dramatic Mirror,* August 19, 1902, 18; *Cambridge Chronicle,* March 28, 1903, 4.

34. *Cambridge Chronicle,* September 10, 1904, 12.

35. *Boston Globe,* October 13, 1905, 6; *New York Sunday Morning Telegraph,* October 15, 1905, 14. An advertisement announcing that Wonderland Park and County Fair would be opening May 30, 1906. appeared in *Billboard,* October 21, 1905, 39.

36. The author of this unjust claim was none other than Floyd C. Thompson himself in an advertisement in *Billboard* magazine touting his own achievements. Advertisement, *Billboard,* October 27, 1906, 37.

37. Atlantic City is usually credited with having the first beachside boardwalk. It opened in 1870. See "Today in History—June 26," Library of Congress, www.loc.gov.

38. "Advantage of a Boardwalk," *White City Magazine*, February 1905, 20.

39. See, in particular, the fire insurance map published in "Boston's New Amusement Park 'Wonderland' at Revere," *The Standard*, March 17, 1906, 260–61, and the Sanborn Fire Insurance Map of Revere, 1906, Massachusetts State House Library, Boston.

40. "Wonderland: Marvelous Growth of the New Dream City," *Portsmouth [NH] Herald*, March 21, 1906, 4.

41. "The Old Mill Gone," *Revere Journal*, August 13, 1904, 1, 6.

42. "The Old Mill Gone," *Revere Journal*, August 13, 1904, 1, 6; "$70,000 Beach Blaze," *Revere Journal*, June 10, 1905, 1, 5.

43. "Boston's New Amusement Park 'Wonderland' at Revere," *The Standard*, March 17, 1906, 260–61.

44. "Fire Protection for Wonderland," *Fire and Water Engineering*, March 31, 1906, 157.

45. *Billboard*, May 5, 1906, 4; "Wonderland, Crowded with Entertainment," *Boston Sunday Post*, June 30, 1907, 31; *Wonderland Souvenir Magazine 1906*, [19].

46. *Billboard*, December 2, 1905, 51. Another story featuring the same illustration appeared in *The Midway*, December 1905. The illustration used by both stories ended up being reproduced as a color postcard for Wonderland, which was sold at the park, even though it did not at all resemble the final appearance of the park. Possibly they had been printed up in quantity in advance, in anticipation of the park's opening.

47. Igorotte natives from the Philippines had already been featured at the 1904 World's Fair in St. Louis and at Coney Island and were sought after by other amusement parks. Clair Prentice, *The Lost Tribe of Coney Island: Headhunters, Luna Park, and the Man Who Pulled Off the Spectacle of the Century* (New York: New Harvest, 2014).

48. *Billboard*, December 2, 1905, 51.

49. As late as February 11, 1906, it was still being reported that the firm of Shea & Moore was building Wonderland; see *Boston Sunday Post*, February 11, 1906, 32.

50. *Boston Post*, March 18, 1906, 19.

51. *New York Times*, October 3, 1906, 14. The *Boston Sunday Post*, May 20, 1906, 22, called Shea and Aldrich "men of the greatest experience, who for years past have made a business of building amusement parks," without saying that they did not do so as their own organization.

52. "Mechanics' Liens," *Brooklyn Daily Eagle*, June 30, 1905, 13.

53. "The Scenograph," *Electrical World* 24, no. 4 (July 28, 1894): 84; *Boston Globe*, October 6, 1894, 4; *Boston Sunday Post*, November 4, 1894, 12; *Boston Sunday Globe*, November 4, 1894, 25; "Electrical Effects at the Chicago Scenitorium," *Western Electrician* 14, no. 8 (February 24, 1891): 85–86.

54. "The World's Fair in Miniature," *Electrical Engineer*, August 1, 1894, 95.

55. A description of the Wonderland electrical system appeared in the *Boston Sunday Post*, July 8, 1906, 15; see also *Portsmouth Herald*, April 10, 1906, 4.

56. "New Amusement Concern," *Brooklyn Daily Eagle*, January 9, 1905, 15; *New York Times*, January 8, 1905, 24.

57. In fact, the board made the claim that Pusterla was the inventor of Creation, which he clearly was not. "Four Weeks to 'Wonderland,'" *Boston Sunday Post*, April 20, 1906, 19.

58. *Boston Post,* March 18, 1906, 19. This is probably the same ride described in the *Boston Sunday Post,* February 11, 1906, 32, as "Love's Rough Journey" (not to be confused with the ride designed by H. H. Pattee and called "Love's Journey"). Pusterla's ride was probably the one described as "Water Carousel," U.S. Patent no. 821,060, granted to A. Pusterla and P. Testi on May 22, 1906, http://patft.uspto.gov.

59. "Plays and Players," *Boston Globe,* February 25, 1906, 37.

60. "Industrial: Eastern," *Iron and Machinery World,* March 17, 1906, 22. Floyd C. Thompson, in setting the company up, announced that its business was to deal "in machinery," evidently to keep its real purpose secret. The certification was on March 1, 1906, as reported in "Table A: Corporations Existing under the Authority of This Commonwealth December 31, 1906," *Report of the Tax Commissioner of the Commonwealth of Massachusetts for the Year Ending November 30, 1906* (Boston: Wright and Potter, 1907), 230. It was officially disbanded in 1910.

61. *Boston Sunday Post,* March 4, 1906, 19.

62. *Boston Sunday Post,* March 4, 1906, 19.

63. There were interesting cultural clashes over the construction of the village. F. U. Shuichi (whose name is given as "Shichi" in some sources) was said to speak English with "tolerable fluency," but his construction tools were unfamiliar to the Boston crews working in the park. "And so, too," reported the *Boston Sunday Post,* March 11, 1906, 19 ("Wonderland's Growth"), "are the specifications for the Japanese Village. The latter, when submitted by Mr. Shichi to the building inspector at Revere, caused that official to remark that they were 'about as plain and significant to the average American as a Japanese war map.'" Nevertheless, Shuichi was able to get them approved. See also "Wonderland to Open Next Wednesday," *Boston Globe,* May 27, 1906, 40, and "Hard at Work in Wonderland Town," *Boston Sunday Post,* March 25, 1906, 25.

64. "Wonderland Nearly Finished," *Boston Sunday Post,* April 8, 1906, 19; "Wonderland Nearing Completion," *Revere Journal,* April 21, 1906, 2; "Beautiful Wonderland Will Open Its Doors to the Public on Memorial Day," *Boston Sunday Post,* April 15, 1906, 10; "Wonderland Bridge," *Boston Globe,* April 8, 1906, 26.

65. *Portsmouth Herald,* April 10, 1906, 4.

66. "Wonderland Opens May 30," *Boston Globe,* May 6, 1906, 42. There was also such a description in "Wonderland, Magic City, Thrown Open," *Boston Herald,* May 31, 1906, 5, and "Wonderland, a Veritable Dream City of Pleasure, Is Almost Completed," *Boston Sunday Post,* May 17, 1906, 19.

67. "Animals Pour In," *Boston Sunday Globe,* May 20, 1906, 14; "Army of Workmen Put Last Touches on 'Wonderland,'" *Boston Sunday Post,* May 20, 1906, 14.

68. "Public Christening for Baby Wonderland Panther-Leopard," *Boston Post,* May 28, 1906, 8.

Chapter 3: Year One—1906 (The Northern Half of the Park)

1. *Boston Globe,* May 31, 1906, 1–2, 4. Wonderland's opening day crowds were impressive especially since they coincided with the opening day and tenth anniversary of the opening of Norumbega Park in Boston. Norumbega broke its own previous attendance record with 25,000 attendees. *Boston Morning Journal,* May 30, 1906, 4; May 31, 1906, 2.

2. "Visited by 100,000—Opening of Wonderland at Revere Beach," *Boston Globe,* May 31, 1906, 4.

3. Hartt, *People at Play,* 43–84, 115–23.

4. *Boston Globe,* May 31, 1896, 18, and many issues afterward.

5. *Boston Post,* February 25, 1906, 14.

6. *Boston Post,* June 28, 1907, 4.

7. The quotations are repeated in *Boston Post,* June 28, 1907, 4.

8. Although there are pictures showing the building, no photograph of the actual carousel seems to exist.

9. *Boston Globe,* February 11, 1906, 44.

10. *Wonderland Souvenir Magazine 1906,* [33–34]. There is a detailed description in the *Boston Post,* June 17, 1907, 7, as well.

11. Attilio Pusterla, "Pleasure Waterway," U.S. Patent no. 776936, filed April 11, 1904, granted December 6, 1904, http://patft.uspto.gov.

12. *Boston Globe,* June 18, 1906, 5; "Outing for J. B. Pearson Co. Employees," *Men's Wear,* August 8, 1906, 62; "For Employees' Welfare," *Textile American,* July 1906, 48; *Wonderland Souvenir Magazine 1906,* [20–23, 25]; *Wonderland Souvenir Program 1908,* [3, 30]; *Boston Sunday Post,* June 17, 1906, 10; *Boston Morning Journal,* June 18, 1906, 5.

13. *Boston Globe,* January 9, 1903, 7; May 10, 1905, 16; March 19, 1905, 71; December 22, 1903, 1; December 18, 1902, 4; *Boston Post,* September 14, 1906, 7.

14. Wonderland 1906 Ledger Book, 120.

15. The Kipling quotation is from his 1892 poem "Mandalay." Arguably this was not the best source for this sentiment, since the speaker in the poem is definitely an unreliable narrator. The Tennyson quote is actually a misquote—"Europe" rather than "England"—from his famous 1835 poem "Locksley Hall."

16. *Boston Globe,* May 31, 1906, 4; May 27, 1906, 40; *Boston Post,* June 4, 1906, 8; July 26, 1906, 8.

17. LaMarcus A. Thompson was not related to either Frederic Thompson, builder of Darkness and Dawn, the Trip to the Moon, and Luna Park, nor to Floyd C. Thompson, builder of Wonderland. Floyd Thompson purchased the rights to a LaMarcus Thompson Scenic Railroad in 1905. *Paterson [NJ] Morning Call,* December 23, 1905, 5.

18. *Wonderland Souvenir Magazine 1906,* [32].

19. H. H. Pattee, "Amusement Device," U.S. Patent no. 826,738, was not granted until after Wonderland opened on July 26.

20. "Richard Savage," Internet Broadway Database, www.ibdb.com.

21. There is a large photograph of Pattee and a biography in *Billboard,* October 27, 1906, 6.

22. He also invented "an improved umbrella for use at the seashore," a new type of Ferris wheel, and a bicycle with its tire pump in the handlebars. *Warrensburgh [NY] News,* October 8, 1891, 1; *New York Herald,* July 4, 1897, 15; *Greensburg [IN] Daily Review,* February 24, 1900, 3.

23. *Canisteo [NY] Times-Republican,* May 31, 1905, 2.

24. *Boston Globe,* May 27, 1906, 40.

25. An image appears in *Billboard,* December 15, 1906, 59, and *Boston Sunday Post,* June 23, 1907, 25.

26. *Boston Globe,* January 2, 1907, 3; *Boston Sunday Post,* January 6, 1907, 26; *Washington [DC] Evening Star,* January 8, 1907, 5; *Boston Morning Journal,* August 18, 1906, 9.

27. *Billboard,* October 25, 1907, 39.

28. Richard Munch, *Harry G. Traver: Legends of Terror* (Mentor, OH: Amusement Park Books, 1982).

29. Munch, *Harry G. Traver,* 22.

30. H. G. Traver and C. W. Nichols, "Amusement Apparatus," U.S. Patent no. 758,341, April 26, 1904; "Traver's Circle Swing at Luna Park (ca. 1904)," Heart of Coney Island, www.heartofconeyisland.com.

31. "The Circle Swing Flying Machine," *Street Railway Review* 14, no. 12 (December 20, 1904): 982–83.

32. *St. Louis Sporting News,* July 26, 1886, 6.

33. The original is in the collection at Central University Libraries, Southern Methodist University, Dallas, TX. For an online version, see "W. C. Manning, Gymnast by SMU Central University Libraries," Sports Blog, August 9, 2012, http://archivedsports.blog spot.com.

34. *Los Angeles Herald,* September 13, 1888, 1.

35. *Cedar Rapids [IA] Evening Gazette,* August 1, 1902, 8; *Sandusky [OH] Daily Star,* August 28, 1901, 3.

36. *Sandusky Ohio Daily Star,* August 28, 1901, 3.

37. "Smokers and Vaudevilles," *New York Athletic Club Journal* 9, no. 1 (January 1902): 16; *New York Dramatic Mirror,* October 6, 1900, 22; June 13, 1903, 3; *Utica [NY] Journal,* March 23, 1902, 5; *Cedar Rapids Evening Gazette,* August 16, 1902, 6; *New York Clipper,* July 16, 1904, 20.

38. *New York Clipper,* October 22, 1904, 804; March 19, 1904, 38.

39. Armstrong was already referred to in 1898 as "the well-known dramatic agent." *Tammany Times* (New York, NY), February 7, 1898, 14.

40. "Bicyclists Greet Billboard in New York," *Billboard,* [n.d.] 1904, 4, copy in private collection.

41. *New York Sunday Telegraph,* April 30, 1905; *New York Dramatic Mirror,* April 29, 1905, 20; January 14, 1905, 11–12.

42. *New York Dramatic Mirror,* December 31, 1904; Robert Grau, *Forty Years Observation of Music and the Drama* (New York: Broadway, 1909), 33. Armstrong was described as "the oldest in service of the vaudeville agents of to-day. He is also a man who has occupied every possible position in the theatrical field during the last thirty years." He began as treasurer to Michael B. Leavitt's All Star Company in 1883. Michael Bennett Leavitt, *Fifty Years in Theatrical Management* (New York: Broadway, 1912), 271.

43. The catalogue of the 1903 Earl's Court exposition is available online at "1903 International Fire Exposition (London: Kelliher and Company, 1903)," https://archive.org. See also Lynn Kathleen Sally, *Fighting the Flames: The Spectacular Performance of Fire at Coney Island* (New York: Routledge, 2006), 49–56.

44. *Billboard*, February 9, 1907, 31.

45. *Boston Morning Journal*, May 26, 1906, 9. See also *Boston Sunday Post*, May 6, 1906, 19.

46. "Wonderland Park, Boston," *Variety*, June 30, 1906, 13.

47. *Wonderland Fire and Flames Souvenir Book 1906*, [5].

48. *Wonderland Souvenir Magazine 1906*, [25].

49. "Giuseppe Creatore," Wikipedia, https://en.wikipedia.org. Creatore himself had performed in Boston the week of May 6, 1906, so many people would have been directly familiar with his style. *Boston Sunday Post*, May 6, 1906, 19.

50. "Salem Cadets Band's Melodies Enchant Wonderland," *Boston Sunday Post*, July 1, 1906, 26; *Wonderland Souvenir Magazine 1906*, [21, 25].

51. We know of the shooting gallery and its location solely because of the 1906 Revere Sanford Insurance Map, Massachusetts State House Library, Boston, and the Wonderland 1906 Ledger Book, 176–77. I have found no record of it in the souvenir books or in any newspaper report of the park.

52. The card-cutting receipts are recorded in the Wonderland 1906 Ledger Book, 253. A description of card cutting appears in C. W. James, *It Was Never a Gamble: The Life and Times of an Early 1900s Hustler* (New York: Writer's Club Press, 2000), 21–23.

53. Box Ball receipts are listed in the Wonderland 1906 Ledger Book, 12–13. It brought in $382.50 over the course of the summer of 1906. An advertisement for a Box Ball court appears in *Billboard*, May 5, 1906, 2.

54. *Wonderland 1906 Ledger Book*, 144–45.

55. According to the Wonderland 1906 Ledger Book, the Dodger ran from June 17 until the park closed. It generated $639.80 of business in that time. Jack Everhart apparently took it over for the 1907 season and placed an advertisement for a new Dodger in the *Boston Post*, May 27, 1907, 11.

56. *Boston Post*, July 24, 1909, 2.

57. There have been several recent webpages devoted to the African Dodger. See Jim Crow Museum, October 2012, Ferris State University, www.ferris.edu. The Snopes website treated it on February 16, 2018, at www.snopes.com. A very comprehensive site with contemporary images showing how widespread and common the attraction was is at AmeriPics, January 10, 2016, https://ameripics.wordpress.com. On the "Dunk Tank" (originally called the "Chocolate Drop" or "African Dip"), see http://davegilson.com.

Chapter 4: Year One—1906 (The Southern Half of the Park)

1. The most informative sources for Kennedy's background are his obituaries: "Kennedy, W. H.," *Billboard*, August 16, 1952, 52; "Requiem Today for Wild West Show Pioneer," *Oklahoman* [Oklahoma City], August 6, 1952, 6.

2. "Paragon Park," *Boston Post*, June 6, 1905, 4.

3. *Billboard*, August 18, 1906, 30; September 1, 1906, 28, 34; September 22, 1906, 30.

4. "Paragon Park," *Boston Post*, June 6, 1905, 4.

5. "Cheyenne Chief Visits the Falls," *Buffalo [NY] Morning Express*, May 12, 1906, 6. Other stories about Toughfeather appear in "Real Indians Here," *Baltimore Sun*, May

21, 1908, 7; "Indian Chief Thinks He Could 'Down' the Mayor," *Baltimore Sun,* May 24, 1908, 11; and "Indians Cash Checks," *Baltimore Sun,* May 29, 1908, 12.

6. The *Wonderland Souvenir Magazine 1906,* [34–35], also calls "Wild Bill" Kennedy a colonel, but honorary titles were almost obligatory at the park. Regarding Chief Toughfeather's being present at Little Big Horn, the most comprehensive list of Indian participants does not include a Toughfeather but does list a Cheyenne named "Two Feathers," which might be the correct form of his name. See Gary Gilbert and Joy Gilbert, "Custer Battlefield Project," Friends of the Little Big Horn Battlefield, www. friendslittlebighorn.com. Toughfeather was in his early seventies in 1906, which would have made him about forty at the time of Little Big Horn.

7. "Mayor Accosted as 'Raffles' at Wonderland," *Boston Post,* July 20, 1906, 9.

8. "Wild West Luncheon," *Boston Globe,* June 27, 1906, 13. Another luncheon was reported in "Gives Banquet at Wonderland," *Billboard,* July 14, 1906, 14.

9. "Wonderland's Popularity," *Fitchburg [MA] Sentinel,* August 7, 1906, 5. See also "Midsummer Shows Draw Crowds to Parks and Theaters: Wonderland," *Boston Post,* August 7, 1906, 4; "Girl Has Thrilling Fight with Bucking Broncho at Wonderland," *Boston Morning Journal,* August 7, 1906, 9; and "Wonderland's Popularity," *Revere Journal,* August 11, 1906, 2.

10. A biography of her may be found in John Rumm, "Girls Gone Wild West," Buffalo Bill Center for the West, March 10, 2014, https://centerofthewest.org.

11. *Billboard,* January 6, 1917, 27; February 24, 1906, 22; "Midsummer Shows: Wonderland," *Boston Sunday Post,* June 17, 1906, 4; "Wonderland's Big Shows," *Fitchburg Sentinel,* June 15, 1906, 8; "Indians, Cow Boys, and Cow Maids at Wonderland Depict Thrilling and Sensational Adventures," *Boston Morning Journal,* July 7, 1906, 9.

12. "Operated on the Alligator," *New York Times,* May 2, 1906, 9.

13. "A New Coney Island Thriller," *Sandusky [OH] Star,* March 23, 1904, 7. The same story appeared in other local papers that month. Another description appears in *Billboard,* March 5, 1904, 8.

14. General descriptions and photographs of Wonderland in its opening days can be found in "The Glorious Awakening of a Truly Wonderland: Greater Boston's New Million Dollar Park," *Billboard,* June 16, 1906, 8; "Gigantic Amusement Enterprise for Boston," *Boston Sunday Globe,* February 11, 1906, 44; "Wonderland Opens May 3—New Amusement Park at Revere Beach," *Boston Globe,* May 6, 1906, 42; "Wonderland to Open Next Wednesday," *Boston Globe,* May 27, 1906, 40; "Wonderland. Magic City, Thrown Open" and "Scenes at New Wonderland Park, Revere," *Boston Herald,* May 31, 1906, 1; "Wonderland Ready to Welcome Hub Crowds Next Wednesday," *Boston Morning Journal,* May 26, 1906, 9; "Boston Is to Have Million Dollar Amusement Enterprise at Revere Beach," *Boston Sunday Post,* February 11, 1906, 32; "Wonderland's Awakening," *Concord [MA] Enterprise,* June 6, 1906; and "Wonderland," *Fitchburg Sentinel,* March 2, 1906, 8.

15. Two books have recently been published about the amazing Martin A. Couney: Dawn Raffel, *Strange Case of Dr. Couney,* and Clare Prentice, *Miracle at Coney Island: How a Sideshow Doctor Saved Thousands of Babies and Transformed American Medicine* (N.p.: Amazon Digital Services, 2016).

16. "Many Novel Features," *Boston Globe,* October 6, 1903, 11; "Exhibit in Mechanics Hall," *Boston Globe,* September 6, 1903, 40; "Mechanics Hall Exhibit," *Boston Globe,* September 27, 1903, 40; "Incubator Babies Thrive," *Boston Globe,* October 14, 1903, 9.

17. "Baby Incubators," *Boston Globe,* June 3, 1904, 10; "Drama and Music," *Boston Globe,* June 7, 1904, 11.

18. "Drama and Music," *Boston Globe,* June 28, 1904, 11.

19. "All Wondering," *Boston Globe,* July 4, 1904, 12; *Revere Journal,* July 9, 1904, 5.

20. The incubators did not actually open until June 6, 1906. See "Infant Incubators Open at Wonderland," *Boston Morning Journal,* June 6, 1906, 5; "Actress Bessie Barriscale Seeks to Adopt 'Midget,' Wonderland's Tiny Incubator Baby," *Boston Post,* September 6, 1906, 3; and *Boston Globe,* June 3, 1907, 5.

21. "The Construction and Operation of Penny Arcades for Service in Railway Parks," *Street Railway Journal* 27, no. 12 (March 24, 1906): 470–71.

22. Nat Burgess was "one of Boston's best-known slot machine men." He also ran arcades on Revere Beach and at Paragon Park in Nantasket. *Billboard,* February 2, 1907, 10. He is listed in the Wonderland 1906 Ledger Book, 132.

23. Later accounts of Gillett's show appeared in the *New York Press,* August 30, 1914, 5, and "Performing Dogs Amuse Crystal Beach Folks," *Buffalo [NY] Courier,* August 28, 1919, 5, among other places.

24. The Wonderland 1906 Ledger Book shows "The South before the War" beginning on July 10 and running through September 16 (220–21). The Gillett Circus at the children's theater is shown as running from opening day through July 9 (28–29).

25. "Wonderland Is Well Worthy of Its Name," *Boston Post,* March 18, 1906, 10.

26. *Washington Post,* July 9, 1905, 35.

27. "Luna Park Will Be 'Made Over,'" *New York Press,* April 24, 1904, 5.

28. Revere Beach already had a "Phantom" submarine ride, built by Herbert N. Ridgeway and run by his Autonomous Boat Company.

29. "Wonderland Crowded with Entertainment," *Boston Post,* June 30, 1907, 31.

30. "Jiu-Jitsu, As It Is Really Used by Japs, Exemplified at Wonderland," *Boston Morning Journal,* August 25, 1906, 9.

31. "Sunday Post Free Wonderland Tickets Eagerly Sought," *Boston Sunday Post,* June 23, 1907, 25. "Virginia Knapp," surprisingly, was a pseudonym. Her real name was Mrs. F. P. Sargent. "Summer Parks," *Variety,* February 24, 1906, 11.

32. Hartt, *People at Play,* 77.

33. "Summer Attractions at the Theaters Well Patronized—at Wonderland," *Boston Sunday Post,* July 3, 1906, 35; "Third Degree at Wonderland Full of Mirth-Provoking Sensations," *Boston Morning Journal,* July 14, 1906, 9.

34. They were operating in 1904 but incorporated in Buffalo, New York. "Incorporations," *New York Times,* April 4, 1905, 16. The directors were L. W. Walter, D. J. Cadotte, and W. H. Winquist. The company operated for twenty years until dissolving in 1926. "Proclamation," *Erie County Independent* [Hamburg, NY], March 11, 1926, 9.

35. "Legal Tangle in Dreamland," *Buffalo Courier,* June 1, 1907, 7, and "Who Owns Concession?" *Buffalo [NY] Morning Express,* June 1, 1907, 8.

36. Hartt, *People at Play,* 76–77.

37. Advertisement, *Boston Post*, July 23, 1906, 8.

38. Horses are not colorblind, but their vision is not quite as good as that of a human. They can see approximately as well as a person with red-green colorblindness.

39. P. Tait, *Wild and Dangerous Performances: Animals, Emotions, Circus* (New York: Palgrave Macmillan, 2011), 39.

40. "Public Christening for Baby Wonderland Panther-Leopards," *Boston Post*, May 28, 1906, 8.

41. "Numidian Lion at Wonderland Said to Be Most Magnificent in Captivity," *Boston Morning Journal*, July 28, 1906, 9.

42. Advertisement, *Boston Morning Journal*, August 17, 1906, 4.

43. *Glen Falls [NY] Morning Star*, December 30, 1895, 8; December 27, 1895, 8; *Lowell [MA] Sun*, June 13, 1899, 21; *Boston Sunday Post*, April 29, 1900, 14. He was also a magician and sleight of hand artist. *Glen Falls [NY] Daily Times*, April 4, 1895, 5. Among his stranger acts was "being nailed to a tree." *Boston Globe*, December 20, 1898, 2; *Boston Sunday Globe*, December 20, 1898, 2.

44. "Aerial Nuptials," *Glen Falls Morning Star*, August 17, 1894, 20; "A Blooming, Blushing Bride," *Glen Falls Daily Times*, August 18, 1894, 2; "A Wedding Trip Skyward," *Johnstown [NY] Daily Republican*, August 22, 1894, 12.

45. *Glen Falls [NY] Daily Times*, June 20, 1895, 4.

46. Intriguingly, La Roux himself was almost killed during a performance at Revere Beach five years before Wonderland opened. His balloon started deflating, so he cut loose the parachute, which just had time to open before he struck first the veranda of a cottage on the beach, then bounced off a picket fence before landing in a pool of water. Spectators, thinking he was dead, were surprised when he got up, apparently unhurt, and went on to another performance that day. "A Close Call—Aeronaut Came Very Near Being Killed," *Lowell Sun*, August 29, 1901, 48.

47. *Boston Sunday Post*, August 5, 1906, 15.

48. Garvin appears to have been local Boston talent. She had performed at Walker's Museum in Boston as "The French Model" in 1905. See "Just before Start of Hair-Raising Balloon Trip," "Sensational Balloon Ascent at Wonderland," and "Drops from Sky Close by Express," *Boston Morning Journal*, July 26, 1906, 1, 2, 3. "Manager Thompson Ballooning," *Revere Journal*, July 28, 1906, 5, states that La Roux was to make the ascent, but this is contradicted by the account in the *Boston Morning Journal*.

49. There is a photograph of Thompson preparing for his balloon flight in "Park Manager Turns Balloonist," *Billboard*, October 6, 1906, 32. It appears to have been taken in the space between the Hell Gate ride and the carousel, with the back of the ballroom and restaurant building visible in the background. The same photo appears on the front page of the *Boston Morning Journal*, July 28, 1906.

50. "Manager Thompson Ballooning," *Revere Journal*, July 28, 1906, 5.

51. "Holds Balloon by the Arms—Floyd C. Thompson Painfully Hurt by Terrible Experience," *New York Press*, July 26, 1906, 1, claimed, "It was only the encouragement of his companion, Mme. LaCroux [*sic*] that prevented Thompson from becoming temporarily insane and dropping far below among the terror-stricken multitude." The report went on to note that "as the balloon shifted its course Mr. Thompson reached for his

hat with his free hand and lost his balance. People who watched the ascent with glasses describe the sight as horrifying. Every one is loud in their praise of Mr. Thompson's nerve."

52. "Near Death in the Sky—Thompson Dangles by One Hand on Balloon Trapeze 5000 Feet in the Air," *Boston Post,* July 26, 1906, 1. The newspaper put the story on its front page, directly below the title, including a sketch of the balloon with La Roux sitting in her trapeze and Thompson dangling from his by both hands (despite the headline).

53. "Holds Balloon by the Arms—Floyd C. Thompson Painfully Hurt by Terrible Experience," *New York Press,* July 26, 1906, 1, claimed that he was attended by two doctors named Dow and Royal, "who applied electrical massage for two hours to restore circulation."

54. "Manager Thompson Ballooning," *Revere Journal,* July 28, 1906, 5.

55. The story was, not surprisingly, picked up by newspapers around the country. See, for example, "Dangled 3000 Feet in Air—Plight of Amateur Aeronaut at Seaside Resort," *Harrisonburg [VA] Daily News,* July 28, 1906, 3, and "Balloonist Makes Thrilling Ascent," *New Castle [PA] News,* August 1, 1906, 2. The story was also reported locally; see "Just before Start of Hair-Raising Balloon Trip," "Sensational Balloon Ascent at Wonderland," and "Drops from Sky Close by Express," *Boston Morning Journal,* July 26, 1906, 1, 2, 3, and "Manager Thompson Ballooning," *Revere Journal,* July 28, 1906, 5.

56. John Winthrop Hammond, "A Tribute to Walter D'arcy Ryan," *General Electric Review* 37, no. 4 (April 1934): 321–22; "Walter D'arcy Ryan," Wikipedia, https://en.wikipedia .org.

57. "An Evening Photographic Production of the Electric Steam Scintillator," *Lynn [MA] Daily Evening Item,* July 17, 1906, 5; "The Scintillator," *Lynn Daily Evening Item,* July 14, 1906, 2; "Harmonious Blending of Tints by Electric Steam Color Scintillator," *Lynn Daily Evening Item,* July 13, 1906, 10; Advertisement, *Lynn Daily Evening Item,* July 12, 1906, 8; *Boston Sunday Post,* July 15, 1906, 15; "Lynn Man's Idea—Ryan's Scintillator Will Illumine Niagara," *Boston Globe,* July 14, 1906, 15.

58. Advertisement, *Lynn Daily Evening Item,* July 10, 1906, 6.

59. "Rail and Boat to Bass Point," *Boston Sunday Post,* July 15, 1906, 15.

60. Hillman, *Looking Forward,* 41–42.

61. "Wonderland," *Boston Sunday Post,* September 9, 1906, 20.

62. "Theater Gossip—Wonderland," *Boston Post,* September 11, 1906, 9; *Boston Post,* September 12, 1906, 12. The original closing date for the first season of Wonderland was to have been September 9, but on September 2 the park announced it would remain open for another week until September 16. The owners may have wanted to "get their money's worth" out of the hiring of the Scintillator. "Wonderland," *Boston Sunday Post,* September 2, 1906, 16.

63. "Old Boston Town Topics Relating to Amusements," *Billboard,* September 29, 1906, 10; "Wonderland Closes Phenomenal Season," *Boston Morning Journal,* September 15, 1906, 9; "Wonderland Season Ends in Blaze of Glory," *Boston Morning Journal,* September 17, 1906, 5; "Drama and Music—Wonderland at Revere," *Boston Globe,* August 26, 1906, 37. Average daily attendance at Wonderland was estimated at twenty thousand. *Boston Morning Journal,* June 16, 1906, 9. But another source set the average

daily attendance at thirty to forty thousand. "Wonderland Is Booming," *Revere Journal*, August 25, 1906, 2. The *Boston Post*, June 6, 1906, 7, reported twenty thousand in attendance at the first Sunday the park was open; for June 10 it was estimated to be sixty thousand. "At Wonderland, 60,000; Revere Beach 150,000; Nantasket 24,000," *Boston Morning Journal*, June 11, 1906, 5. A crowd of sixty thousand was also reported in "Crowd of 60,000 in Wonderland Gates," *Boston Morning Journal*, June 25, 1906, 3. The crowd on July 4, 1906, was estimated at 50,000 to 75,000. "Wonderland's Wondrous Popularity," *Portsmouth [NH] Herald*, July 6, 1906, 5.

64. *Boston Post*, September 20, 1906, 10.

65. *Boston Post*, September 14, 1906, 7.

66. *New York Deaf and Mutes Journal* [Mexico, NY], October 25, 1906.

Chapter 5: The Rise and Fall of Floyd C. Thompson

1. *Wonderland Souvenir Magazine 1906*, [11].

2. Floyd was actually born not in upstate New York but in the town of Cedar Falls, Iowa. His family had moved out there the year before, and his father started the Bank of Cedar Falls. Five years later they abruptly returned to New York, amid accusations of embezzlement. "Business Houses, Professional Men, &c.—Bankers," *Cedar Falls [IA] Gazette*, December 30, 1870, 2; *Waterloo [IA] Courier*, December 13, 1876, 8.

3. Presently Bethany, New York. *Attica [NY] Daily News*, March 3, 1926, 12.

4. *Albany College of Pharmacy, 13th Commencement Exercises Program*, March 13, 1894, Albany College of Pharmacy and Health Sciences, Albany, NY. Floyd C. Thompson of Albany is listed as one of twenty graduates, but he is not listed among the class officers, executive committee, or valedictorian. See also "College of Pharmacy," *Hudson [NY] Daily Evening Register*, March 14, 1894, 2.

5. *Catskill [NY] Recorder*, May 31, 1895, 2. It seems likely that the pharmacy was the one his father had just opened, possibly intending it to be a family business. "Up the State," *Merck's Market Report* 4, no. 7 (April 1, 1895): 140.

6. "Weddings Announced," *Albany [NY] Times-Union*, October 8, 1895, 1; "Hymneal—Thompson-Burdick" and "Marriages—Thompson-Burdick," *Catskill Recorder*, October 18, 1895, 2; "Burdick-Thompson," *Albany Times-Union*, October 15, 1895, 1.

7. "Births," *Windham [NY] Journal*, July 18, 1899, 2.

8. "New Corporations," *New York Times*, October 21, 1900, 25; "New Corporations," *New York Times*, November 2, 1900, 10; "News of the Month—New York," *Western Druggist*, November 1900, 643; "Stock Companies Incorporated," *Rochester [NY] Democrat and Chronicle*, October 21, 1900, 9; "Incorporated at Albany," *New York Tribune*, October 21, 1900, 7.

9. "Catskill Company," *Albany Times-Union*, November 1, 1900, 1; "Catskill Medical Company," *Hudson Daily Evening Register*, November 1, 1900, 2.

10. *Albany Times-Union*, June 19, 1901, 1.

11. *Albany Times-Union*, July 21, 1897, 1; "Northern New York," *Plattsburgh [NY] Press*, July 23, 1897, 11.

12. "Trade Notes," *Geyer's Stationer* 29, no. 6985 (March 22, 1900): 7.

13. Thompson and his family are listed as living in Manhattan in the New York 1905 census. Manhattan AD 19, ED 11, Digital Folder 004518315.

14. *Polk's (Trow's) New York Copartnership and Corporation Directory*, March 1904, 251.

15. *Annual Reports for 1904 Made to the Seventy Seventh General Assembly of the State of Ohio* (Columbus, Ohio: F. J. Heer, 1904), part 1:517.

16. Advertisement, *Pacific Medical Journal* 46 (January–December 1903): 44.

17. *The Trow Copartnership and Corporation Directory of the Boroughs of Manhattan and the Bronx, City of New York*, March 1906, 716; *Electrical World and Engineer* 43 (June 4, 1904): 1107; "New York Incorporations," *New York Times*, May 19, 1904, 11.

18. One of these was likely the "Pressure Regulator" he had applied to patent in 1902. F. M. Ashley, "Pressure Regulator," U.S. Patent no. 824,681, June 26, 1906, http://patft.uspto.gov.

19. *Middletown [NY] Daily Argus*, April 8, 1904, 1.

20. A New Coney Island Rises from the Ashes of the Old," *New York Times*, May 8, 1904, 5. See also "Advertisement," *New York Times*, May 8, 1904, 29; *New York Times*, July 4, 1904, 7; "Cars Collide for Fun," *Technical World Magazine* 6, no. 1 (September 1906): 79; "The Leap-Frog Railway," *Scientific American*, July 8, 1905, 29–30; and P. K. Stern, "Railway and Railway Car," U.S. Patent no. 814245, March 6, 1906.

21. "Stern's Duplex Railway, American Mutoscope and Biograph 1905 H64925," YouTube, www.youtube.com; "Stern's Duplex Railway (Leapfrog Railway)," https://imgur.com.

22. Local papers claimed that Thompson had long been interested in show business, saying that he has been seduced by the lure of the "Byron Spaun tented shows on the west side [of Catskill], a 'stonethrow' from druggist Thompson's place of business," and that "the man of drugs finally felt the show bee in his bonnet and started off through the country as a medicine man, traveling with wagons and with a handful of variety performers. Later he closed out his drug business at Catskill and entered the employ of a New York drug house." "Manager $1,000,000 Dollar Park—Former Catskill Druggist Vice President of Boston Amusement Resort," *Cobelskill [NY] Index*, November 29, 1906, 1.

23. "Steeplechase Park Plans," *New York Sun*, November 4, 1904, 14; "The Stadium Company of New York," *Rome [NY] Daily Sentinel*, November 10, 1904, 4; "Stadium Company Organized," *New York Herald*, December 1, 1904, 12.

24. "Stadium Company Incorporated," *New York Evening Post*, November 30, 1904, 1.

25. The sale by George Tilyou of Steeplechase Park was such a seismic event that you would think it would be well-covered in the historical literature. Yet the only source discussing it is a single article in a relatively obscure magazine. See [James Abbate], "Steeplechase Park, Sold in 1904?" *National Amusement Park Historical Association News* 35, no. 1 (2014): 3–5. Contemporary sources on it include "Steeplechase Park Plans," *New York Sun*, November 5, 1904, 5; *Billboard*, November 1904, 7; *Brooklyn Daily Eagle*, December 1, 1904, 6; *Brooklyn Daily Standard Union*, November 5, 1904, 4; "Big Change at Coney Island," *New York Dramatic Mirror*, November 12, 1904, 17; "New Syndicate Buys Steeplechase Park," *Brooklyn Daily Standard Union*, November 2, 1904, 5; "Big Resort Sold," *New York Daily Tribune*, November 3, 1904, 14; "Steeplechase Park Sold?" *New York Sun*, November 2, 1904, 1; "The Stadium Co. of New

York," *Rome Daily Sentinel,* November 30, 1904, 4; *Brooklyn Daily Standard Union,* December 1, 1904, 3; *Iron and Machinery World* 96, no. 24 (December 10, 1904): 28; "Stadium Company Incorporated," *New York Evening Post,* November 30, 1904, 1; *New York Morning Telegraph,* December 23, 1904, 10; "Stadium Company Has Lease of Park," *New York Morning Telegraph,* December 25, 1904, 1; *New York Herald,* December 1, 1904, 12; and "Coney Island Deal Now Off," *New York Morning Telegraph,* February 6, 1905, 2. The sale is recorded in *Real Estate Record and Builder's Guide* 74 (October 29, 1904): 939.

26. *New York Morning Telegraph,* December 23, 1904, 10.

27. *New York Morning Telegraph,* February 6, 1905, 2; *Billboard,* February 11, 1905, 2.

28. "New York Incorporations," *New York Times,* January 8, 1905, 24.

29. *New York Times,* February 5, 1905, 15.

30. "Warrant for Private Reason," *New York Sun,* May 26, 1905, 8; "Paid in Wind, He Says, for Parachute Stock," *New York Morning Telegraph,* May 26, 1905, 8.

31. "Judgments," *New York Times,* September 13, 1905, 6; "Judgments," *New York Times,* September 14, 1905, 5.

32. "Judgments," *Real Estate Record and Builder's Guide* 76 (September 16, 1905): 457.

33. Notable newspaper accounts praising Thompson's efforts appeared in *Billboard,* June 9, 1906, 8 (which had a large portrait picture of Thompson); "Amusement Week Reviewed—News from the Big Towns," *Billboard,* July 7, 1906, 4; "One Summer Attraction Leaves Boston Theater—Wonderland Parks Remarkable Success Is Almost Startling," *Billboard,* August 4, 1906, 6; and *Billboard,* December 15, 1906, 92. No comparable articles giving credits to any other park officials appeared in any of the papers during Wonderland's operation. In the *New York Dramatic Mirror,* June 9, 1906, 19, Thompson claimed to be vice president as well as general manager of Wonderland.

34. "Vanity Fair and Floyd C. Thompson," *Billboard,* October 20, 1906, 32; *New York Dramatic Mirror,* September 29, 1906, 22.

35. *Billboard,* October 21, 1905, 6.

36. *Billboard,* October 20, 1906, 4. Another announcement appears, buried in small print in the center of the page, in the *Boston Post,* October 12, 1906, 6.

37. "Point of Pines, Boston, Mass.," *Billboard,* January 12, 1907, 31. There was a conceptual sketch and description of the Point of Pines park in the same issue; other images and descriptions of the proposed park appeared in the *Boston Globe,* January 20, 1907, 37, and *Boston Sunday Post,* January 20, 1907, 35. The bathhouse for 7,500 bathers was reported in the *Boston Post,* October 29, 1906, 7. See also *Cambridge Chronicle,* March 11, 1905, 15, for the early history of Paradise.

38. "The Social Whirl Wins with Boston Theatregoers," *Billboard,* October 27, 1906, 37. The same issue also ran a news story about Thompson's new venture at Point of Pines on page 4. A report in the *New York Dramatic Mirror,* October 27, 1906, 10, reported that he went to New York to seek funding for the park.

39. *Billboard,* November 3, 1906, 37; November 10, 1906, 37.

40. "Business Troubles—Out of Town," *New York Times,* December 9, 1906, 21.

41. "Business Troubles," *New York Times,* December 9, 1906, 21.

42. *Variety,* January 5, 1907, 12.

43. He was named president of the Point of Pines Construction Company in the *New York Clipper,* January 26, 1907, 1289.

44. "Seattle," *New York Dramatic Mirror,* August 3, 1907, 9.

45. *Seattle Star,* September 26, 1907, 8; September 27, 1907, 1, 3; "Seattle," *New York Dramatic Mirror,* October 12, 1907, 11; *New York Clipper,* October 26, 1907, 684; *Billboard,* October 19, 1907, 42.

46. *Spokane [WA] Press,* August 21, 1907, 4.

47. *Seattle Republican,* October 25, 1907, 3. *New York Clipper,* November 2, 1907, 1102, stated that the site had closed "for an indefinite period." The Seattle Eden Musée reopened just before Christmas with a new manager and a new set of attractions, but it was swamped with debt and closed for good on Valentine's Day in 1908. See *Seattle Star,* February 15, 1908, 3. Yet another attraction called the Eden Musée, this one modeled more closely on the one in New York, opened in Seattle in June 1908.

48. "Seattle, Wash.," *Billboard,* November 23, 1907, 4.

49. 1908 Los Angeles directory, cited in Bill Counter, "Wonderland," Los Angeles Theaters, https://losangelestheatres.blogspot.com.

50. *Los Angeles Times,* January 4, 1908, 13. Typically, although it was stated that there were many investors, Thompson was the only one named.

51. *Los Angeles Times,* March 8, 1908, 35; March 12, 1908, 8; March 23, 1908, 8; March 26, 1908, 22.

52. He acted as a booking agent for Glen Park, New York. *Billboard,* June 6, 1908, 53.

53. Private communication with the Albany College of Pharmacy and Health Sciences.

54. Gail Chumbley, personal communication; Florida Death Index 1877–1998, certificate 26568.

55. "Ebenezer Echoes," *Aurora [IN] Dearborn Independent,* January 18, 1884, 2.

56. Frank Elmer Locke, Find a Grave, www.findagrave.com; *Eclectic Medical* Journal 92 (April 10, 1931): 228; "Eclectic Medical Institute of Cincinnati Matriculation Records," Lloyd Library and Museum, https://lloydlibrary.org.

57. "Locke-Cole Wedding," *Maysville [KY] Evening Bulletin,* April 5, 1893, 2; *Maysville [KY] Public Ledger,* April 5, 1893, 1.

58. Gail Chumbley, personal communication. Their progress can be documented in a number of newspapers from Kentucky, Indiana, and California.

59. *Los Angeles Herald,* February 17, 1907, 10; March 24, 1908, 12; *Los Angeles Times,* June 2, 1907, 72.

60. "Carnival News," *Billboard,* October 28, 1911, 25.

61. *Billboard,* April 6, 1912, 23.

62. "Incorporations," *Indianapolis Star,* September 25, 1914, 14; "Tips for New Business—Central States," *Iron Trade Review,* October 15, 1914, 740.

63. "These Rabbits Fail to Leap," *Chicago Tribune,* April 2, 1915, 18.

64. "'Jack Rabbit' Promoters Again Held as Swindlers," *Chicago Sunday Tribune,* "Jack-rabbit Plant Myth, Investors Say," *Chicago Examiner,* April 3, 1915, 1; "Dannenberg Accused in 'Hydrocraft' Stock Deal," *Chicago Examiner,* April 4, 1915, 1; "U.S. Hearing Shows Hydrocraft Stock," *Chicago Examiner,* April 6, 1915, 9.

65. "Four One-Act Plays Will Be Given in Jackson Heights," *Brooklyn [NY] Daily Star,* February 26, 1925, 12. Thompson's descendants have a copy of the program from a performance the following month in their possession, along with a copy of the play.

66. The extension could not have been for very long because another show opened in the same theater on December 9. That the run was extended is recorded in *Billboard,* November 15, 1919, 8, and "Where's Your Wife?" Internet Broadway Database, www .ibdb.com. Thompson's own entry is at "Thompson, Floyd C.," Internet Broadway Database. This show is his only recorded credit. See also "Show Producing Is Mecca of Managers New at Game," *New York Dramatic Mirror,* 1919, 1652, copy in author's possession; "'Where's Your Wife' Is Novel and Entertaining," *New York Clipper,* October 15, 1919, 16; and *Billboard,* October 18, 1919, 7. Alexander Woolcott in his review was not impressed. Woolcott, "The Play," *New York Times,* October 6, 1919, 15.

67. "Greeted on Broadway," *Billboard,* October 25, 1919, 21.

68. *Billboard,* December 11, 1920, 15; "Billboard Callers," *Billboard,* February 19, 1921, 59; *Billboard,* June 4, 1921, 63.

69. "Billboard Callers," *Billboard,* January 20, 1922, 86; *Billboard,* March 18, 1922, 109; "In Bankruptcy," *Brooklyn Daily Star,* March 5, 1924, 12; *Billboard,* February 14, 1925, 95.

70. I am grateful to Gail Chumbley, great-granddaughter-in-law of Floyd C. Thompson, for sharing these photographs with me.

71. *Brooklyn Daily Star,* June 3, 1925, 13.

72. "Deaths in Queens," *Brooklyn Daily Star,* August 4, 1925, 9; *Attica [NY] Daily News,* August 6, 1925, 1.

73. "Floyd Chaddock Thompson" and "Ashley Cooper Thompson," Find a Grave. Floyd's mother is buried there as well, as are other family members.

Chapter 6: Year Two—1907

1. *Billboard,* May 25, 1907, 12; *New York Clipper,* August 24, 1908, 721.

2. "Higgins and Perry to Manage Wonderland," *Boston Post,* December 25, 1906, 7; "Junction and West Cambridge," *Cambridge [MA] Chronicle,* December 28, 1906, 2. On December 8, 1906, Perry moved from Cambridge to Revere in order to be closer to work and might have known about his promotion at that time. *Cambridge Chronicle,* December 8, 1906, 18.

3. "Wonderland, Revere Beach's Beauty Spot, Ready to Open Memorial Day," *Boston Post,* May 29, 1907, 9.

4. The Wild West show was only booked through August 1, 1906. *Billboard,* July 21, 1906, 34. Kennedy's shows were noted as being booked for an "indefinite" period of time in the *New York Telegraph,* July 23, 1905, 11; July 30, 1905, 11; and August 6, 1905, 12. Kennedy's show was reported to be in Greenfield, Massachusetts, in *Billboard,* September 22, 1906, 15, and in the *Greenfield [MA] Gazette and Courier,* September 1906, 5.

5. *Concord [MA] Enterprise,* October 3, 1906, 7.

6. "Summer Parks," *Variety,* February 24, 1906, 11.

7. "Wonderland," *Boston Sunday Post,* May 26, 1907, 29; "Sunday Post Readers Plan to

Invade Wonderland at Revere Next Week with Sunday Post's Free Tickets," *Boston Post*, May 30, 1907, 4; "Free Ticket to Wonderland in Each Sunday Post This Month," *Boston Sunday Post*, June 2, 1907, 29. Stickler's Federal Construction Company ran advertisements for the Velvet Coaster in *Billboard*, 1905–6. The ride originated at Chicago's Riverside Park. See David W. Francis and Diane Demali Francis, *The Golden Age of Roller Coasters in Vintage Postcards* (Chicago: Arcadia Press, 2003), 30.

8. "Free Ticket to Wonderland in Each Sunday Post This Month," *Boston Sunday Post*, June 2, 1907, 29.

9. The miniature railway circled the area where the Wild West show had been. See "Wonderland," *Cambridge Chronicle*, June 30, 1908, 3. You can also make out the tracks in the panoramic shot from the top of the Shoot the Cutes published in "Wonderland Crowded with Entertainment," *Boston Sunday Post*, June 30, 1907, 31. The Wonderland advertisements in the *Boston Post* for June 1907 said simply that it went through "the most picturesque part of the park." Tunnel no. 23 was probably where the tracks passed underneath the grandstand against the outer fence of the park. The grandstand stayed up for several years.

10. "Wonderland Open," *Revere Journal*, May 25, 1907, 8; Joe Roman, *Listed: Dispatches from America's Endangered Species Act* (Cambridge, MA: Harvard University Press, 2011), 92.

11. "Beachey's Airship and Other Attractions Delight Big Crowds at Wonderland," *Boston Post* June 1, 1907, 9; "Wonderland Now Open," *Revere Journal*, June 1, 1907, 5.

12. A biography of Lincoln Beachey is Frank Marrero, *Lincoln Beachey: The Man Who Owned the Sky* (San Francisco: Scottwall Associates, 1997). See also "Lincoln Beachey," National Aviation Hall of Fame, www.nationalaviation.org; "Lincoln Beachey," Wikipedia, https://en.wikipedia.org; and Carla Courtney, "Lincoln J. Beachey: The Tragic Rise and Fall of the Master Birdman," Disciples of Flight, October 3, 2016, https://disciplesofflight.com.

13. Advertisement, *Boston Sunday Post*, May 26, 1907, 29; "Wonderland, Revere's Beauty Spot, Ready to Open Memorial Day," *Boston Post*, May 29, 1907, 9; Advertisement, *Boston Morning Journal*, May 30, 1907, 5; Advertisement, *Boston Morning Journal*, June 1, 1907, 8. A picture of Beachey working on the engine of his craft appeared in "Sunday Post Readers Plan to Invade Wonderland at Revere Next Week with Sunday Post's Free Tickets," *Boston Post*, May 30, 1907, 4.

14. "Bold Aeronaut, Drifting to Sea, Is Rescued by Fishermen and Airship Towed Safe into Port" and "Drifting Out to Sea Is Rescued," *Boston Post*, June 7, 1907, 1, 3; "Boston Sees First Skyship Flight—Beachey Circles State House Dome" and "Most Thrilling Journey in Mid-Air," *Boston Morning Journal*, June 7, 1907, 1. These articles have several photographs and a map of Beachey's route.

15. "Beachey's Skyship Flies Every Day This Week," *Boston Morning Journal*, June 10, 1907, 11.

16. "Crowds of Sunday Post Free Ticket Holders Invade Wonderland," *Boston Sunday Post*, June 26, 1907, 7.

17. "Eugene Fielding the Star of Orchard Park Water Sports," *Boston Post*, August 22, 1902, 3; *Cambridge Chronicle*, August 30, 1902, 3.

18. "Summer Stage—Entertainments at Wonderland," *Boston Globe*, June 25, 1907, 2.

19. *Boston Post,* July 13, 1907, 10; *Boston Morning Journal,* July 11, 1907, 14; "Old-Home Week, Theater Bills—Wonderland, Revere Beach," *Boston Globe,* July 28, 1907, 35; "Wonderland," *Revere Journal,* July 13, 1907, 2.

20. The film has recently been restored and is available on home video and on internet services. See "The Hold-Up of the Rocky Mountain Express," YouTube, www.youtube .com.

21. "Free Ticket to Wonderland in Each Sunday Post This Month," *Boston Post,* June 2, 1907, 29. Other announcements about the Abbey appeared in "Wonderland to Open Gates on Memorial Day to Thousands of Patrons," *Boston Post,* May 26, 1907, 29; "Wonderland, Revere Beach's Beauty Spot, Ready to Open Memorial Day," *Boston Post,* May 29, 1907, 9; and "Wonderland—Famous Resort Will Open Memorial Day," *Boston Globe,* May 26, 1907, 39.

22. Fortunately, a description of the construction of the Battle Abbey building exists. The construction for the building was apparently done not by Aldrich & Shea but by the Angus MacDonald Construction Company of 161 Devonshire Street in the Back Bay neighborhood of Boston. The next year the construction supervisor, Arthur Waldo Joslin, wrote an article entitled "Estimating Cost of Buildings," *Building Age,* April 1908, 128–29. Joslin later incorporated the material into a book. In chapter 22, he gave an example of how to estimate the costs for a typical building and used Battle Abbey as an example. Joslin, *Estimating the Cost of Buildings: A Systematic Treatise on Factors of Costs and Superintendence,* 2nd ed. (New York: David Williams, 1913), 128–31.

23. "Great List of Attractions for Sunday Post Guests at Wonderland," *Boston Sunday Post,* June 16, 1907, 21.

24. "If it's not true, at least it's a good story." Carl Beck, "Extract from 'At Christmastime in Florida,'" *Post Graduate,* September 1906, 856–68. It seems that Tom used the same nail-impaling feature of alligators as the one exhibited by Harry Welsh's alligator at Luna Park.

25. "Wonderland to Open Gates on Memorial Day to Thousands of Patrons," *Boston Sunday Post,* May 26, 1907, 29.

26. "Wonderland—Famous Resort Will Open Memorial Day," *Boston Globe,* May 26, 1907, 29; "Wonderland, Crowded with Entertainment," *Boston Sunday Post,* June 30, 1907, 31; and Advertisement, *Boston Sunday Post,* June 2, 1907, 39, all said eight hundred alligators.

27. "Crowds of Sunday Post Free Ticket Holders Invade Wonderland," *Boston Sunday Post,* June 26, 1907, 7.

28. "Wonderland to Open Gates on Memorial Day to Thousands of Patrons," *Boston Sunday Post,* May 26, 1907, 29.

29. "Wonderland to Open Gates on Memorial Day to Thousands of Patrons," *Boston Sunday Post,* May 26, 1907, 29.

30. "Sunday Post Readers Plan to Invade Wonderland at Revere Next Week with Sunday Post's Free Tickets," *Boston Post,* May 30, 1907, 4, had a picture of Salisbury.

31. "Sea Cow and Her Baby Dead," *Boston Post,* June 24, 1907, 7. See also "Sunday Post Readers Plan to Invade Wonderland at Revere Next Week with Sunday Post's Free Tickets," *Boston Post,* May 30, 1907, 4.

32. "Sea Cow and Her Baby Dead" and "Crowds of Sunday Post Free Ticket Holders Invade Wonderland," *Boston Sunday Post,* June 26, 1907, 7.

33. "An Attractive Parade—Beautiful Ponies and Cute Dogs Galore," *Logansport [IN] Daily Pharos,* May 6, 1895, 4. See also "Ready for the Opening," *Kokomo [IN] Daily Tribune,* April 2, 1897, 8.

34. "Circus History—Brief Bits—Blake's Dog and Monkey," Circus History, www.circus history.org.

35. "Sipe Sells Out," *Kokomo Daily Tribune,* January 18, 1899, 4.

36. There are numerous stories about Blake's "Simian City" in the *White City Magazine* in 1905, including issues no. 2, pp. 30–31; no. 3, p. 48; and no. 4, pp. 46–48. The souvenir magazine from Chicago's White City Amusement Park can be found online at "White City Magazine," Archive.org, https://archive.org.

37. Advertisement, *Variety,* August 14, 1909, 36.

38. Charles Willard possibly first satisfied his mischievous need for popular entertainment not with music but with writing. A comic poem attributed to Charles D. Willard appeared in the *San Francisco Chronicle* in 1894 and was widely reprinted in newspapers in the Midwest. "The Views of Uncle Josh," *Ottumwa [IA] Daily Democrat,* October 12, 1888, 6. Two humorous stories also appeared in newspapers in the 1890s. "Fourth Cousins" appeared in the *Athens [OH] Messenger and Herald,* July 25, 1895, 3; "The Earlier Bird" appeared in the *Easthampton [NY] Star,* February 2, 1894.

39. "Musical Novelty at Pantages," *Sacramento [CA] Union,* February 6, 1911, 5.

40. Advertisement, *Las Vegas Daily Optic,* October 31, 1899, 4; Advertisement, *Los Angeles Herald,* November 17, 1899, 2; Advertisement, *Daily Reno Nevada State Journal,* March 16, 1900, 3; *Reno [NV] Evening Gazette,* March 20, 1900, 1; "Greater America," *Woodland [CA] Daily Democrat,* February 19, 1900, 1; "Resulted in Loss," *Reno Evening Gazette,* March 21, 1900, 2; "Lost on the Benefit," *Daily Nevada State Journal* [Reno], March 22, 1900, 3; "An Individual Company," *Woodland California Daily Democrat,* February 15, 1900, 1. "Greater America" gives an early description of the Willards' act.

41. A picture of the "Wonderland Ladies" appeared in the *Boston Post,* June 28, 1907, 4.

42. "Navigable Airship the Attraction for Which Thousands Waited," *Boston Morning Journal,* May 31, 1907, 5.

43. "Beachey Leaves Wonderland Soon," *Boston Post,* June 8, 1908, 9. This article also included a photograph of the stage with Willard's instruments spread out on display at Wonderland.

44. "Willard's 'Temple of Music,'" Vaudeville America, http://vaudevilleamerica.org.

45. In an intriguing parallel, there has been a team of performers on Deagan aluminum chimes at Disney World since 1971.

46. *Revere Journal,* May 25, 1907, 5.

47. "Beachey's Airship and Other Attractions Delight Big Crowds at Wonderland," *Boston Post,* June 1, 1907, 9; *New York Clipper,* August 4, 1906, 640; "Music Hall," *Boston Post,* June 24, 1902, 5.

48. "High Wire King at Wonderland," *Boston Morning Journal,* July 16, 1907, 11.

49. "Beachey Leaves Wonderland Soon," *Boston Post,* June 8, 1907, 9.

50. Walter Starr Wentworth was born in either 1832 (as certified in his Massachusetts death

certificate, Massachusetts State Vital Records, 1841–1920 Register no. 69, p. 115) or July 22, 1835, as given by his gravestone (Find a Grave, www.findagrave.com). But he consistently gave his age as about ten years older (or his birthdate as ten years earlier) in newspaper stories. He gave his birthdate as July 22, 1825, in the *New York Clipper*, September 11, 1909, 782, 790, 792. In the *Strand* magazine in 1896, he gave his age as "about seventy years of age" when he was about sixty-one or sixty-four. Framley Steelcroft, "Some Peculiar Entertainments I," *Strand* 11 (1896): 328–35. In another 1909 story, he gave his age as eighty-nine, when he was really only seventy-four or seventy-seven. Frank Marshall White, "Some Old Stage Folk at Home," *The Passing Show Magazine*, October 1909, 810–15. There are a great many more examples.

51. "Walter Starr Wentworth," Find a Grave. A biography of Walter appeared in *New York Clipper*, September 11, 1909, 782, 790, 792.

52. Advertisement, *Buffalo [NY] Evening News*, April 26, 1890, 2; "At Wonderland," *Buffalo Evening News*, April 22, 1890, 1; Framely Steelcroft, "Some Peculiar Entertainments," *The Strand* 11 (1896): 328–35; "'Daddy' of Contortionists Supple as a Snake at 77 Years," *Galveston [TX] Sunday News*, September 28, 1902, 12. This article is essentially the same as "'Daddy' of Contortionists Supple as a Snake at 77 Years," *New York Herald*, September 28, 1902, 5, right down to the illustration, which copies the photos in the *Herald* story.

53. *New York Sun*, May 23, 1904, 5; "The Grand Central Theater, Troy NY," *New York Clipper*, October 6, 1877, 223.

54. *Wheeling [WV] Daily Intelligencer*, June 21, 1877, 2.

55. "Sold His Body for $100," *Washington [DC] Evening Star*, August 19, 1902, 9; "'Daddy' of Contortionists Supple as a Snake at 77 Years," *New York Herald*, September 28, 1902, 5.

56. "Guests of the Sunday Post Crowd Wonderland and Enjoy the Features of Revere's Famous Park," *Boston Post*, June 4, 1907, 9.

57. *New York Clipper*, July 13, 1907, 565; "Frank Todd," *New York Dramatic Mirror*, July 13, 1907, 8; "Frank Todd," *New York Herald*, July 5, 1907, 5; "Deaths," *Boston Post*, July 4, 1907, 2.

58. "Circus Is Here Again," *New York Herald*, April 3, 1896, 10; "Pretty Rose Wentworth," *New York Times*, April 28, 1895, 16.

59. I am grateful to Bob Kitchen of the Fall River Historical Society, Fall River, MA, for providing this information. There are a very few notices of her performing under her name "Maude Allington." See "Circus Comes to Town," *Buffalo Evening News*, December 26, 1936, 10 (a retrospective written by O. Henry); "Great Equestrian Acts," *Connersville [IN] Times*, August 7, 1895, 6; and John Daniel Draper, "Rose Wentworth—A Circus Legend," *Bandwagon* 57, no. 4 (July–August 2013): 16–25.

60. "Town Personalities: Ex-Circus Star Recalls the Time British King Pulled Her Hair," *Indiana Weekly Messenger*, (Indiana, PA), October 7, 1937, 14.

61. *New York Post*, June 14, 1896, 11.

62. *New York Times*, April 10, 1894, 8.

63. "Rehearsal in the Arena," *New York Sun*, April 15, 1894, 1.

64. "Pretty Rose Wentworth," *New York Times*, April 28, 1895, 16.

65. Advertisement, *Boston Post*, August 15, 1907, 10; *Boston Post*, August 10, 1907, 31.

66. "Wonderland," *Boston Post*, August 27, 1907, 5.

67. "Incubators at Wonderland Greatest Attraction of All," *Boston Sunday Post*, September 1, 1907, 21, credits Perry as producer.

68. "Alice Sees Wonderland—She Arrived, Not through Looking Glass, but By Way of Revere," *Boston Post*, September 5, 1907, 11.

69. "Alice Sees Wonderland—She Arrived, Not through Looking Glass, but By Way of Revere," *Boston Post*, September 5, 1907, 11; "Wonderland," *Revere Journal*, August 31, 1907, 2; "Wonderland," *Boston Sunday Post*, September 8, 1907, 19; "Alice in Wonderland," *Revere Journal*, September 7, 1907, 4.

70. "Wonderland," *Boston Sunday Post*, September 15, 1907, 25.

71. "W. C. Manning to Sail for England," *New York Clipper*, April 3, 1908, 194; "Revere Beach," *Revere Journal*, May 15, 1909, 5.

72. Advertisement, *Billboard*, December 14, 1907, 36; "The National Amusement Park Association," *Street Railway Journal*, January 25, 1908, 129.

Chapter 7: Year Three—1908

1. "Wonderland—Boston's Mammoth Resort Opens in Splendor Today," *Boston Morning Journal*, May 23, 1908, 2.

2. "Wonderland, Revere—Opens Soon with Many New Attractions," *Boston Globe*, May 17, 1908, 38; "Summer Shows—Wonderland Opens at Revere Beach Today," *Boston Globe*, May 23, 1908, 14; "Wonderland," *Boston Sunday Post*, May 17, 1908, 24; *Cambridge [MA] Chronicle*, May 23, 1908, 14. It may be significant that the Tremont Theater in Boston ran Franz Lehár's operetta *The Merry Widow* that summer. *Boston Globe*, August 16, 1908, 33. A special press tour of the park was given on June 8. "At Wonderland—Massachusetts Editors Enjoy Afternoon Outing Monday," *Concord [MA] Enterprise*, June 10, 1908, 6.

3. "Wonderland," *Boston Post*, June 9, 1908, 9; "Wonderland," *Boston Post*, June 23, 1908, 9.

4. "For Sale," *Boston Globe*, November 29, 1907, 11.

5. "In Bohemia—Holly Club Is the Newest of Boston's Table d'Hôte Restaurants," *Boston Post*, February 1, 1908, 2.

6. "Boston's Best Restaurant," *Boston Sunday Post*, May 3, 1908, 11.

7. "Restaurant's Creditors Act—McDonald Company in Financial Difficulties," *Boston Globe*, February 11, 1908, 4.

8. "For Sale," *Boston Post*, November 29, 1907, 11; "Restaurant's Creditors Act," *Boston Post*, February 11, 1908, 4; *Boston Sunday Post*, May 3, 1908, 11; "Boston's Best Restaurant," *Boston Post*, May 16, 1908, 42; "Boston Chefs and Their Favorite Dishes," *Boston Sunday Post*, December 27, 1908, 2.

9. *Wonderland Souvenir Program 1908* [9]; "Wonderland," *Newton [MA] Graphic*, May 22, 1908, 4; *Boston Globe*, June 3, 1900, 19; "Gets Nine Licenses," *Boston Globe*, July 1, 1902, 4; "Many Friends Present—Mr. and Mrs. Charles E. Davidson Celebrate Their Silver Wedding at Their Medford Home," *Boston Globe*, December 31, 1904, 7; "Society Plays

Whist for Cause of Charity," *Boston Globe,* August 7, 1901, 7. This last one has a picture of Davidson.

10. "Wonderland," *Cambridge Chronicle,* July 4, 1908, 10; "Boston, Mass.," *Billboard,* July 11, 1908, 7.

11. "Pawnee Bill Writes," *Billboard,* August 8, 1908, 24–25. See also *Lowell [MA] Sun,* July 30, 1908, 28.

12. "A Mexican Park Scene," *Billboard,* April 27, 1907, 14.

13. "Wonderland," *Billboard,* June 6, 1908, 6; "Wonderland, Revere—Opens Soon with Many New Attractions," *Boston Globe,* May 17, 1908, 38.

14. "Pawnee Bill Writes," *Billboard,* August 8, 1908, 24–25.

15. A copy of this ticket is in the author's possession.

16. Advertisement, *Billboard,* March 21, 1908, 11.

17. Advertisement, *Billboard,* September 11, 1909, 11.

18. Advertisement, *Billboard,* April 11, 1908, 52.

19. "Wonderland," *Cambridge Chronicle,* July 4, 1908, 4.

20. *Baltimore Sun,* May 31, 1908, 12.

21. *Boston Sunday Globe,* May 17, 1908, 38; *Boston Sunday Post,* May 17, 1908, 24.

22. Jeffry Klenotic, "'The Sensational Acme of Realism': 'Talker' Pictures as Early Cinema Sound Practice," in *The Sounds of Early Cinema,* ed. Richard Abel and Rick Altman (Bloomington: Indiana University Press, 2001), 156–66.

23. Amy H. Croughton, "Scanning the Screen," *Rochester [NY] Times-Union,* July 14, 1944, 9A.

24. "College Chums," YouTube, www.youtube.com.

25. "Wonderland," *Boston Post,* May 16, 1908, 32.

26. "Wonderland," *Cambridge Chronicle,* May 30, 1908, 15.

27. For example, "Port Jervis Elks—Guests of the Darktown Fire Brigade," *Middletown [NY] Daily Argus,* May 7, 1902, 1; "Big Spectacle for the Point," *Sandusky [OH] Daily Register,* May 25, 1907, 1; "Big Liza Made 'Em All Take Notice," *Sandusky Daily Register,* July 11, 1907, 2; "The Fireman's Parade," *Middletown [NY] Orange County Times,* October 5, 1900, 3.

28. Advertisement, *Billboard,* November 12, 1910, 63. A biography of her in Spanish is Antonio Orlando Rodrigues, *Chiquita* (Doral, FL: Alfaguarra/Santillana, 2008). There is a Wikipedia entry for her, but it gets some facts incorrect, including the date of her death. "Espiridiona Canda," Wikipedia, https://en.wikipedia.org. A brief biography appears in Ian Brabner, "Autographed Cabinet Photograph of Carnival Entertainer Chiquita, The Doll Queen," Rare Americana, www.rareamericana.com. Another appears in Margaret Creighton, *The Electrifying Fall of Rainbow City: Spectacle and Assassination at the 1901 World's Fair* (New York: Norton, 2016), 29, 32, 35–40, 156, 169, 191, 203, 215–17, 231–37, 244–46.

29. "Hobson Did Not Kiss Chiquita," *Buffalo [NY] Evening News,* July 1, 1901, 1.

30. "Chiquita Kidnaped?" *Buffalo [NY] Courier,* November 2, 1901, 7.

31. A photograph taken at Ridenouer Studio in Philadelphia labeled her "Mrs. Anthony C. Woeckener," showing her with a young man who might be Anthony Woeckener.

"Mrs. Anthony C. Woeckener of Erie, Pennsylvania, Better Known as Chiquita the Doll Queen," Library of Congress Prints and Photographs Division, www.loc.gov.

32. Chiquita had nearly been killed in a fire in Baltimore in February 1901 that killed three hundred of Bostock's animals. Chiquita was rescued by being lifted and carried from her room but the traumatic experience made her hysterical and finally rendered her unconscious. Circus folk would not take kindly to anyone who might start another such blaze. "300 Died in Big Zoo Fire," *New York Morning Telegraph*, February 1, 1901, 10.

33. "Little Chiquita Was Married Last Night," *Buffalo Evening News,* November 2, 1901, 8; "Chiquita, the Midget, Married," *Rome [NY] Daily Sentinel,* November 4, 1901, 1.

34. "Was Marriage of Chiquita the Result of a Plot?" *Buffalo Courier,* November 4, 1901, 5; "Probing Chiquita's Marriage," *Buffalo Courier,* November 5, 1901, 7.

35. Despite these public displays of fatherly concern, Bostock's real feelings were very different. According to Margaret Creighton, he hit Chiquita so hard when they were first together after her return that she fell to the ground senseless. Creighton, *Electrifying Fall of Rainbow City,* 205.

36. "For Chiquita's Heart," *Baltimore Sun,* November 9, 1901, 2; "Bostock Sued and Arrested," *Buffalo Courier,* November 9, 1901, 7; "Wants His Doll Wife," *Oswego [NY] Daily Times,* November 9, 1901, 1.

37. Advertisement, *Boston Globe,* December 7, 1901, 11.

38. "His Tiny Bride Lost to Tony Woeckner," *Buffalo Evening News,* January 9, 1902, 1.

39. "Tony Woeckner," *Sinclairville [NY] Commercial,* January 10, 1902, 1.

40. "Another Chapter in 'The Marriage of a Midget,'" *Buffalo Evening News,* March 8, 1902, 45; *Sherman [NY] Chataqua News,* March 8, 1902, 2.

41. "Chiquita's Adventures," *Silver Springs [NY] Signal,* August 28, 1902. But according to Margaret Creighton, Tony never got a ticket to Glasgow. Creighton, *Electrifying Fall of Rainbow City,* 233.

42. "Chiquita Makes a Plunge," *Batavia [NY] Daily News,* August 28, 1902, 1; "Smallest Woman in Earth Has Big Row with Manager," *New York Morning Telegraph,* August 29, 1902, 9.

43. "Ciquita's Programme," Sideshow World, www.sideshowworld.com. The program is from the National Export Exposition in Philadelphia, September 14–November 30, 1899.

44. The definitive biography of Pawnee Bill is probably Shirley, *Pawnee Bill.* It has been faulted recently as being too credulous and willing to believe tall tales. See Alyce Vigil, *The Big Break: Race and Gender in Pawnee Bill's Historic Wild West, 1888–1913* (M.A. thesis, University of Southern Oklahoma, 2013). See also Eric Willey, "*One of Our Own: Pawnee Bill's Life as Viewed by Bloomington Residents,*" *Bandwagon* 60, no. 4 (2016): 72–90.

45. Don Russell, *The Lives and Legends of Buffalo Bill* (Norman: University of Oklahoma Press, 1979), 447. See also "Wild West Girls Are Not Amazons," *Boston Morning Journal,* May 29, 1908, 5.

46. We have an excellent record of what the "set" of Pawnee Bill's show looked like because a photographer named Erwin E. Smith, who wanted to go west and photograph

cowboys and document the closing of the American frontier, was then studying photography at the School of the Museum of Fine Arts in Boston. The appearance of Pawnee Bill's show at Wonderland in Revere gave Smith the opportunity to do so without leaving Boston. His collection of photographs is part of the Library of Congress collection now on deposit in the Amon Carter Museum of American Art in Fort Worth, Texas. Smith ultimately went on to take over two thousand photographs of the Old West, creating one of the best records of the passing way of life.

47. "Wonderland," *Boston Sunday Post,* July 26, 1908, 15.

48. *Wonderland Souvenir Program 1908,* [12]. See also *Variety,* June 27, 1908, 12, and *Billboard,* August 1, 1908, 17. A brief description appears in "Genuine 'Round Up' Every Day at Wonderland Shows," *Boston Globe,* July 19, 1908, 41. Admission to the show was twenty-five cents. See Advertisement, *Boston Globe,* July 20, 1908, 10.

49. "Interesting Indians—Notable in the Village at Wonderland," *Boston Globe,* June 15, 1908, 2.

50. "Wonderland," *Cambridge Chronicle,* July 11, 1908, 10.

51. "Summertime Shows—Wonderland," *Boston Post,* June 23, 1908, 12.

52. "Pawnee Bill on Trail," *Boston Post,* August 15, 1908, 2.

53. "Indians Attend Immaculate Conception Church Anniversary," *Boston Post,* August 24, 1908, 4.

54. The official biography of Kellermann is Gibson with Firth, *Original Million Dollar Mermaid.* A children's biography of her is Shana Corey, *Mermaid Queen: The Spectacular True Story of Annette Kellerman, Who Swam Her Way to Fame, Fortune, and Swimsuit History* (New York: Scholastic, 2009). In later years, Kellermann often dropped the second "n" at the end of her surname.

55. "When I was a girl I was a cripple from calcium deficiency. So little was known about diet that my parents didn't think it was important to make me drink milk," Kellermann said to a reporter in 1950. Lydia Lane, "'Ageless' Swimmer Gives Health Rules," *Los Angeles Times,* April 9, 1950, B9.

56. The suit was manufactured by Asbury Mills in New York from 1920 to 1960. "Annette Kellerman Brand Swimsuit," Powerhouse Museum of Applied Arts and Sciences (New South Wales, Australia), https://collection.maas.museum; "Swimming Tights by Annette Kellerman," The Vintage Traveler, August 3, 2016, https://thevintagetraveler .wordpress.com. Nevertheless, these suits were explicitly banned in some places into the 1920s. *Washington [DC] Evening Star,* April 25, 1921, 1. In fact, it was still deemed indecent at a trial in 1943. Jean Preer, "Esquire v. Walker: The Postmaster General and the 'Magazine for Men' Part 3," *Prologue Magazine* 23, no. 1 (Spring 1990), www .archives.gov.

57. "Miss Annette Kellerman," *Revere Journal,* June 8, 1907, 3. It was evidently a sort of syndicated feature, for it appeared also as "Miss Annette Kellerman," *Plattsburgh [NY] Daily Press,* August 14, 1907, 2.

58. A "behind the scenes" photograph shows the "Scenic" building from the Thompson Scenic Railway in the northeast corner of the park. It probably dates after the first year of the park. It appears to show a new structure scaffolding behind the railway building, although it does not look much like a diving structure. If it were part of the

Kellermann pool area, the entrance would have been behind the Velvet Coaster and the Hell Gate building.

59. "Diabolo with Miss Kellermann," *Boston Post,* September 3, 1908, 14; "Diabolo Tennis Is Coming to Summer at Revere," *Boston Post,* May 18, 1908, 2. Another picture of her with the Diabolo Tennis apparatus appears in "Annette Kellerman on the Ballfield (1907)," Wikimedia Commons, https://commons.wikimedia.org.

60. "Wonderland," *Boston Sunday Post,* July 26, 1908, 1.

61. "A Great Feat," *Boston Post,* July 31, 1908, 6; Harry B. Center, "Turn of the Tide Cost Girl Victory," *Boston Post,* July 31, 1908, 1; "Annette Kellermann to Make Her Daring Swim Tomorrow," *Boston Post,* July 29, 1908, 9.

62. "Alice in Wonderland," *Boston Post,* September 1, 1908, 3; "'Alice in Wonderland' Proves a Most Brilliant Spectacle," *Boston Post,* September 2, 1908, 4. The latter also includes a picture.

63. See "Bathing Suit Caused Arrest," *Boston Post,* July 23, 1906, 5, and "Baltimore Society Belles Pinched," *Idaville [IN] Observer,* July 31, 1908, 7. But there is no contemporary evidence that Kellermann herself was ever arrested for this.

64. "Annette Kellerman Fined $5," *New York Press,* December 3, 1909, 8, reported her being fined for speeding while driving in New York City. See also "Culbertson Caught the 'Diving Venus,'" *Brooklyn [NY] Daily Eagle,* July 29, 1909, 2, and "Annette the Water Queen Goes Behind the Sergeant's Desk and Blushingly Gives Up Her Fine," *Oakland [CA] Tribune,* August 14, 1909, 12.

65. Annette Kellermann, "My Story," undated manuscript, MLMSS 6270/1, Mitchell Library, State Library of New South Wales, Australia.

66. While most people have uncritically accepted the story as true, even going so far as to rationalize reasons that no records exist, not everyone has. The Massachusetts Department of Conservation and Recreation (DCR) has placed the following notice on its website: "The DCR Archives often receives inquiries regarding Australian Swimmer Annette Kellerman's August 1, 1907, arrest on Revere Beach. Unfortunately, none of the surviving records of the Metropolitan Park Commission makes reference to Kellerman's arrest by the Metropolitan Park Police. During World War II the Massachusetts Administration and Finance Office encouraged state agencies to participate in paper recycling efforts in a 1944 bulletin, There is evidence that possibly some of the records of the Annette Kellerman incident were destroyed by the MDC Revere Beach Reservation Police Station as part of this paper recycling program." Sean M. Fisher, "A Guide to Related Archival Collections Outside of the DCR Archives Pertaining to the Metropolitan Parks System, the Metropolitan Water Works System, and the State Forests and Park System," section entitled "Annette Kelleman (1886–1975) Massachusetts DCR April 8 2009 and June 9 2015 and 1907 Arrest on Revere Beach," p. 42, www.mass.gov. However, a paper recycling effort by the DCR cannot explain the absence of records in contemporary newspapers.

An article in the *Boston Globe* repeated the story as part of the publicity campaign for *Million Dollar Mermaid.* Ishbel Johns, "Boston Arrest a Mistake, Says Annette," *Boston Globe,* October 11, 1953, A3. In 2015, Kristine Toussaint queried the Revere police department and reported, "Lieutenant Amy O'Hara of the Revere Police

Department couldn't find any information about the 1907 arrest on old logbooks, but she could still tell that the event was monumental." Kristine Toussaint, "This Woman's One-Piece Bathing Suit Got Her Arrested in 1907," boston.com, July 21, 2015. It should also be pointed out that other accounts—even by Kellermann herself—say that the arrest occurred elsewhere. The caption of a photograph of Kellermann with Esther Williams in the *Oakland Tribune*, September 28, 1952, 51, states that it happened at "Bradley Beach" in New Jersey in 1907. Louella Parsons said that it happened in Atlantic City, New Jersey, in a column in 1951. See *Lowell Sun*, February 5, 1951, 10.

67. *Lowell Sun*, March 16, 1909, 9; "Wife Names Miss Kellerman," *New York Times*, March 13, 1909, 1.

68. "Beauty, Beer, and Beatings Home Woe Trio," *Des Moines [IA] Daily News*, March 17, 1909, 2; "Fair Swimmer Weeps over Charges" and "Pattee Spurns Charges," *Oakland [CA] Sunday Tribune*, March 14, 1909, 13, 15.

69. "Miss Kellermann Rouses Wife's Ire," *New York Herald*, March 13, 1909, 1; "Fair Swimmer in Divorce," *Middletown Daily Argus*, March 13, 1909, 3.

70. "Made Faces at Wife" and "Says Annette Kellerman Drank Beer with Husband," *Boston Post*, March 13, 1909, 1, 14.

71. "Beautiful Diver Sobs Her Denial in Divorce Suit," *Philadelphia Inquirer*, March 14, 1909, 1; "Tearfully Denies Drinking Beer with Another's Husband," *Oakland Tribune*, March 13, 1909, 4.

72. "Fair Swimmer Weeps over Charges," *Oakland [CA] Sunday Tribune*, March 14, 1909, 13, 15; "Pattee Spurns Charges," *Boston Sunday Post*, March 14, 1909, 10.

73. "Pattee Spurns Charges," *Boston Sunday Post*, March 14, 1909, 10.

74. *Lowell Sun*, March 16, 1909, 9.

75. An advertisement for "100 young ladies who have had experience in stage dancing" appeared in the *Boston Sunday Post*, July 26, 1908, 11, asking them to send age, height, weight, and experience to Eugene L. Perry at Wonderland. The first rehearsals were held August 10, as reported in "Wonderland," *Boston Post*, August 11, 1908, 4.

76. A photograph of the "Alice in Wonderland" cast in costume—the only photograph we have from the show—appeared in "'Alice in Wonderland' Proves a Most Brilliant Spectacle," *Boston Post*, September 2, 1908, 4. Other descriptions appeared in "Alice in Wonderland," *Boston Globe*, September 1, 1908, 4; "Last Week of Wonderland," *Boston Globe*, September 15, 1908, 6; and *Newton Graphic*, September 4, 1908, 7.

77. "Alice in Wonderland," *Boston Globe*, September 1, 1908, 4.

78. *Boston Post*, September 11, 1908, 6.

79. *Variety*, September 5, 1908, 10.

80. "Wonderland," *Boston Sunday Post*, September 20, 1908, 23.

81. "Perry Divorce Case," *Cambridge Chronicle*, October 3, 1908, 3.

82. According to *Variety*, March 6, 1909, 10, some parks that closed as a result of the panic were in Beachwood, Philadelphia, and Johnstown, Pennsylvania, as well as "White City" in Louisville, Kentucky.

83. "Fate of Park in Balance—Wonderland's Poor Season May Result in Dismantling Resort," *Boston Sunday Post*, October 11, 1908, 10.

Chapter 8: Year Four—1909

1. Advertisement, *Billboard,* January 16, 1909, 19.

2. "Wonderland to Go to Auction," *New York Clipper,* February 6, 1909, 1.

3. "Wonderland at Auction," *Boston Globe,* January 30, 1909, 14.

4. "Wonderland Is Sold for $50,000," *Boston Post,* March 9, 1909, 9.

5. The main entrance to Wonderland and its administration building were located on Walnut Avenue in Revere.

6. *Report of the Tax Commissioner of the Commonwealth of Massachusetts* (Boston: Wright and Potter, 1911), 421. Revere is located in Suffolk County.

7. *New York Clipper,* April 17, 1909, 24. Descriptions of the reorganization are given in undated papers in a private collection.

8. *New York Clipper,* November 9, 1908, 25; April 3, 1909, 194.

9. The *Revere Journal,* June 5, 1909, 3, called it "the most unique merry-go-round in America."

10. *"1915" Boston Exposition Official Catalogue and the Boston 1915 Year Book—Old Art Museum Copley Square November 1–27 1909* (Boston: "1915" Boston Exposition Company, 1909), copy in University of Wisconsin, Madison. Airplanes listed on p. xv.

11. See *"1915" Boston Exposition Official Catalogue and the Boston 1915 Year Book.* J. J. Higgins is listed on p. viii.

12. Advertisement, *Christian Science Monitor,* May 1, 1909, 5.

13. "Amusement Notes," *Boston Globe,* May 22, 1909, 7; "Wonderland Opens for the Season Today," *Boston Post,* May 29, 1909, 14; "Wonderland," *Boston Sunday Post,* May 23, 1909, 23; "Thousands Saw the Sights of Wonderland," *Boston Sunday Post,* May 30, 1909, 5.

14. *Greenfield [MA] Gazette and Courier,* August 29, 1908, 4.

15. "Wonders at Wonderland," *Greenfield [MA] Recorder,* July 14, 1909, 7; *New York Clipper,* June 8, 1907, 10.

16. "Contest Now Over—N. J. Lawler to Be Appointed Postmaster," *Greenfield Recorder,* October 7, 1914, 1.

17. "Wonderland," *Boston Sunday Post,* May 23, 1909, 23; "N. J. Lawler's Work at Wonderland," *Greenfield Gazette and Courier,* September 25, 1909, 4.

18. "Wonderland Open," *Boston Globe,* May 29, 1909, 3; "Wonderland Lights Up," *Boston Globe,* May 30, 1909, 3; "Thousands Saw the Sights of Wonderland," *Boston Sunday Post,* May 30, 1909, 5.

19. *Billboard,* March 7, 1908, 5; November 6, 1909, 25; "Another Big Act Crowds the Gaiety," *Mount Vernon [NY] Daily Argus,* April 23, 1910, 2; Advertisement, *Mount Vernon Daily Argus,* April 22, 1910, 9; April 23, 1910, 12; "Lyric Vaudeville," *Rome [NY] Daily Sentinel,* February 28, 1911, 2.

20. *New York Dramatic Mirror,* July 15, 1905, 521; *Buffalo [NY] Courier,* July 8, 1906, 44; July 10, 1906, 8. Emma's last name was variously misspelled as "Shalen" and "Shakan," but it was properly "Chacon."

21. "Prof. Ernest Brengk at the Orpheum," *Oakland California Tribune,* November 11, 1907, 14.

22. "Keith's Theater," *Boot and Shoe Recorder* [Boston], October 26, 1898, 141; *Boston Post,* August 24, 1897, 5.

23. "Cart before the Horse," *Bluefield [WV] Daily Telegraph,* May 10, 1912, 4; *Syracuse [NY] Herald,* April 7, 1923, 145; *Berkeley [CA] Daily Gazette,* April 19, 1919, 5; *Bridgeport [CT] Telegram,* January 27, 1922, 29; *Lowell [MA] Sun,* January 29, 1917, 8.

24. *Variety,* July 31, 1909, 7; "Wonderland," *Boston Sunday Post,* June 13, 1909, 28; "New Features at Wonderland," *Cambridge [MA] Chronicle,* June 19, 1909, 11.

25. This was the story of Cinderella and her golden slipper. "Wonderland," *Boston Post,* July 20, 1909, 4. Most people are familiar with Perrault's version, with its ethereal glass slipper, from countless storybooks and, of course, from Rogers and Hammerstein's version and the Disney cartoon. But the golden slipper was as legitimate a version, the story told by the Brothers Grimm. There is, besides, another reason to use a golden slipper—it shows up better on stage, especially when sparkling under innovative electric lighting. It was much the same reason that the MGM movie version of *The Wizard of Oz* changed the iconic silver slippers that the Wicked Witch of the East wore (and which ended up on Dorothy Gale's feet) to ruby slippers: they looked better in Technicolor.

26. *Boston Sunday Globe,* July 8, 1900, 18; "'Pinafore' on the Chute Grounds' Lake," *Boston Sunday Globe,* July 10, 1900, 2; "Last Week of the Opera Company at Lakeview," *Lowell Sun,* August 11, 1902, 5.

27. "Lakeview Theatre," *Lowell Sun,* June 19, 1903, 10.

28. "Wytche Hazelle," *Boston Sunday Post,* May 6, 1900, 14.

29. "Wonderland," *Boston Sunday Post,* July 18, 1909, 27; "Wonderland," *Boston Sunday Post,* August 29, 1909, 29.

30. "Wonderland," *Boston Sunday Post,* July 11, 1909, 27.

31. *Boston Post,* January 13, 1913, 2.

32. "Wonderland's New Show," *Boston Globe,* July 13, 1909, 8.

33. "Spitefulella" and "Vixenella" sound like clumsy creations for this production, but these names actually have a long history for the evil stepsisters in Cinderella, going back to stage versions in the nineteenth century. The names appear in an 1855 English version of Giacomo Puccini's opera *La Cerentola (Cinderella).* They earlier appeared in another English version by M. Rophino Lacy in 1831 (reprinted in John Graziano, ed., *Italian Opera in English* [1931; reprint New York: Garland, 1994], 3:3–64). The names are the invention of the translators, since in Puccini's opera the sisters are named Clorinda and Tisbe (and there is no slipper, only a bracelet).

34. "Wonderland," *Boston Sunday Post,* July 18, 1909, 27; *Boston Globe,* July 13, 1909, 8; *Boston Post,* July 14, 1909, 11.

35. *New York Clipper,* July 24, 1909, 620; *Boston Globe,* July 13, 1909, 8.

36. "Wonderland's Attractions," *Boston Globe,* August 29, 1909, 37.

37. *Boston Post,* July 20, 1909, 4.

38. "Wonderland's Attractions," *Boston Globe,* July 25, 1909, 35.

39. Advertisement, *Boston Post,* July 28, 1909, 11.

40. *Boston Post,* August 7, 1909, 11.

41. Advertisement, *Boston Post,* August 21, 1909, 11.

42. "Wonderland," *Boston Sunday Post*, September 5, 1909, 24.

43. Irving Berlin, *The Complete Lyrics of Irving Berlin*, ed. Robert Kimball and Linda Emmett (New York: Knopf, 2001), 7–8.

44. A 1909 recording of the song, sung by Edward Favor, can be found at Onkel Greifenklau, YouTube, April 12, 2015, www.youtube.com. He pronounces "Salome" as "SAH-loam." No recording of Brice performing the song seems to exist, but an idea of what her "Yiddish Indian" act must have been like can be inferred from the 1932 Betty Boop cartoon *Stopping the Show*.

45. "Wonderland," *Boston Post*, September 5, 1909, 24.

46. "Wonderland's Attractions," *Boston Globe*, August 29, 1909, 37.

47. A picture of ninety-year-old Gertrude Fitzgerald appeared in the June 23, 1980, issue of *New York Magazine*, which reported that the nonagenarian was still singing and dancing. Thus, she would have been nineteen in 1909. The article noted that she had been with Ziegfeld's Follies. Gerry Hirshey, "Sunshine Girls and Boys on 46th Street," *New York Magazine*, June 23, 1980, 15–16.

48. This cannot be the still-familiar song "It's a Long, Long Way to Tipperary," which was made popular during World War I, because that song was not written until 1912. There were other songs with "Tipperary" in the title that predated 1909, however, such as the nineteenth-century "The Tipperary Recruiting Song," William Ames Fisher's 1905 "Sweet Tipperary," or the earlier "Sweet Is Tipperary."

49. "Wonderland," *Boston Globe*, August 24, 1909, 8.

50. See Frank Dumont, *One Night in a Medical College* (New York: Robert M. DeWitt, ca. 1877).

51. "Wonderland's Finale," *Boston Sunday Globe*, September 12, 1909, 43; "Wonderland," *Boston Sunday Post*, September 12, 1909, 28; "Last Days at Wonderland," *Revere Journal*, September 11, 1909, 2; "Crowds at Wonderland," *Revere Journal*, September 4, 1909, 2.

52. *Christian Science Monitor*, October 20, 1909, 12.

53. "Wonderland," *Boston Sunday Post*, July 10, 1910, 37.

54. Thomas Kirwan, "Growth and Development of Revere Beach," *Revere Journal*, August 14, 1909, 10.

Chapter 9: Finale—1910

1. "Amusement Notes," *Boston Globe*, June 11, 1910, 14; "Reopening of Wonderland," *Boston Globe*, June 12, 1910, 43.

2. "Revere Beach," *Revere Journal*, June 18, 1910, 5; "Reopening of Wonderland," *Boston Globe*, June 12, 1910, 43; *Boston Globe*, June 19, 1910, 52.

3. "Wonderland Park Opens," *Boston Globe*, June 18, 1910, 4.

4. "Wonderland Park Opens," *Boston Globe*, June 18, 1910, 4; "Wonderful Achievements by Intrepid Airman," *Boston Globe*, August 14, 1910, 43.

5. "Big Sunday Crowd," *Revere Journal*, June 25, 1910, 2; "Wonderland, Revere Beach," *Boston Globe*, August 23, 1910, 4; "Wonderland, Revere Beach," *Boston Globe*, August 16, 1910, 11; "Summertime Amusements—Reopening of Wonderland," *Boston Globe*,

June 12, 1910, 43. The balloon could take four passengers at a time. The discovery that some oil wells held large reserves of helium had just been discovered in 1903, and large-scale production of helium for balloons did not begin until World War I. All early ballooning was done with hot air or with hydrogen.

6. "Amusement Notes," *Boston Globe,* June 18, 1910, 4.

7. Lawrence, *Little Stories,* 10. The letter originally appeared in the *Exeter News Letter,* probably in 1910.

8. Advertisement, *Boston Post,* August 12, 1910, 13.

9. Morris K. Jesup was a banker, philanthropist, and onetime president of the American Museum of Natural History. He bankrolled Peary's last expedition.

10. Advertisement, *Boston Post,* July 1, 1910, 14. See also *Boston Post,* June 28, 1910, 6, and "Summer-Time Amusements—Matt Henson at Wonderland," *Boston Globe,* July 3, 1910, 49.

11. "Summer-Time Amusements—Matt Henson at Wonderland," *Boston Globe,* July 3, 1910, 49.

12. *Cleveland Gazette,* January 22, 1910, 3; "Peary's Negro to Give Lecture," *La Crosse [WI] Tribune,* February 7, 1910, 4; *Boston Globe,* October 3, 1910, 8.

13. "Peary Ungrateful, Says Matt Henson," *Syracuse [NY] Post-Standard,* March 11, 1910, 7. See also "Henson and Peary," *Syracuse Post-Standard,* March 17, 1910, 4.

14. *Syracuse [NY] Daily Journal,* October 7, 1911, 4; *Syracuse Post Standard,* October 10, 1911, 12.

15. "Here's the Woman Who Can Beat Any Mere Man at Pool Playing," *Oswego [NY] Palladium,* April 2, 1910, 11. W. W. disliked the term "pool," which, he explained, came from the practice of betting on the outcome. The Kings strove to keep the image of the game high-toned.

16. "Pleasant Wonderland," *Boston Globe,* July 10, 1910, 44.

17. *Syracuse Post Standard,* March 20, 1917, 8; *New York Press,* May 12, 1910, 5; *Joplin Missouri Morning Tribune,* December 8, 1912, 14; *Sandusky Ohio Star-Journal,* December 26, 1912, 7.

18. "Wonderland, Revere Beach," *Boston Globe,* August 28, 1910, 46; "Wonderland, Revere Beach," *Boston Globe,* August 30, 1910, 11; "Wonderland, Revere Beach," *Boston Globe,* June 19, 1910, 52. The last tells of a "colored baby being added to the incubator collection."

19. Advertisement, *Boston Post,* June 14, 1910, 8.

20. "Everybody Swims but Not Father," *Boston Sunday Post,* September 13, 1908, 27.

21. *Japan Times and Mail* (Tokyo), August 3, 1912, 801–2. See also "Old Lady Swims Five Miles," *Sheboygan [WI] Daily Press,* September 5, 1912, 6; "A 1.3 Mile Trip Made in 45 Minutes—Daughter Finishes Second," *Chillicothe [MO] Constitution,* July 15, 1912, 2, 65; and "She Swims Nearly Five Miles," *Honolulu Star Bulletin,* August 2, 1912, 5.

22. Wonderland's springs, surprisingly for a salt marsh, had provided the water used to fill the Kellermann pool and probably most of the water attractions.

23. *New York Clipper,* February 6, 1909, 1.

24. "The Big Show at Revere," *Billboard,* August 6, 1910, 17; Advertisement, *Boston Post,* July 31, 1910, 36; "Monitor and Merrimac at Revere," *Boston Sunday Post,* July 31, 1910, 37; "Historic Battle at Revere," *Boston Sunday Post,* August 7, 1910, 37.

25. "The Irish League—Arranges for Its Annual Excursion to Revere," *Lowell [MA] Sun,* July 30, 1910, 33.

26. Advertisement, *Boston Post,* September 3, 1910, 12. An advertisement in the *Boston Post,* September 5, 1910, 14, announced that it was the last day Wonderland would be open.

27. "Wonderland to Close," *Boston Globe,* September 4, 1910, 41.

28. "Promises to Beat Records," *Boston Globe,* September 4, 1910, 6.

29. "Miniature Almanac" and "Showers, the Forecast," *Boston Globe* September 5, 1910, 9, 16.

30. "For Sale," *Boston Sunday Post,* September 11, 1910, 22; "For Sale," *Boston Sunday Post,* October 2, 1910, 23; "For Sale," *Boston Sunday Post,* September 4, 1910, 8; "For Sale," *Boston Sunday Post,* November 6, 1910, 14; "For Sale," *Boston Sunday Post,* October 23, 1910, 14; "For Sale," *Boston Sunday Post,* October 30, 1910, 14; "For Sale," *Boston Sunday Post,* October 30, 1910, 14. See also *Boston Sunday Post,* October 23, 1910, 14, and November 6, 1910, 14.

Chapter 10: After the Ball Was Over—1911 and Beyond

1. Although Nazzaro and Nazzaro, *Revere Beach's Wonderland,* 59, and all the internet sites based on it, and McCauley's *Revere Beach Chips,* 93, claim that Wonderland's final season was 1911, there are no advertisements or notices for Wonderland in the year 1911. "The Observant Citizen," *Boston Post,* July 14, 1911, 11, explicitly stated that Wonderland did not open that summer.

2. An advertisement for "recording electric meters" in "first class condition" that had been used at Wonderland appeared in *Billboard,* December 9, 1911, 63.

3. "All Aboard for Revere Beach!—How They Pried the Lid Off Last Week," *Boston Sunday Post,* May 7, 1911, 31.

4. Advertisement, *Boston Globe,* April 21, 1912, 23.

5. "The Observant Citizen," *Boston Post,* April 11, 1914, 14.

6. "The Observant Citizen," *Boston Post,* October 13, 1917, 12.

7. "Seek Lower Taxes on Wonderland Property," *Boston Post,* July 22, 1911, 8; *Boston Sunday Globe,* July 23, 1911, 36; *Christian Science Monitor,* July 22, 1911, 19.

8. "Need Not Buy Wonderland," *Boston Post,* September 1, 1911, 7; *New York Dramatic Mirror,* September 13, 1911, 11, 12.

9. Advertisement, *New York Herald,* April 11, 1912, 16.

10. "'Wonderland Park's New Residential Section," *Boston Sunday Post,* July 27, 1919, 28.

11. "Boy Drowns in Pit," *Boston Globe,* August 7, 1914, 11.

12. *Boston Globe,* October 6, 1919, 9; *Boston Sunday Post,* May 23, 1920, 22.

13. "Revere Police Get Autoists," *Revere Journal,* October 13, 1917, 5.

14. "More Than 250,000 Visit Revere Beach on Sunday," *Boston Globe,* May 23, 1921, 3.

15. "Wonderland Dog Racetrack to Close," WBUR, August 19, 2010, www.wbur.org.

16. "Wonderland Station," Wikipedia, https://en.wikipedia.org.

17. Advertisement, *New Boston,* April 1911, 658.

18. Advertisement, *System: The Magazine of Business,* March 1912, 225; Advertisement,

Farm Journal, January 1912, 10; Advertisement, *Country Gentleman,* January 6, 1912, 22.

19. U.S. Census 1930, Jacksonville, FL, precinct 10A, book 7141, sheet 11B.

20. "John Joseph Higgins," Find a Grave, www.findagrave.com.

21. "Death of Harold Parker Early Today," *Boston Globe,* November 29, 1916, 9; "Harold Parker," Find a Grave; "Memoirs of Deceased Members—Harold Parker," *Journal of the Boston Society of Civil Engineers,* December 1917, 443–44.

22. "Aliens to Be Held for Service," *Christian Science Monitor,* October 31, 1917, 10; "In Other Places," *New York Sun and Herald,* April 5, 1920, 9. He is reported as living in Miami-Dade in the U.S. Census for 1940, www.archives.com.

23. "For Common Council, Ward 9," *Boston Globe,* December 9, 1908, 11; "Light Infantry Veterans," *Boston Sunday Globe,* November 21, 1920, 85; "James Walker," Find a Grave.

24. "New Jersey," *Billboard,* May 22, 1909, 30; "Two Bostonians Marry," *Variety,* October 16, 1909, 8.

25. *New York Dramatic Mirror,* September 13, 1911, 16; "Eugene L. Perry Selected," *Billboard,* February 10, 1917, 13; "Perry Quits Riverside," *New York Clipper,* August 8, 1917, 1; "Employees Honor Perry," *New York Clipper,* August 15, 1917, 6; "Eugene L. Perry," Find a Grave.

26. "Court House Murals Cause New Debate," *Syracuse [NY] Herald,* March 26, 1937, 16; "Deaths—Attilio Pusterla," *Philadelphia Inquirer,* May 3, 1941, 8; *New York Sun,* May 2, 1941, 28; Attilio Pusterla, "Flying Machine," U.S. Patent no. 1,009,895, November 28, 1911, http://patft.uspto.gov.

27. Advertisement, *Christian Science Monitor,* May 10, 12, 28, 1910; Dudley S. McDonald, death certificate, August 17, 1916, Massachusetts State Vital Records, 1841–1920 Register 30, p. 410.

28. "Louis Bopp Kills Self," *Variety,* March 22, 1923, 8; "Louis Bopp," Find a Grave.

29. "Boston's Winter Garden," *Boston Post,* November 15, 1908, 14; "Girl Swimmer Out with Challenges," *Boston Post,* June 24, 1909, 12; "Luna Park," *Boston Post,* July 4, 1909, 23; *Billboard,* August 14, 1909, 24; "Women Swimmers in Contest Today," *Boston Post,* June 14, 1909, 2; "Diving Girls at Broadway Palace—Stage Mermaids Disporting in 10,000 Gallon Tank," *Saratoga Springs [NY] Saratogan,* June 22, 1914, 2; "New Flatbush Theater," *Brooklyn [NY] Daily Eagle,* December 13, 1914, 15; Salem, Mass," *Variety,* August 15, 1913, 31. See also *New York Clipper,* May 2, 1914, 23.

30. *Billboard,* September 4, 1920, 61; *Catalog of Copyright Entries: Musical Compositions* (Washington, DC: Government Printing Office, 1914), part 1, vol. 11, no. 2, p. 25494. Pattee had written comedies as well—*Dora's Joke* in 1901 and *Initiated* in 1912. *Catalogue of Title Entries of Books and Other Articles Entered* (Washington, DC: Government Printing Office, 1901), 28:91; *Dramatic Compositions Copyrighted in the United States, 1870 to 1916* (Washington, DC: Government Printing Office, 1918), 1:1074.

31. New York City Marriage Records, 1829–1940, September 10, 1914; U.S. Census 1920, Bronx Borough, ward 5401, sheets 6B, 7A.

32. "Florida," *Billboard,* June 24, 1922, 80; Advertisement, *Billboard,* November 19, 1921, 99; "Three Acres of Joy," *Billboard,* November 19, 1921, 76.

33. "Herbert H. Pattee," New York City, New York Municipal Deaths, 1795–1949, June 18, 1936.

34. Jim McHugh, "Traver Found His Inspiration in Seagulls, Money in Big Crowds," *Billboard,* April 17, 1943, 45, 52; "Harry Travers Life Resembled His Roller Coasters," Newsgroup Archive, https://rec.roller-coaster.narkive.com; Richard Munch, *Harry G. Traver: Legends of Terror* (Mentor, OH: Amusement Park Books), 1982; "The Circle Swing," *Street Railway Journal,* October 8, 1904, 18A; "The Traver Circle Swing Company," *United States Investor,* April 16, 1904, 590–91; "The Circle Swing Flying Machine," *Street Railway Review,* December 20, 1904, 982–83.

35. "Joseph Giacomo Ferari," Wikipedia.

36. "Carnival for Revere Beach," *Billboard,* March 16, 1912, 22; *New York Dramatic Mirror,* May 15, 1912, 19; Advertisement, *Boston Evening Globe,* May 1, 1918, 12; "Park News—Park Manager's New Enterprise," *Billboard,* October 24, 1914, 20; "W. C. Manning Planning—Spectacular Exhibition for 1919," *Billboard,* December 7, 1918, 28; Advertisement, *Billboard,* July 26, 1919, 106; *Billboard,* July 9, 1921, 69; "W. C. Manning—Undergoes Successful Operation," *Billboard,* October 22, 1921, 84.

37. U.S. Census 1930, Revere, Massachusetts, sheet 1B.

38. "James J. Armstrong Dies—Was Dean of All Vaudeville Agents," *Billboard,* February 9, 1918, 7.

39. *Billboard,* July 4, 1908, 38; "Telegraphic News—Cincinnati," *New York Dramatic Mirror,* July 6, 1907, 8; *Billboard,* July 6, 1907, 20, 27.

40. *New York Clipper,* September 26, 1914, 10. Kennedy had not been absent for very long. *Billboard,* March 15, 1913, 50, reports him performing in "Kennedy's Wild West and Frontier Days" in Arkansas. See also *New York Clipper,* May 17, 1913, 17.

41. "Atkinson Show in Arizona," *Billboard,* March 14, 1925, 76.

42. "Kennedy, W. H.," *Billboard,* August 16, 1952, 52; "William H. Kennedy," Find a Grave; "Requiem Today for Wild West Show Pioneer," *Oklahoman* [Oklahoma City, OK], August 6, 1952, 6.

43. "Robert J. Blake Dead," *Kokomo [IN] Daily Tribune,* June 26, 1916, 1; *Variety,* June 9, 1916, 8; *Variety,* June 23, 1916, 10; "Robert J. Blake," Find a Grave.

44. Advertisement, *Billboard,* June 3, 1922, 100; Advertisement, *Billboard,* August 17, 1918, 33.

45. Harry Goldman, *Kenneth Strickfaden: Dr. Frankenstein's Electrician* (Jefferson, NC: McFarland, 2017), 25–27.

46. Bob Davidsson, "The Life and Times of Palm Beach's 'Alligator Joe,'" Origin and History of the Palm Beaches, July 5, 2017, http://pbchistory.blogspot.com; Jim Broton, "Florida's Warren Frazeee, the Original 'Alligator Joe,'" *Tequesta* 68 (2008), www.historymiami.org.

47. Lisa Yannucci, "Lincoln Beachey—A Jump Rope Rhyme about a Pilot," Mama Lisa Blog, October 17, 2011, www.mamalisa.com.

48. There is an account of him still performing in the *New York Clipper,* March 2, 1912, 10.

49. "Walter Starr Wentworth," Find a Grave.

50. "Rose Wentworth Retiring," *Billboard,* April 25, 1914, 4. Rose had previously claimed that she was retiring in an announcement in *Variety,* November 13, 1909, 17.

51. "Rose Wentworth Gives Party," *Billboard,* December 19, 1925, 64; "Town Personalities: Ex-Circus Star Recalls the Time British King Pulled Her Hair," *Indiana [PA] Weekly Messenger,* October 7, 1937, 14.

52. "Retired Bareback Queen, 70, Knows She Can Ride 'Em," *Billboard,* October 20, 1945, 53.

53. "Hippodrome at Columbia Park," *Buffalo Courier,* July 22, 1909, 15.

54. "Clown Tells of Shattered Romance," *Urbana Illinois Courier-Herald,* October 10, 1913, 6.

55. "Annette Kellerman Wed to J. R. Sullivan, Manager," *New York Press,* December 1, 1912, 2.

56. Bob Thomas, "Miss Kellerman Says 'Bikini' Is on Way Out," *Gloversville and Johnstown [NY] Morning Herald,* February 16, 1952, 19.

57. Kellermann's biography is told at length in Annette Kellermann, "My Story," undated manuscript, MLMSS 6270/1, Mitchell Library, State Library of New South Wales, Australia; Gibson with Firth, *Original Million Dollar Mermaid;* "Annette Kellermann," The Silents Are Golden, www.silentsaregolden.com; "The Form Divine," *Salamanca [NY] Republican Press,* July 20, 1963, 4 (reporting on her seventy-fifth birthday); and Paul Bentley, "The Kellerman Archive Bears Fruit," The Wolanski Project, April 8, 2005, www.twf.org.au.

58. Shirley, *Pawnee Bill,* 232–33; *Elmira [NY] Star Gazette,* February 9, 1942, 6.

59. "Pan-American Midway Midget Dies in Mexico," *Smethport-MKean County Democrat* (Smethport, PA), April 26, 1928, 6; *Billboard,* August 6, 1932, 46.

60. *Catalogue of Copyright Entries,* part 3, *Musical Compositions,* new series (Washington, DC: Government Printing Office, 1913), vol. 8, part 2, no. 11, p. 1409.

61. Matthew A. Henson, *A Negro Explorer at the North Pole* (New York: Freeman A. Stokes, 1912).

62. Lowell Thomas, "First at the Pole," *New York Herald Tribune,* April 2, 1939, 3.

63. Bradley Robinson, *Dark Companion* (New York: K. M. McBride, 1947).

64. "Prodigious Henson," *Elmira Star-Gazette,* March 18, 1955, 6; "Matthew Henson," Wikipedia.

SELECTED BIBLIOGRAPHY

Allen, Thomas S. *Wonderland Waltz Song*. Boston: Walter Jacobs Music, 1906.

Chumbley, Gail. *River of January*. Nampa, ID: Point Rider, 2014. A memoir of Helen Thompson and Montgomery Chumbley, the daughter and son-in-law of Floyd C. Thompson, by Helen's daughter-in-law.

Civitello, Linda. *Baking Powder Wars: The Cutthroat Food Fight That Revolutionized Cooking*. Urbana: University of Illinois Press, 2017.

Craig, William J., and the Revere Society for Cultural and Historic Preservation. *Revere*. Charleston, SC: Arcadia Press, 2004.

Draper, John. "Rose Wentworth: A Circus Legend." *Bandwagon* 57, no. 4 (2013): 16–25.

Gibson, Emily, with Barbara Firth. *The Original Million Dollar Mermaid: The Annette Kellerman Story*. London: Allen and Unwin, 2006.

Hartt, Rollin Lynde. *The People at Play: Excursions in the Humor and Philosophy of Popular Entertainments*. Boston: Houghton Mifflin, 1909.

Higgins, John J., John T. Burnett, and Eugene V. R. Thayer. Sale of land to Walnut Avenue Company, March 20, 1909. Suffolk, MA, Registry of Deeds, book 3349, pp. 515–18. Massachusetts State Archives, Boston.

Hillman, H. W. *Looking Forward: The Phenomenal Progress of Electricity in 1912*. Northampton, MA: Valley View, 1906.

Kitchen, Robert. "Rose Wentworth: A Rose by Any Other Name." *Bandwagon* 59, no. 3 (2015): 18–29.

Lawrence, Harry V. *Little Stories*. Boston: Spartan Press, 1914.

Lee, George S. Sale of land to John J. Higgins, May 2, 1905. Suffolk, MA, Registry of Deeds, book 3040, pp. 258–60. Massachusetts State Archives, Boston.

Lieberman, William. *The Train on the Beach: Forgotten Railroads That Transformed Winthrop, Orient Heights, and Revere Beach Massachusetts*. St. Petersburg, FL: Book Locker.com, 2017.

Mathias, Christopher R., and Kenneth C. Turino. *Nahant*. Charleston, SC: Arcadia Press, 1999.

McCauley, Peter, ed. *Revere Beach Chips: Historical Background from The Revere Journal*, 2nd edition. 1996; reprint Revere, MA: Revere Society for Cultural and Historic

Preservation, 2017. A collection of articles and photographs from the *Revere Journal* and elsewhere

Nazzaro, Edward, and Frederick Nazzaro. *Revere Beach's Wonderland: The Mystic City by the Sea.* Melrose, MA: Privately printed, 1983.

Poole, Daniel. Sale of land to John J. Higgins, May 2, 1905. Suffolk, MA, Registry of Deeds, book 3040, pp. 263–64. Massachusetts State Archives, Boston.

Raffel, Dawn. *The Strange Case of Dr. Couney: How a Mysterious European Showman Saved Thousands of American Babies.* New York: Blue Rider Press, 2018.

Schmidt, Leah A. *Revere Beach.* Charleston, SC: Arcadia, 2002.

Shirley, Glenn. *Pawnee Bill: A Biography of Major Gordon W. Lillie.* Albuquerque: University of New Mexico Press, 1958.

Shurtleff, Benjamin. *The History of the Town of Revere.* Boston: Beckler Press, 1937.

Silverman, Stephen M. *The Amusement Park: 900 Years of Thrills and Spills and the Dreamers and Schemers Who Built Them.* New York: Black Dog and Leventhal, 2019.

Wonderland Company. Sale of land to John J. Higgins, John T. Burnett, and Eugene V. R. Thayer, March 19, 1905. Suffolk, MA, Registry of Deeds, book 3349, pp. 502–15. Massachusetts State Archives, Boston.

Wonderland Fire and Flames Souvenir Book 1906. Boston: T. J. Hennessy, 1906. Private collection.

Wonderland Fire and Flames Souvenir Book 1907. Boston: T. J. Hennessy, 1907. Private collection.

Wonderland 1906 Ledger Book. Private collection.

Wonderland Souvenir Magazine 1906. Edited and compiled by William H. Walsh. *Boston: Libbie Show Print,* 1906.

Wonderland Souvenir Program 1908. Boston: Waters Press, 1908. This work exists in at least two slightly different versions, with differing content and photographs. Private collection; Otis House, Historic New England, Boston.

INDEX